DATE DUE

MAY 2 6 98			
OC 1 8 '99			
NO 8 '99			
NO2 9 99			
3 0'00			
NV 22 0			

Climbing the Hill

K

CLIMBING THE HILL

Gender Conflict in Congress

Karen Foerstel
and Herbert N. Foerstel

Westport, Connecticut
London

Library of Congress Cataloging-in-Publication Data

Foerstel, Karen.
    Climbing the Hill : gender conflict in Congress / Karen Foerstel
and Herbert N. Foerstel.
        p.   cm.
    Includes bibliographical references and index.
    ISBN 0–275–94914–1 (alk. paper)
    1. Women in politics—United States. 2. Women legislators—United
States. 3. United States. Congress—Officials and employees.
4. Sex discrimination against women—United States.   I. Foerstel,
Herbert N. II. Title.
HQ1391.U5F64   1996
320′.082—dc20   95–37651

British Library Cataloguing in Publication Data is available.

Library of Congress Catalog Card Number: 95–37651
ISBN: 0–275–94914–1

First published in 1996

Praeger Publishers, 88 Post Road West, Westport, CT 06881
An imprint of Greenwood Publishing Group, Inc.

Printed in the United States of America

The paper used in this book complies with the
Permanent Paper Standard issued by the National
Information Standards Organization (Z39.48–1984).

10 9 8 7 6 5 4 3 2 1

Contents

Photo essay follows Chapter 3

Chapter 1

A History of Struggle

HUMBLE BEGINNINGS

In 1866, Elizabeth Cady Stanton, a pioneer for woman suffrage, ran as an independent candidate for Congress from the 8th District in New York. Running on a platform of free speech, free press, free trade, freed men, and universal suffrage, she received a total of 24 votes. Six years later she was arrested for the crime of voting in the national election of 1872.

Women have come a long way since then, with the election of 28 new women to Congress in 1992 the crowning achievement to date. But were just 28 women out of a 1992 freshman class of 110 any cause for celebration? A look at the daunting, often demeaning path that women have trod toward Capitol Hill may explain the giddy optimism that surrounded the 1992 elections.

Many of the early women in Congress were tokens. Some were appointed rather than elected, and many came to their office by way of "special elections" designed to fill the remainder of the term for a seat left vacant by the death or retirement of a spouse or other congressional incumbent. Often, the woman filling out the term was required to agree not to seek further office. Terms of only a few months were not unusual.

Some political analysts claim that too much has been made of the "matrimonial connection" for women in Congress, since, historically, the majority of seats left vacant by death have *not* been filled by the wife of the deceased. This misses the point that during the early history of women in Congress, succession to the seat of a deceased incumbent, particularly a spouse, was not only a frequent occurrence, it was the method of access for the overwhelming majority of women. Five of the first eight women in Congress came by their seats through the death of an incumbent. Up to

World War II, 19 of the 32 women who had served in Congress came there by filling the remainder of the term of a deceased incumbent. In addition, one woman was elected to Congress after first being named Democratic national committeewoman as a tribute to her late husband. Another woman succeeded to her husband's term after his imprisonment on charges of conspiracy to transport liquor. Even after World War II many women continued to enter Congress through exceptional circumstances. Indeed, up to 1970, women filling out the term of a deceased incumbent still represented the majority of all women who had served in Congress.

A PROUD PIONEER

Against this background of controlled and patronizing access to political power, the early accomplishments of some highly motivated women in Congress are particularly impressive. Indeed, the very first woman to enter Congress was one of the most independent and principled politicians, male or female, ever to grace Capitol Hill. Jeannette Rankin (R-Mont.) was elected to Congress in 1916, four years before American women were even allowed to vote. She was sworn in on April 2, 1917, a fitting precursor to the confident and committed women who are today shaking things up on Capitol Hill.

As a young woman in Montana, Rankin lived the robust western life, accompanying her father on trips to his lumber camp, where she cooked for crews of 50 or 60. Indeed, Rankin later attributed her political success to the egalitarian attitudes of rugged Montana. "We got the vote in Montana," she said, "because the spirit of pioneer days was still alive. Men thought of women in the same terms as they thought of themselves."[1]

Rankin's family was Republican, intellectually inclined, and politically minded. Her father had served as the local county commissioner, and her brother Wellington, active in the Progressive Party, became state attorney general. Before Jeannette entered politics, she had seen the hard realities of America. She was shocked by a tour of Boston's slums. She worked among the poor of San Francisco's Latin Quarter. In 1908, she spent a year at the New York School of Philanthropy, an institution whose progressive philosophy claimed that American women suffered because they had no voice in creating the power that ruled over them.

Rankin became a leader in Montana's suffrage movement, and later served as a lobbyist in a dozen states and on Capitol Hill. When she decided to enter the GOP congressional race in Montana, her brother Wellington managed her campaign. He warned her that the prejudice against sending a woman to Congress was the biggest problem facing them. During her exhausting campaign, Jeannette Rankin took her message to the people by touring every village and town in Montana. She traveled by train, buggy, car, and horseback, promising to work for a women's suffrage amendment, an eight-hour work day for women, improved health care for mothers and children, and prohibition. She was the only Republican to win major elective office in Montana that year. More important, she became the first woman elected to *any* national representative body in the world.

After her election, the newspapers presented a confusing image of the nation's first congresswoman. Some referred to her as a "cowgirl," despite her sophistication and university education. One newspaper called her an "Amazon," though she was not large in stature. She was described as 33 years of age, though she was actually 36. But from the beginning of her career, most of her trouble with the press concerned matters of war and peace. During her campaign for Congress, she had expressed opposition to American involvement in the war in Europe. The *New York Times* responded with an editorial assurance that the war would continue despite the weariness and protests of women.

On April 5, 1917, when Senate Joint Resolution Number One was introduced, declaring that a state of war existed between the German Imperial Government and the government of the United States, the newly arrived Rankin was under heavy pressure to support the resolution. Even her brother Wellington urged her to "vote a man's vote" and warned that she couldn't be elected again if she voted against the war. Nonetheless, when her name was called during the roll-call vote, she rose and said softly, "I wish to stand by my country, but I cannot vote for war. I vote no."[2]

The *New York Times* described Rankin as weeping copiously during the roll call, but witnesses sitting near her said she was composed and shed no tears. Forty-nine of Rankin's colleagues had joined her in rejecting President Wilson's request for a declaration of war, yet the press singled her out for criticism, suggesting that she alone had been cowardly and disloyal. The *Nation* wrote: "[I]t is unfortunate that Miss Rankin's first important vote on the floor should have been one in which she could not with an easy conscience voice the prevailing sentiment of her own district or of the country at large, for her attitude on the war issue can never be expunged from the record, however earnestly she may devote her energies hereafter to the national cause."[3]

On the contrary, Rankin's pacifist principles were quite appropriate to the energetic and successful pursuit of her broader "feminist" agenda. Early in the first session of the 65th Congress, she cosponsored a resolution for a constitutional amendment granting women the right to vote. When the House Judiciary Committee tried to bottle up the measure, Rankin successfully introduced legislation creating a 13-member Woman Suffrage Committee, on which she became the ranking minority member. Rankin was then chosen to lead the floor debate on suffrage. But the press was as hostile to Rankin and the woman suffrage leaders as it was to pacifists. The *Times* wrote: "We are justified in judging their sobriety of judgement, the fitness of the mass for political life, from the utterances of these leaders. 'A woman in Congress,' said Miss Rankin after her election, 'will be like a suffrage banner on parade.' What does the country read on that banner? 'I want to stand by my country, but I cannot vote for war.' "[4]

Opponents of women's suffrage claimed that it would produce masculine women, feminine men, and the eventual decay of American civilization, but under Rankin's leadership the House approved the amendment by *exactly* the two-thirds vote required. Unfortunately, the Senate did not pass the amendment, effectively killing it for the 65th Congress. But women across the nation urged the defeat of antisuffrage senators, and by mid–1919, the Woman Suffrage Amendment went to the states for ratification. Ironically by then Jeannette Rankin was no longer in Congress to cast a final supporting vote. In 1918, a redistricting action by the Montana legislature would have forced Rankin, a Republican, to run for the House in a largely Democratic district. To avoid such geographical restraints, she ran for the Senate. In the Republican primary she lost by 1,714 votes, but chose to run in the general election as the candidate of the newly formed National Party, a coalition of Socialists, Prohibitionists, Progressives, and farmers.

In her campaign, Rankin appealed to women by pointing to her congressional record on women's rights. Her opponents, predictably, targeted her opposition to the war. She was characterized as unpatriotic, despite her campaign slogan, "Win the War, and Make the World Safe for Humanity." In an election that took place less than a week before the signing of the armistice, Rankin ran a distant third, but her defeat did not exile her from Capitol Hill. For the next 20 years she worked as field secretary of the National Consumer's League, lobbying for federal wage-and-hour laws, for a child-labor amendment, and for the maternity and infancy bill she had introduced under her own name in the 65th Congress. She also worked with the Women's International League for Peace and Freedom and the Women's Peace Union, lobbying for a constitutional amendment "forbidding the United States from preparing for, or engaging in war." She later became legislative secretary for the National Council for the Prevention of War, urging Congress to adopt a policy of neutrality. In 1940, as she approached 60 years of age, Jeannette Rankin announced that she would run again for the U.S. House of Representatives. Her platform slogan was, "Prepare to the limit for defense; keep our men out of Europe." In an endorsement of Rankin, New York mayor Fiorello La Guardia wrote: "This woman has more courage and packs a harder punch than a regiment of regular line politicians."

In the November election, Rankin won by more than 9,000 votes, and was the lone Republican to win national office in Montana. On December 8, 1941, the day after the Japanese attack on Pearl Harbor, the U.S. Senate approved President Roosevelt's request for a declaration of war by an 82-to-0 vote. The House attempted to suspend the rules and approve the war resolution without a vote. Only Jeannette Rankin objected, but each time she rose to speak she was ruled out of order. Finally, when her name was called during the first roll-call vote, Rankin spoke a clear "No," adding, "As a woman I can't go to war, and I refuse to send anyone else."[5]

The following day, the *Washington Post* wrote: "After she voted, there was a small procession of solemn-faced colleagues back up the aisle to her seat. They spoke earnestly to her, in the benign manner of men who strive to change a woman's mind . . . but at the end of each conversation, she always shook her head."[6]

Thus, with Rankin's lone dissenting vote, Congress declared war. As she left the Capitol, hostile crowds forced her to seek refuge in a phone booth, "cornered like a rabbit," after which the police had to escort her to her office, where she spent the afternoon behind locked doors. William Allen White, publisher of the *Emporia Gazette*, wrote: "Probably 100 men in Congress would have liked to do what she did. Not one of them had the courage to do it. . . . When in one hundred years from now, courage, sheer courage, based on moral indignation, is celebrated in this country, the name of Jeannette Rankin, who stood firmly in folly for her faith, will be written in monumental bronze, not for what she did but for the way she did it."

Rankin later told a friend that her vote against the war had been guided by her philosophy of life, a philosophy which could not be changed by an incident. She repeated an old adage of the suffrage movement: "You can trust the woman who believed in suffrage, but you can never trust the woman who just wanted to vote."[7]

Rankin's second term in Congress effectively ended on December 7, 1941. After her unpopular vote against the war, she knew she could not be reelected, and her financial situation was dire. In a letter to a colleague in the peace movement she said she was not willing to risk everything on an election that would probably leave her with no office and heavy debt.

Jeannette Rankin retired from electoral politics at the end of her second term, but she lived out her life in consistent pursuit of two ideals: peace and women's rights. At the age of 88 she was still traveling across the nation, speaking at rallies opposing the Vietnam War. In a speech she declared, "It is unconscionable that 10,000 boys have died in Vietnam and I predict that if 10,000 American women had mind enough they could end the war. . . ."[8] The "Jeannette Rankin Brigade" became a prominent women's group opposing the Vietnam War, and when the Brigade marched on Washington in 1968, Rankin led a delegation of women, including Mrs. Martin Luther King, Jr., to present a petition to House Speaker John McCormack.

A PROMISE DENIED

In the 27 years spanning Jeannette Rankin's initial election to and final departure from Congress, 32 other women were elected to the House and Senate. None could match Rankin's principled activism, perhaps because they saw the price she paid. In 1920, just a year after Rankin first left Congress, the 19th Amendment, for which she had worked so strenuously, was passed and ratified by the states, giving women the right to vote. But any hopes that women would now transform Capitol Hill were quickly dashed. That same year, Alice M. Robertson (R-Okla.) became the second woman ever elected to Congress and the first elected while women had the vote. She was an antisuffragette who maintained that exchanging a woman's "privileges" for a man's "rights" was a poor bargain.

"Apparently neither she nor her party regarded her candidacy seriously," wrote the *New York Times*. "She did not leave Muskogee, her home, and merely advertised her cafeteria and her candidacy in the same modest cards in the newspapers. Lo, the overwhelming Republican landslide swept her into the House—its only woman member."[9] The *Times* made clear that Robertson bore no resemblance to Jeannette Rankin: "She is no tender Miss Rankin. She wouldn't have wept and she wouldn't have voted No on the declaration of war with Germany. An ardent Rooseveltian, she says that 'we ought to have gotten in a long time before we did.' She tells us that the men 'voted for her but bet against her.' "[10]

Early in her first term, Robertson incurred the wrath of women's groups around the country when she refused to support the Sheppard-Towner Bill, a measure originally authored by Jeannette Rankin, which was designed to reduce the number of deaths of mothers and newborn infants. Robertson said sternly, "The 'sob stuff' claim that 680 babies die every day from the failure in enacting this bill . . . is absurd." She also voted against the creation of a federal Department of Education, explaining that, unlike the North, southern states would never accept the seating of colored schoolchildren next to whites.

Despite her extreme conservatism and apparent insensitivity to women's issues, Robertson maintained her popularity in Oklahoma until she made a mistake reminiscent of Rankin. She opposed the payment of a bonus to World War I veterans. She was subsequently defeated at the polls.

The third woman to enter Congress was Rebecca Latimer Felton (D-Ga.), the nation's first female senator. Hers was a token appointment, part of a cynical process manipulated by the political ambitions of the men around her. On September 26, 1922, when controversial Georgia senator Thomas Watson died, Governor Thomas Hardwick chose to appoint a woman for the period until the next Congress convened. Because Congress was not in session, Hardwick saw a political opportunity to offer a sop to the newly enfranchised women who had been outraged at Watson's vote against the 19th Amendment and Hardwick's own opposition to woman suffrage. Though his political ambitions would be ultimately unsuccessful, Hardwick himself hoped to win the vacant seat before the "interim" woman could set a foot on Capitol Hill. He appointed Rebecca Latimer Felton, an aged widow whom he characterized as a "noble Georgia woman now in the sunset of a splendid, useful life." Hardwick disingenuously added, "It is unfortunate that an elected successor will prevent her from being sworn in."

During her appointment ceremonies, Mrs. Felton said, "The biggest part of this appointment lies in the recognition of women in the government of our country. It means, as far as I can see, there are now no limitations upon the ambitions of women. They can be elected or appointed to any office in the land."

Many newspapers around the country characterized Governor Hardwick's appointment of Felton as, at best, an empty gesture, but most were more blunt in examining the governor's motives. The *Pittsburgh Gazette-Times* stated: "He did not appoint a woman because he has respect for women in politics, but actually to smooth his own path to the Senate." The *St. Louis Star* was downright morbid: "Other Governors who may be studying the health charts of U.S. Senators should take full note of Governor Hardwick's strategy."

In her letter of acceptance to Hardwick, the 87-year-old widow seemed to acknowledge Hardwick's political ploy as she expressed her appreciation "on behalf of the thousands of Georgia women who will reward you at the ballot box." At the official ceremony of appointment, the governor admitted that he had been opposed to women's suffrage, but said now that it was the law of the land, he would support it. He told Felton that even though her tenure would end before she could be sworn in, she should be satisfied that her name would appear on the official roster of U.S. senators. Little did Hardwick know that the octogenarian widow had her own plan to crash the men's club called the U.S. Senate.

Women across the country began a public lobbying effort to have Mrs. Felton officially seated among her senatorial colleagues. This could only be done if the president called a special session of Congress, or if the Senate consented to swearing her in before the elected successor was seated. President Harding was overwhelmed with letters and telegrams urging him to allow Mrs. Felton to be sworn in, but he decided that it would be too expensive to summon Congress just to seat a single senator.

In the meantime, Walter Franklin George won the Georgia Democratic primary for the vacant Senate seat, ending Governor Hardwick's political aspirations. In Georgia, the primary victory was tantamount to election, so women's groups quickly shifted their pressure to George. Assuming that he would be elected, they asked him to defer the presentation of his credentials to allow Mrs. Felton to be sworn in. George pointed out that, by law, the term of an appointed senator ends the day a successor is elected.

At this point, Mrs. Felton turned once more to President Harding, sending him a personal note asking that he reconsider his decision against calling a special session of Congress. Harding ignored her request, but, by apparent coincidence, he accomplished the same thing when he subsequently convened a special session to allow the passage of an administration-sponsored ship-subsidy bill. Here was the opportunity Mrs. Felton had been waiting for.

Senator-elect George said he would have to be present on the opening day of the special session, but he was willing to allow her to present her credentials before his, if she could somehow gain access to the Senate chambers. He warned her that the objection of a single senator could deny her the right to be sworn in.

Greeted by cheers from a gallery crowded with women, Rebecca Felton arrived in the Senate more than an hour before Vice President Calvin Coolidge called the special session to order on November 20, 1922. Just 12 minutes later the meeting was adjourned. Mrs. Felton posed for photographers, holding high her certificate of confirmation and vowing to return the following day for her formal seating. The second-day proceedings were again viewed by a gallery packed with women who watched Georgia senator William J. Harris rise to ask if any senator objected to Mrs. Felton taking the oath of office. Hearing no formal objection, the president pro tem then asked the clerk to read Mrs. Felton's credentials, after which she was sworn in to the accompaniment of applause from the gallery.

The following day, Senator Rebecca Felton answered the roll call and rose to address the assembled senators in the first and last speech of her career. As for the men who had cynically attempted to manipulate her appointment for their political gain, Felton had only the kindest words. She admitted that the state of Georgia had been "very slow in reference to her promises with respect to woman's suffrage," but she proudly proclaimed that "one chivalric governor went to the front and said, 'Send that old lady there and let her look at the Senate for even a day.' "

She thanked the senator-elect from Georgia, Mr. George, saying, "He has been most chivalric. . . . I am at home in the Senate for one day." She had kind words for America's women as well. "I want to say further that I commend to your attention the 10,000,000 women voters who are watching this incident. . . . Let me say, Mr. President, that when the women of the country come and sit with you, though there may be but a very few in the next few years, I pledge you that you will get ability, you will get integrity of purpose, you will get exalted patriotism, and you will get unstinted usefullness."[11]

Senator-elect Walter F. George was immediately sworn in. The last item of business before the session ended was a resolution directing the secretary of the Senate to pay Rebecca Felton $287.67 for compensation for her one day of service, plus $280 for mileage.

BEYOND A SINGLE TERM

The fourth and fifth women to join Congress, Winnifred Mason Huck (R-Ill.) and Mae Ella Nolan (R-Calif.), continued the seeming tradition of one term and out, and their brief appearances on Capitol Hill were uneventful. However, they were followed by a spate of congresswomen with staying power. Most of these new members had shed the pacifism that characterized earlier women in Congress, espousing instead a traditionally "masculine" commitment to military strength.

Florence Kahn (R-Calif.), the wife of Julius Kahn, Broadway actor turned congressman, served as her husband's campaign aide until his death in 1924, at which time she was elected to succeed him. Once in Congress, she was assigned to Military Affairs, the committee formerly chaired by her husband. The *Pictorial Review* wrote of Florence Kahn, "Congress treats her like a man, fears her, admires her and listens to her."[12] She was a public patriot whose legislative legacy included an act creating the Gold Star Mothers. She also drew up legislation to widen the authority of the FBI. Director J. Edgar Hoover, then widely regarded as a misogynist, publicly proclaimed Mrs. Kahn "The Mother of the FBI." Kahn often advised women running for office to "obliterate sex in politics." This notion of gender-blind politics was to dominate two generations of women in Congress, who seemed to conclude that overt feminism was a prescription for defeat at the polls and ineffectiveness in a male-dominated Congress. Not until 1936, when the New Deal swept most conservative Republicans from office, did Florence Kahn leave Capitol Hill.

— Mary Teresa Norton (D-N.J.), elected in 1924, was America's first Democratic congresswoman and the first to be elected from the East. She drew her political power from Boss Frank Hague, who ran New Jersey's powerful Democratic machine. She had worked in a variety of jobs in his organization, and after the passage of the 19th Amendment, Hague thought she would be a popular candidate with women in his district. He was right. Norton had never been a suffragette, but she easily won election to Congress, beginning a 26-year career on Capitol Hill. She became the first woman to head a House legislative committee, the first to act as chairman of a state Democratic committee, and the first to be appointed chairman of a subcommittee on resolutions and platforms by the National Democratic Committee.

Norton declined the honor of being nominated for vice president of the United States in 1932, disappointing many women, but during World War II she became a strong advocate for females. In a speech she stated, "Women of the United States have never used their power. Very few of them realize what power they have. If the women of this country organize to their full strength they can do anything they want to. They can make sure their grandsons never have a World War to fight. Women can have their way . . . but they must organize."[13] She introduced the first constitutional amendment to repeal the Volstead Act (Prohibition) and served as the unofficial mayor of Washington, D.C. She is most remembered for her work as chair of the Labor Committee, in which capacity she helped pass the Fair Labor

Standards Act of 1938, establishing a minimum wage and maximum work hours. In 1950, approaching 75 years of age, she declined to run for another term.

‒ Edith Nourse Rogers (R-Mass.), the first congresswoman from New England, used the matrimonial connection to reach Congress and the military connection to remain there for almost 36 years. During World War I, while her husband, Rep. John Jacob Rogers (R-Mass.), was briefly serving in the field artillery, Mrs. Rogers went overseas with a contingent of civilian volunteers. Returning to Washington, she disdained the growing suffrage movement to spend her time assisting in veterans' hospitals, earning her the title "Angel of Walter Reed." In March 1925, her husband died shortly after beginning his seventh term in the House, and Mrs. Rogers, represented as a gallant, grieving widow, easily won the special election to succeed him. By 1947, she became chairman of the Veterans' Affairs Committee, and bills passed under her political stewardship created a nationwide network of veterans' hospitals, the GI Bill of Rights, the Women's Auxiliary Army Corps, and similar women's military services within the navy, coast guard, and marine corps. She became an aggressive Cold Warrior, advocating American withdrawal from the United Nations if "Red China" was admitted to that body. She died two days before the 1960 primary election, in which she was running unopposed for a 19th consecutive term.

⌣ Katherine Langley (R-Ky.) came to Congress in 1926 after her husband, Rep. John Wesley Langley, a veteran Kentucky congressman, was locked up in the federal penitentiary in Atlanta on a felony conviction for illegally transporting and selling whiskey. Mrs. Langley's comfortable election victory was openly attributed to the loyalty of Kentucky mountain folk to her husband, but she was returned to Congress in 1928 by a larger vote than she had received in her first election victory. She quickly began lobbying President Coolidge to grant clemency to her husband. When that clemency was granted, it was with the understanding that he never again seek office. However, in 1929, John Langley chose to disregard that understanding as he announced his intention to regain his former House seat. When Mrs. Langley said she had no intention of stepping down for her husband or anyone else, the result was a publicly aired domestic quarrel that doomed the political futures of both husband and wife. When election day arrived, it was Mrs. Langley's name that appeared on the ballot, but many Republicans stayed away from the polls, ensuring victory for the Democratic candidate.

‒ The politics of Prohibition and the Depression resulted in short terms for most congresswomen during the next decade. One prominent exception was Hattie Caraway (D-Ark.), the 16th woman in Congress and the first woman *elected* to the Senate (Rebecca Felton had been *appointed* in 1922). Her husband, Sen. Thaddeus Caraway, had died during his second term in office, and Arkansas law required a special election to fill the remainder of his term.

Hattie Caraway was initially appointed to her husband's seat, pending the special election, and when local Democratic leaders could not agree on a male candidate, Mrs. Caraway was nominated. In the one-party politics of the deep South, nomination meant election, and thus, without making a single appearance as a candidate, Mrs. Caraway won a seat in the Senate.

The press made clear that her election was nothing more than a gracious act by Arkansas' Democratic leaders. When she was given the same desk that the first woman senator, Rebecca Felton, had briefly used years earlier, she commented, "I guess they wanted as few of them contaminated as possible."[14] Her time in the Senate chamber was spent quietly reading or knitting. She cast her Senate votes strictly on the basis of how her husband would have voted. At the time of her nomination for the special election she had agreed not to be a subsequent candidate, but as the general election approached, she changed her mind, shocking the many male candidates, including the governor who had extracted her promise to retire.

Hattie Caraway had only one Capitol Hill ally, the controversial, populist Louisiana senator Huey Long. Caraway's early campaign platform bore some resemblance to Long's policies of tax reform and redistribution of the wealth, and one week before the primaries, Huey Long announced that he would tour Arkansas on behalf of Mrs. Caraway. She had suddenly became a "serious" candidate. Long's campaign convoy consisted of a black limousine, two sound trucks, and four vans for transporting campaign posters and literature. These, along with a host of energetic young campaigners, brought a circus atmosphere to traditionally staid Arkansas politics. Hattie Caraway had never addressed a public gathering, yet on the platform with Huey Long she spoke before 39 crowds in counties across Arkansas. In an amazing turnabout, she swept to victory at the polls, winning almost as many votes as the combined total of the six men running against her.

Being the first woman elected to the Senate by popular vote did not change her commitment to follow her husband's legislative legacy: farm relief, flood control, and opposition to special-interest lobbies. She also supported the entire range of New Deal reforms. In 1938, she won another six-year term to the Senate, this time without help from Huey Long, who had been assassinated in 1935. In 1943, she became cosponsor of the proposed Equal Rights Amendment, because she felt there was too much prejudice against women in politics.

In practice, because she continued to pursue her deceased husband's agenda, she was not taken seriously on Capitol Hill, or in Arkansas. She ran a distant fourth in her 1944 bid for a third term.

NEW DEAL WOMEN

During FDR's unprecedented 13 years in the White House, 23 women, 16 of them Democrats, joined Congress. Surprisingly, most of the Democrats were defeated after a single term. The longest incumbency for a New Deal Democrat belonged to Caroline O'Day (D-N.Y.), who in 1934 defeated a Republican woman for a congressional seat in New York. O'Day fully endorsed FDR's policies, but her ultimate victory at the polls may have turned on Eleanor Roosevelt's personal appearance on her behalf. O'Day's political background featured early involvement with the suffrage movement, including efforts alongside Jeannette Rankin to obtain the vote for New York women. Before and after her election to Congress, she, like Rankin, was a tireless worker for peace, serving as vice-chairman of the Women's International League for Peace and Freedom. She retained her seat in Congress for four consecutive terms and had the unique experience of defeating Republican women in all four elections. As was the case with Rankin, her pacifism was an unreliable political platform, and her political career effectively ended with the Japanese attack on Pearl Harbor.

It was the fading popularity of FDR's policies in the late 1930s that brought Republican women with staying power to Capitol Hill. In 1938, the GOP put up its most isolationist, anti–New Deal congressional candidate, Jessie Sumner (R-Ill.). Her Illinois constituency shared her views, and sent her to four terms in the House, but her colleagues in Congress regarded her views as extreme. She advocated appeasement with Hitler, demanded that D-Day be postponed, and denounced the United Nations, casting 1 of only 15 votes against United States membership. Still, had she not decided in 1946 to return to her Illinois law practice and banking interests, she might have continued her tenure in Congress.

In October 1939, when Rep. Chester Bolton (R-Ohio) died while in office, local Republican leaders were reluctant to consider his wife Frances as a candidate to succeed him. Reminded that the wealthy Mrs. Bolton's $125,000 donation had assured that the Republican National Convention would be held in Cleveland in 1936, the party gave her its support. She said, "I had worked so closely with my husband that when I was asked to run for election to fill his unexpired term, I did not hesitate to do so, certain that I could fulfil that year more nearly as he would have done than anyone else." In the special election in February 1939, she defeated her Democratic challenger by an almost 2-to-1 margin. Yet just nine months later, after Mrs. Bolton had completed the term of her late husband, the local Republican leadership did its best to discourage her from running in the regular election. In part because of the opposition, she decided to run, explaining, "The men so much wanted to get me out that I determined they would have to put up with me."[15]

Bolton was a champion of equal rights, and did not believe in distinguishing between the sexes on the basis of their duties, opportunities, or privileges, including their military obligations. She advocated that women be included in the military draft, saying, "I am afraid that gallantry is sadly out of date, and as a woman I find it rather stupid. We can easily guard against any threat to marriage and the home. . . . Women's place includes the saving of that home."[16]

In 1952, as she campaigned for a seventh term, her 36-year-old son, Oliver, was also running in Ohio's 11th District. Both won, and became the only mother-son team ever to serve concurrently in Congress. The "Dean of Congresswomen" title soon passed to her from Edith Nourse Rogers, and she became the ranking minority member on the Foreign Affairs Committee and chairman of Ohio's Republican delegation. During the legislative debates on civil rights in the 1960s, she sought to cover women under the federal ban against discrimination. She had always claimed that women, particularly congresswomen, had to work twice as hard as men for their accomplishments. "The Lord, after creating the world, put a man in charge of it," she said. "He messed everything up, so the Lord turned everything over to a woman, and He gave her everything He had given man, plus two more things; pain, so she would understand what creation is, and laughter, so that she could stand that and man."[17]

Bolton was 83 years old when she began her 15th and final campaign for Congress in 1968. Due to a shift in population and some gerrymandering, her district had become overwhelmingly Democratic, and she lost a hard-fought race that sent her into retirement.

Margaret Chase Smith was the first Republican female senator, the first woman to win election to both houses of Congress, and the first to be elected to the Senate without having been appointed to fill a vacancy. After Rep. Clyde Smith (R-Maine) died of a heart attack in April 1940, his widow, Margaret Chase Smith (R-Maine), became a candidate in the special June election to fill the unexpired term. During her campaign, she called on a wide network of supporters, mostly women, with whom she had worked as a member of her husband's staff. She won both the special election and the September general election by sizable margins, beginning a 32-year career in Congress that included lengthy terms in both the House *and* Senate. From the beginning, Smith showed a strong commitment to military strength, and in 1940, unlike most Republicans in the House, she voted for selective service, the arming of American merchant ships, and lend-lease. After Pearl Harbor she introduced legislation creating the women's naval service called the WAVES.

On labor issues Smith was more liberal, voting with the Democrats against an antistrike bill and supporting broader Social Security coverage and higher federal salaries. In response to Republican critics who opposed her centrist views, she said the American people wanted neither a "Big Business" Republican Party nor a "Labor" Democratic Party. Her constituents in Maine supported her position and seemed prepared to return her to the House indefinitely, but in 1947 she announced her candidacy for the Senate seat of retiring Wallace White. Party leaders and political experts said she was stepping out of her class. To win a Senate seat, they claimed, required a political machine, heavy campaign funding, business support, and connections with powerful people. She had none of these.

Party leaders suggested that she run for the governorship instead of the Senate, but she took on the GOP hierarchy, facing three well-known and well-financed men in the senatorial primary. On Friday, February 13, 1948, while campaigning in frigid Bangor, Maine, she slipped and fractured her arm. She went to a hospital where her broken arm was set, and by morning she was back on the campaign trail. At noon she addressed a group of men's clubs in Rockland, 60 miles away, and that night she attended another meeting 90 miles down the coast. The voters regarded her misfortunes on that day as symbolic of her courage, and her campaign quickly gathered steam.

During the campaign, critics within her own party called her a New Dealer and even a communist. Nonetheless, women voted in record numbers in the June 1948 Republican primary, helping Smith to win more votes than the combined total of her three opponents. In the September general election she won 70 percent of the total vote, overwhelming her Democratic opponent.

Margaret Chase Smith's finest hour occurred early in her first Senate term when she stood, virtually alone, in public opposition to the excesses of Sen. Joe McCarthy (R-Wisc.). McCarthy had been bullying and smearing political figures and private citizens with such success that most senior members of Congress were unwilling to confront him, but on July 1, 1950, Smith rose to speak against him in the Senate. She said Congress had been "debased to the level of a forum of hate and character assassination sheltered by the shield of congressional immunity. . . . I speak as a Republican. I speak as a woman. I speak as a United States senator. I don't want to see the Republican Party ride to a political victory on the four horsemen of calumny—fear, ignorance, bigotry and smear." Though she never mentioned his name, it was clear to the scowling McCarthy and the rest of the assembled senators that "McCarthyism" was finally being confronted.[18]

It took several years before Congress finally showed the will to "censure" McCarthy, but Smith's speech was the beginning of the end of his politics of intimidation.

Meanwhile, Margaret Chase Smith continued to receive accolades from the press and solid voter support. Her 1960 election campaign marked the first time that two women had competed for a Senate seat. Richard Nixon, opposing John F. Kennedy in the presidential race, visited Maine on Smith's behalf and said, only half in jest, that among Maine voters he was hoping to hang on to Margaret's skirts. Indeed, she not only defeated her opponent, but received 15,000 more Maine votes for the Senate than Nixon received for the presidency.

During President Truman's administration, Smith had been asked by a reporter, "I know you don't want to be President, Senator Smith, but suppose you woke up one morning and found yourself in the White House, what would you do?" Smith responded soberly, "Well, I'd go straight to Mrs. Truman and apologize, and then I'd go home."[19] In 1964, the idea of Margaret Chase Smith in the White House was taken much more seriously. Her pride and assertiveness had its highest political expression in January 1964, when she announced her candidacy for the presidency of the United States. She was nominated at the Republican National Convention in San Francisco, and the number of convention delegates voting for her was second only to the number received by the party's eventual nominee, Sen. Barry Goldwater.

In her book, *Declaration of Conscience*, Smith expressed concern that her advocacy of women in the military might lead the public to regard her as "a feminist concentrating on legislation for women." She wrote, "[I]f there is any one thing I have attempted to avoid it is being a feminist. I definitely resent being called a feminist."[20] Still, she always fought against any restrictions on the aspirations of women.

During the Cold War, Margaret Chase Smith's hawkish attitudes appealed to a broad national constituency and helped to establish her international reputation. Former Soviet leader Nikita Khruschev once called her "the devil in the disguise of a woman." She gradually became the leading spokesperson for the opposition to the Kennedy administration, and her authority was largely associated with her aggressive military stance. But Smith's independence often led her to stray from party orthodoxy. In 1970 she criticized the attempts of the Nixon administration to repress dissent. She also opposed the administration's proposal for a supersonic transport plane, a new antiballistic missile system, and the nominations of Clement Haynsworth and G. Harrold Carswell to the Supreme Court. In 1972, the 74-year-old Smith was defeated at the polls in her attempt for a fifth term in the Senate. At the time of her retirement, she was the ranking Republican on the Senate Armed Services Committee, the number three Republican on the Appropriations Committee, and the second-ranking Republican on the Aeronautical and Space Committee. After leaving office, she lectured widely and wrote for newspapers and magazines. She died on May 29, 1995, at the age of 97.

Clare Booth Luce (R-Conn.) was one of the most influential political women in American history. As a 19-year-old she joined the National Woman's Party, enlisting new converts and gaining publicity for the women's movement. After a six-year marriage to multimillionaire George Tuttle Brokaw, she joined the staff of *Vanity Fair* magazine and became executive secretary to a new political party, the National Party. She worked with people like Donald Freeman (managing editor of *Vanity Fair*) and James Forrestal (subsequently the nation's first secretary of defense) to draft the new party's platform, which was designed to wrest the nation from the economic policies of both the Republicans and the Democrats. However, her visit to the 1932 Democratic National Convention, intended to lure dissidents into the National Party, resulted in her conversion to the New Deal of Franklin Roosevelt. She became a friend of presidential adviser Bernard Baruch, joining the select group of FDR intimates and facetiously calling herself "the lowly kitchen maid of the New Deal cabinet." Eventually, however, she rejected the New Deal's inclination toward a planned economy, and threw her support to the Republican opposition.

After her marriage to Henry Robinson Luce, the wealthy founder and publisher of *Time, Life,* and *Fortune,* she became the most prominent feminine supporter of Wendell Willkie, the Republican businessman who challenged FDR in 1940. Her speech before 22,000 people at a Willkie rally in Madison Square Garden established Clare Booth Luce as a national political figure whose influence would endure long after Willkie had departed the scene.

At Connecticut's 1942 Republican state convention, she won nomination to represent the 4th Congressional District by an 84-to-2 vote. In her campaign for the House seat she attacked Roosevelt's domestic policies and his conduct of the war, and Willkie returned her past favors by speaking on her behalf. On election day she won by a comfortable margin.

Oregon's influential *Salem Capital Journal* wrote: "In Representative Clare Boothe Luce of Connecticut the Republicans have found their ablest campaign orator next to Wendell Willkie, and she is perhaps more subtle than the latter, a better master of satired invective and phrase-coiner—using the rapier rather than the broadsword." In her first speech as a congresswoman, she attacked Vice President Henry Wallace's "global thinking" as "globaloney," a term that was quickly picked up by the nation's newspapers. Her second speech characterized Roosevelt's policies as "dazzle-dust" thrown into the people's eyes. Her record in the 78th Congress included proposals for a European alliance (later achieved through the creation of NATO), independence for India, racial equality in the armed services, and a condemnation of the Daughters of the American Revolution for preventing black singer Marian Anderson from performing in Constitution Hall. Despite her intense political activity and accomplishments, the press could not resist publicizing the fact that a public-opinion poll on "America's most beautiful pair of legs" found Clare Boothe Luce second only to Marlene Dietrich. Luce characterized such publicity as "New Deal propaganda designed to distract attention from the end of me that is really functioning."[21]

In her bitter 1944 reelection campaign, Luce won by a slim margin against a female challenger, Margaret Connors. Connors had the strong backing of FDR and prominent members of his administration, but Luce disparaged them as carpetbaggers. She blamed Pearl Harbor on FDR, and took a virulently anticommunist stance that proved to be a precursor to America's Cold War policies. Her postwar legislative initiatives included bills to support jobs for veterans, to eliminate job discrimination against minorities, and to establish civilian control over atomic energy.

In 1946, at the height of her political power, Clare Booth Luce announced that she would not seek reelection to the House. Many felt that a Senate seat would have been hers for the asking, but she chose instead to return to writing and lecturing, exercising considerable political power through the media and behind the scenes. In 1952 she made more than a 100 speeches on behalf of presidential candidate Dwight D. Eisenhower, and after his election she was appointed as ambassador to Italy. In subsequent years she cochaired Citizens for Goldwater during Barry Goldwater's run for the presidency, and she strongly backed Richard Nixon's campaigns.

Helen Gahagan Douglas (D-Calif.) was called "the Democrat's answer to Clare Boothe Luce." Like Luce, she was glamorous and intellectual, and her life was full of drama and achievement. She was named one of the "12 smartest women in the world" by the editors of the *Book of Knowledge* and one of the 20 women who exert the greatest influence on American life in a poll by *Pageant Magazine*. Like Luce, she had switched her party affiliation, but in the opposite direction. She was a convert from Republicanism, an advocate of social change, and an aggressive opponent of fascism.

As a ten-year-old child, Douglas decided to become a great actress, and years later she left college for the stage, against her parents' wishes. She soon appeared in a series of Broadway hits, and then briefly left the stage to study voice in preparation for operatic roles. In 1937, during a concert tour of Europe, she recognized the growing Nazi threat to that continent and the world. Back home, she was shocked at the pitiable plight of the migrant farmers streaming to California from the Depression-racked Dust Bowl. She attributed her concern for social justice to her grandmother, whose family had operated an "underground railroad" for runaway slaves before the Civil War, and who had scandalized Troy, Ohio, in 1870 by demanding that women be allowed to use the public library.

The international threat of fascism and the domestic spectre of the Depression led Douglas to politics. She later recalled, "I didn't decide I wanted to get into public affairs. . . . The current of the times . . . carried me."[22] In 1939, President Roosevelt appointed Douglas to the National Advisory Committee of the WPA, and her work with other New Deal agencies led to a friendship with Eleanor Roosevelt and frequent visits to the White House. Douglas made over 150 speeches in support of the Roosevelt-Wallace ticket in 1940 and she was a delegate to the Democratic National Convention in Chicago. In 1942, her work in support of pro-Roosevelt congressional candidates in California picked up four House seats, despite heavy Democratic losses elsewhere in the country.

In 1944, with the retirement of Rep. Thomas Ford, Douglas became the choice of California Democratic leaders to run for his seat. During her campaign she received support from such disparate groups as Hollywood movie stars, migrant workers, and organized labor, and she won the election by almost 4,000 votes. Once in office she fought successfully for the United Nations and the Marshall Plan, and against a bill that would have given control of atomic energy to the military. On October 4, 1945, Douglas delivered a major speech entitled "The Atomic Age," in which she argued that a policy of atomic secrecy would not only be futile, but would provide a false sense of security. "[O]ur faith in the future," she warned, "cannot be built upon the sands of isolationism, or on the false security of any secret weapon. It must be built upon the rock of international good faith, upon the brotherhood of man."

Douglas coauthored the McMahon-Douglas Bill, placing atomic patents under civilian control, and the Federation of Atomic Scientists (FAS) called that bill the most important piece of legislation ever passed by Congress. William A. Higinbotham, head of the FAS, thanked her for her "outstanding contribution," noting that few others had been "so keenly aware of the crisis which faces us and the world. None has been more courageous in assuming public responsibility."[23]

Helen Douglas wrote and introduced the first legislation to protect the rights of citizens appearing before congressional committees, such as the House Un-American Activities Committee (HUAC). Because of her support for liberal causes, she became the target of Cold Warriors and social conservatives. The Daughters of the American Revolution called her a "nigger lover" because she championed black soldiers during World War II.

After three terms in the House, Douglas chose to run for the Senate seat held by Democrat Sheridan Downey, who withdrew from the race before the Democratic primary. In the general election she faced Rep. Richard Milhous Nixon, who accused her of being "soft on communism" because of her vote against funding HUAC, on which he served. Nixon continued this theme in his campaign, frequently quoting her out of context. For example, in one of her speeches, Douglas had emphasized that communism had no place in American society, and Americans should therefore not allow the "irrational fear of communism" to blind us to our real problems. In his speeches, Nixon misrepresented her views by saying only that Helen Douglas considered the fear of communism to be irrational. The Nixon campaign directed personal harassment and threats against Douglas and her campaign workers and organized a phone bank of "anonymous" callers who would simply say, "I think you should know Helen Douglas is a Communist," and then hang up. One study indicated that these volunteers made approximately 500,000 such calls. This broad campaign of what came to be known as "red smear" tactics swept Nixon to a surprise victory, propelling him to national prominence and ending Helen Douglas's political career.

She returned to the theater, starring in the Broadway production of *First Lady* (1952), *Family Reunion* (1954), and *One Plus One* (1956). In 1963 she published a book, *The Eleanor Roosevelt We Remember*, and continued to travel and lecture on the failure of American policies to serve the national interests.

WOMEN'S RIGHTS

Between the end of World War II and 1960, 27 women were added to Congress. The postwar reordering of national priorities led most of them to a domestic focus and issue-oriented politics. Women's rights was one such issue, and Katharine St. George (R-N.Y.) was the first postwar woman to make sexual discrimination a major part of her agenda. In 1946, she defeated three male opponents to join the 80th Congress, and for the next 18 years she maintained control of her district, running against seven different men and one woman. She was a conservative Republican, wife of a wealthy businessman, and her campaign called for making every union member a "capitalist." She became the first woman ever named to the powerful Rules Committee, which controls the passage of bills to the House floor, and she worked hard to abolish all forms of discrimination against women. She was initially chosen to lead the fight for the Equal Rights Amendment (ERA) in Congress, and years later she recalled her motivation in stewarding the ERA. "I always felt—and I spoke about it many, many times—women were discriminated against in employment. They were not paid the same thing for the same job. . . . That's what I objected to. I didn't want anything more than that. I think women are quite capable of holding their own *if* they are given the *opportunity*."[24]

St. George eventually passed the congressional leadership on the ERA to Rep. Martha Griffiths (D-Mich.), who brought the battle to its culmination. Griffiths had won election to the House in 1954, and over the next 20 years she won reelection ten times, by pluralities as high as 80 percent. She was quickly appointed to terms on the committees of Banking and Currency and Government Operations, and she became the first woman in history to join the presitigious Ways and Means Committee, which drafts the nation's legislation. She spent 13 years on Ways and Means, working with 24 men who were described as "holdovers from the brass spittoon era, . . . still loftily imbued with the theory [that] woman's place is in the kitchen."

On Ways and Means she was in a strategic position to influence laws affecting women. Among the legislation bearing her name or influence were a bill prohibiting sex discrimination in consumer credit, a bill allowing divorced mothers and motherless children to receive certain Social Security benefits, and the protection of women under the Civil Rights Act of 1964. She said, "The drafters of the [Social Security] law really believed, in my opinion, that a woman's work was worth nothing. . . ." As for Title VII of the Civil Rights Act, she said, "I made up my mind that all women were going to take one giant step forward, so I prepared an amendment that added 'sex' to the bill." [25]

But Griffiths's monumental achievement was the passage of the Equal Rights Amendment (ERA), which would guarantee that "equality of rights under the law shall not be denied or abridged by the United States or by any State on account of sex." Because the ERA has not yet been ratified by the states, Rep. Griffiths's hopes have not been fully satisfied, but she has accomplished all that is within the power of Capitol Hill. She sponsored the ERA and twice shepherded it through the House. Like the Woman Suffrage Amendment, which sat in congressional committees for over 40 years before its passage, the ERA was introduced in every Congress for nearly half a century before being passed and sent to the states for ratification in 1972. Rep. Griffiths's initial battle was to acquire the requisite 218 signatures to remove the bill from the Judiciary Committee and for this she had to call in a number of political IOUs. Louisiana's Hale Boggs, then Democratic whip, was opposed to the ERA, but he agreed to sign as Number 200, if Griffiths could get the first 199 signatures. "You may be sure," Griffiths recalls, "that when I had Number 199 signed up, I rushed to his office, and Hale Boggs became Number 200."[26] Soon thereafter, Griffiths acquired the necessary 218 signatures, well within the required 40-day period.

Rep. Griffiths's hard work paid off in the House, which passed the ERA by 315 to 15 in 1970, but the Senate allowed it to die when the chamber adjourned that year without acting on the measure. Griffiths began anew the following year, winning the House by 354 to 23 and, this time, winning Senate approval by 84 to 8. In 1974, Griffiths declined to be a candidate for renomination to an 11th term, but even in retirement she continued to lobby state legislatures for ratification and enactment of the ERA.

Rep. Edith Green (D-Ore.) was another congresswoman who worked throughout her career to end discrimination against women. Her only close race for Congress was her first one, in 1954, when she won with a plurality of just 9,608. In 1956 she won reelection by over 65,000 votes, and in her 20-year career it was not unusual for her to win majorities of 70 percent. Her legislative focus was the nation's education, and she soon became the second-ranking member of the Education and Labor Committee and the chairman of its Special Subcommittee of Education. Her considerable influence in Congress might have been even greater had she not turned down three opportunities to run for the Senate. Because fellow Oregonian Wayne Morse was chairman of the Senate Subcommittee on Education, she knew she would not be appointed to that committee. She was also deterred by the high cost of campaigning and her unwillingness to raise money with "strings attached."

Among Green's legislative initiatives to combat sexual discrimination was the Equal Pay Act of 1963. She complained incredulously that it took eight years to persuade Congress that a woman doing identical work with a man ought to be paid the same salary. She was also responsible for a key provision in the 1972 Omnibus Higher Education Act, which prohibited institutions accepting federal financial support from discriminating on the basis of sex. Her office staff was mostly female, and she was keenly aware of discrimination against female staff and members. She believed women on Capitol Hill were victims of psychological warfare systematically waged by men who considered politics their exlusive domain.

In the 1970s, Green's mistrust of big government alienated her from the Democratic Party. Although virtually assured of continued reelection, she decided not to run in 1974, and in 1976 was a cochair of Democrats for Gerald Ford.

Rep. Coya Knutson's (D-Minn.) tribulations on Capitol Hill are a good example of the kind of sexual stereotyping that even the ERA won't prevent. When Knutson came to Capitol Hill after an upset victory over six-term incumbent Rep. Harold Hagen (D-Minn.), she left behind her alcoholic husband, Andy, to look after their little hotel in Oklee, Minnesota, where Coya had cooked the food and waited on tables. Her domestic problems back home did not intrude on her political fortunes in Washington until near the end of her second term in Congress, when her husband wrote a letter describing himself as lonely and neglected. "[O]ur home life has deteriorated to the extent that it is practically nonexistent," he wrote. "I want to have the happy home that we enjoyed for many years prior to her election." Andy then issued a press release accusing his wife of improprieties with her young administrative assistant, and threatened a $200,000 alienation of affections suit. The press seized upon these hot allegations, with *Life* magazine featuring several of Coya's constituents saying "a woman's place is in the home," not in Congress.

Andy later recanted many of his charges, but his letter of apology was too late to save Coya's career. In 1958, she was the only Democratic incumbent in the country to lose her seat to a Republican. A month after her defeat, Coya and Andy appeared before the special House Elections Subcommittee, which was investigating the charge that she had been the victim of a political conspiracy. Andy testified that "friends" had persuaded him to write the notorious letter and that Coya's rivals in the Democratic primary were among those friends. He further testified that his press release had been drafted by the campaign manager for the Republican candidate who subsequently defeated Coya. The subcommittee unanimously agreed that "the exploitation of the family life of Mrs. Knutson was a contributing cause to her defeat," but it could find no direct evidence of a plot.[27]

Many in the press decried the double standard applied to Coya Knutson. Columnist Doris Fleeson said Rep. Knutson was marked as fair game simply because she was a woman. "The lesson," wrote Fleeson, "is that, as a practical matter, women are held to a far higher standard of accountability in politics than men are."[28]

Coya Knutson ran for Congress one more time in 1960, but was defeated. Her accomplishments during her two terms in Congress were overshadowed by the slander and intrigue that brought her down. She had been the first woman to serve on the Agriculture Committee, where she worked to help farmers and save the family farm. Among her legislative accomplishments were a bill creating a federal student-loan fund and a bill funding cystic fibrosis research. The latter resulted in the perfection of a serum to counteract the disease.

PUBLIC HEALTH, CONSUMER AFFAIRS, AND THE ENVIRONMENT

The health and safety of the American public and the protection of our environment became the focus of intense debate in the 1960s, and women in Congress often framed that debate. When Iris Blitch won a surprise victory in the 1954 Georgia Democratic primary and followed with an easy victory in the general election, she brought to Congress the hard line of the conservative South on social issues. But as a member of the Public Works Committee, she expressed strong views about environmental protection. She conducted a one-woman crusade to save Georgia's Okefenokee Swamp from drought and fire, resulting in safeguards such as low-sill dams on connecting waterways. She also sponsored an amendment to the Water Protection and Flood Prevention Act that gave small property owners federal financial assistance for water-conservation projects. Medical problems forced her retirement from Congress in 1963, but she maintained her interest in the life and environment of her district.

Rep. Leonor K. Sullivan (D-Mo.) was a congressional pioneer in consumer affairs. She had worked as a member of her husband's staff during his years in Congress, and after his death in 1951, she served for one year on the staff of another congressman before deciding to run in the Democratic primary for her husband's seat. She was ignored by the Democratic leadership, and her party-endorsed opponent condescendingly claimed, "I know Lee Sullivan, and if you'll elect me I'll give her the top position in my office."[29] Mrs. Sullivan's campaign emphasized her experience as a congressional staffer and the need for a woman's voice on Capitol Hill. She defeated seven men in the primary election and gained twice as many votes as her GOP opponent in the general election. She was reelected 11 subsequent times, usually without opposition in the primaries. In her general elections she won by margins ranging from 65 percent to 79 percent.

Years before men like Ralph Nader made a name for themselves, Leonor Sullivan was known as the nation's consumer advocate. She became chairman of the Banking and Currency Subcommittee on Consumer Affairs, where she crusaded against harmful food additives, deceptive advertising, contaminated meat, and hidden finance charges. In 1961 she introduced a

41-page omnibus bill covering *all* foods, drugs, and cosmetics. When warned that powerful commercial interests would be united against her, she said there were thousands of women who needed protection from food and cosmetics containing carcinogens. Her comprehensive bill was never passed, though she reintroduced it in every Congress. Nonetheless, a series of consumer-protection laws eventually passed by Congress accomplished, in piece-meal fashion, much of what she had advocated. The legacy of her legislative initiatives included the banning of carcinogens in food; compulsory federal inspection of poultry; pretesting of all chemical additives used in food; stricter control over the manufacture and sale of pep pills and barbiturates; and the Fair Credit Reporting Act, protecting consumers against false or malicious information from credit bureaus.

Sullivan was also responsible for the passage of food-stamp legislation. When operational funds for its implementation were withheld, Sullivan wrote to President-elect John F. Kennedy, reminding him that as a senator he had supported her plan. Indeed, under the Kennedy and Johnson administrations, her food-stamp plan was implemented and expanded nationwide.

Sullivan retired from Congress in 1976 and was succeeded by Richard A. Gephardt, the current Democratic leader.

Rep. Florence Dwyer (R-N.J.) began her lengthy congressional career in 1956 with an upset victory in her New Jersey district. Once in Congress, she worked for consumer protection and equal pay for women. She was an important influence in the creation of the Environmental Protection Agency and the Department of Transportation. For 16 years, Florence Dwyer concentrated on issues of consumer protection, women's equality, and procedural reform in the House of Representatives. She was a chief sponsor of the act creating the Consumer Protection Agency and another act that sought to eliminate discriminatory lending practices.

Though she fought against sexual discrimination in government, Dwyer did not make gender an issue in her own campaigns, claiming, "I have never campaigned as a woman; if I can't take on any man running against me, I don't deserve to represent the women and the men of this county." She said a congresswoman must "look like a girl, act like a lady, think like a man, speak on any given subject with authority, and most of all work like a dog."[30]

In the 1960s, Dwyer led a group of Republicans who sought to enlarge the Committee on Rules and thereby diminish the influence of southern Democrats and conservative Republicans who had blocked social and civil-rights legislation. Dwyer never faced a serious challenge to her seat, but in 1972, shortly before her 70th birthday, she announced that she would not be a candidate for reelection.

Rep. Julia Butler Hansen (D-Wash.) spent almost 22 years in the Washington state legislature before entering the U.S. House of Representatives

in 1960. She brought with her to Congress her life-long concern about
ecology. Throughout her seven terms in the House, she struggled with those
corporate interests that had irresponsibly exploited and profited from
public land for generations. While serving on the Interior and Insular
Affairs Committee she worked to protect and maintain our national forests,
parks, and other federal land, and to improve the quality of life of Native
Americans. She also urged the use of antipollution devices to control
industrial wastes. In February 1974, Rep. Hansen announced that she
would not run for an eighth term and she resigned on the last day of the
year.

Maurine Neuberger (D-Ore.) was another in that long line of women
who followed a deceased husband into Congress, but many, including her
husband, had always thought she was the better politician of the two. Just
two days before the March 11 filing deadline in 1960, Oregon senator Dick
Neuberger's sudden death forced a quick and difficult decision on his
widow, Maurine. Confident that her husband would have wanted her to
run for his Senate seat, she acquired several thousand signatures on peti-
tions to put her name on the ballot. She had served in the state legislature
for two terms, and she had proved her ability as a campaigner. A few years
earlier, in a magazine article titled, "My Wife Put Me in the Senate," her
husband had written, "Wherever I went campaigning with Maurine, I did
much better at the polls than where I stumped the countryside alone. My
crowds were larger; their enthusiasm seemed more genuine. . . . To some
degree I suspect that her performance proves the old maxim that 'the best
politics is no politics.' If anyone ever violated every standard political rule,
that person is my wife." Her husband concluded, "There is not a doubt in
my mind she could win any office the state has to offer, including the one
which I occupy."[31]

After his death, Maurine Neuberger proved her husband correct, winning the May 1960 primary over four male challengers and defeating the
Republican in November by almost 70,000 votes. While serving on the
Commerce Committee, she cosponsored a truth-in-packaging bill that required commercial products, such as cosmetics, to list ingredients on their
labels. She initiated a nationwide antismoking campaign, enraging the
tobacco industry and anticipating the subsequent surgeon general's report
linking smoking to lung cancer. As a result, Congress gave the Federal Trade
Commission the authority to regulate cigarette advertising and labeling.

Early in her political career, Maurine Neuberger wrote: "In politics, the
woman's mission is to champion the particular aspirations of her sex, but
to expect no quarter in doing so. She is in for a rude awakening if she enters
public life thinking her male associates will defer to her opinions merely
because she is a woman. . . . Without sacrificing any of the qualities which
make women attractive in men's eyes, she must stand by her convictions
and uphold the interests of her sex. And when questions involving eco-

nomic dominance and political power are at issue, not only will she have no preference because of her sex, but she probably will be considered fair game for that reason."[32]

Near the end of her six-year term in Congress, Sen. Neuberger began to appear politically vulnerable. When she remarried in 1964, the press faulted her for retaining the name Neuberger, claiming that she was trading on the name of her late husband. She was also criticized for lending the Oregon flag to participants in the Selma civil-rights march. In November 1965 she announced that she would not seek reelection, saying that she was able to voluntarily leave Congress after 25 years in public service because politics was not her whole life. Indeed, she subsequently served as chairman of the Citizens' Advisory Council on the Status of Women, and she lectured on government at Radcliffe College. She also remained active in the American Cancer Society's campaign against smoking.

A LOSING CAUSE?

In 1962, 40 years after Jeannette Rankin's brief but inspiring intrusion on the men's club called Congress, the total number of women serving in the Senate and House combined was just 20. The good news was that these 20 women represented an all-time high for Congress. The bad news was that each successive election in the 1960s was to further *reduce* this embarrassing "high point." By 1969, there were only 11 women in all of Congress. "There are three times as many whooping cranes as congresswomen," complained one female member of the House. "While many things are being done to protect the rare, long-legged bird, nobody seems concerned about our being an endangered species."[33]

Why had the agonizingly slow but steady gains of women in Congress seemingly been reversed? Some noted the small number of women running for office. Others cited apathy, or even hostility, among women voters toward women candidates. But an impersonal variable called the "opportunity factor" may have largely determined the success or failure of women candidates, then as now. The names, reputations, and seniority of powerful incumbents scared off would-be female candidates and defeated the upstart women who dared to challenge them. The positive side of this phenomenon was the reelection of most female incumbents, by substantial margins. And, of course, among the six new women elected between 1963 and 1969 there were some noteworthy names.

Charlotte Reid (R-Ill.) won election to the House in 1962, following the death of her husband, the Republican nominee. She had been a professional singer who, during the late 1930s, had entertained millions of radio listeners as the featured vocalist on Don McNeill's popular show, "Breakfast Club." As a freshman in Congress, Reid's prominence was made clear when she received 19 invitations to campaign for Republican candidates. She won reelection in 1964, stressing her conservative views on economy in government, reduced federal power, and "peace with honor" in Vietnam. In 1965, she became the first member of Congress to be cleared by the Defense Department to visit the Vietnam war zone. Before leaving for Saigon she spoke reassuringly of the "loyal Americans" who supported the war. When she returned from her four-day tour of Vietnam, she telephoned the families of servicemen she had met, assuring them that their sons and husbands felt it was their duty to secure a victory over the Communists. Such reassurances were soon proved hollow.

In Congress, Reid sponsored a resolution to rescind the Supreme Court ruling outlawing public school prayer, and though she never considered herself a feminist, she gave a speech in favor of the Equal Rights Amendment. She was appointed to the Interior and Insular Affairs Committee because the chairman thought a woman's view was needed. "Men respect our opinions and ideas," she stated. "Small as our numbers are, we create a needed balance in the complicated business of adapting our governmental processes to the requirements of a changing society."[34]

In October 1971, Charlotte Reid departed Congress to accept appointment to the Federal Communications Commission, becoming only the second woman to serve on the seven-member panel.

Patsy Mink (D-Hawaii) stood in stark contrast to the conservative, hawkish Charlotte Reid. Mink had been active in Democratic Party politics in Hawaii and the drive for Hawaiian statehood. In 1959, the year Hawaii was admitted to the Union, she lost her first bid for the U.S. House of Representatives, but in 1964 she became the first woman from Hawaii to enter Congress.

Mink joined Congress as the Johnson administration was escalating American military involvement in Vietnam. As President Nixon subsequently increased that involvement, she committed herself to the antiwar movement. She advocated amnesty for men who had evaded the draft and executive clemency for military personnel discharged for protesting the war. Her position against the war cost her votes in her district, which housed military installations vital to the local economy, and her GOP opponent in 1968 questioned her patriotism. Mink responded by characterizing Nixon's pursuit of the war as a racist policy that approved the slaughter of Asians by Asians.

In addition to her antiwar activities, Mink had aggressively fought for equal opportunity for women. When President Nixon nominated George Harold Carswell for the Supreme Court, she was the first opposition witness and the only member of Congress to oppose him on the grounds that he would constitute an affront to American women. She cited Carswell's refusal, while serving as an appeals court judge, to consider a woman's complaint that she was denied a job because she had young children. Not only did her testimony eventually result in the rejection of the

Carswell nomination, but it caused the Justice Department to ask the Supreme Court to consider the appeal of the mother rebuffed by Carswell.

Mink frequently found herself confronted with sexual discrimination within her own party. When she urged the Democratic Party's Committee on National Priorities to consider more women for leadership and policy-making positions, she was confronted by another committee member, Edgar Berman, Vice President Hubert Humphrey's personal physician. Dr. Berman claimed that women's executive and leadership potential was limited by the hormonal influences of the menstrual cycle and menopause. "Suppose," he asked, "that we had a menopausal woman President who had to make the decision of the Bay of Pigs or the Russian *contretemps* with Cuba at the time?" He warned that such a woman would be "subject to the curious mental aberrations of that age group."

Needless to say, Mink was outraged. In a subsequent letter, she demanded Berman's ouster from the committee, calling him a "bigot" who had demonstrated "the basest sort of prejudice against women." She said, "His use of the menstrual cycle and menopause to ridicule women and to caricature all women as neurotic and emotionally unbalanced was as indefensible and as astonishing as those who still believe, let alone dare state, that the Negro is physiologically inferior." The widely publicized incident resulted in Dr. Berman's resignation from the committee, but in departing he claimed to have been crucified on the cross of women's liberation. He characterized Mink's anger as "a typical example of an ordinarily controlled woman under the raging hormonal imbalance of the periodical lunar cycle."[35]

Undeterred by such caricatures of her sex, Mink continued to address sexual discrimination on Capitol Hill and elsewhere. Among the approximately 500 allegations of sexual discrimination received by her office each year was one pointing out that U.S. Post Office regulations barred women from positions as postal inspectors. Mink protested to the postmaster general, and within two weeks women's applications for such positions were being accepted.

In 1971, Rep. Mink accepted an invitation from Oregon Democrats to enter their 1972 presidential primary, the only primary in which all Democratic presidential contenders were represented. She gave the following reasons for running: "Without a woman contending for the Presidency, the concept of *absolute equality* will continue to be placed on the backburner as warmed-over lip service. My candidacy offers a real and tangible alternative, based—if any one word can be singled out—on humanism." She won only 2 percent of the vote in the Presidential primary, but the experience convinced her that there would be a woman vice president sooner than might otherwise have been the case.[36]

As a member of the Education and Labor Committee, she drafted legislation barring sexual discrimination in schools and institutions of higher learning. The bill she sponsored in 1972 called for curricular changes that would avoid the narrow role-conditioning of girls that was common in public schools. She also used her personal influence to persuade textbook publishers to produce texts portraying women in nontraditional roles.

In 1976, Mink decided to seek the Democratic nomination for the Senate rather than run for a seventh term in the House. She lost that contest to Spark Matsunaga (D), but was subsequently appointed by President Jimmy Carter as an assistant secretary of state in 1977 and 1978. She then served three years as president of the Americans for Democratic Action, and returned to Hawaii where she served on the Honolulu City Council from 1983 to 1987. In 1990, she returned to Capitol Hill, winning a special election to fill the seat left vacant by Daniel Akaka, making her only the third woman to return to the House after being defeated. She also won the subsequent general election to join the 102nd Congress, and was reelected in 1992 and 1994.

Margaret Heckler (R-Mass.) was another young congresswoman who rose to prominence from among the tiny group of women elected during the 1960s. In 1966, it took a lot of courage for her to challenge former GOP House Speaker Joseph Martin, who had represented the 10th District in Massachusetts for 42 years. The GOP leadership, including Massachusetts Governor John Volpe, refused to support the 34-year-old Heckler against the 81-year-old Martin. In her campaign, Heckler was careful to avoid direct reference to Martin's advanced age and decreased vigor, instead emphasizing her own youth, energy, and desire to serve. Such characteristics stood in contrast to Martin, who had missed 50 percent of the meetings in the preceeding session of Congress.

Heckler won the primary by 3,200 votes, but then faced an even more difficult battle against her Democratic opponent, popular attorney Patrick Harrington, Jr. Stumping for the Harrington campaign were national stars, including Vice President Hubert Humphrey and the Kennedy brothers, Robert and Edward. Making things worse, Heckler's district contained 81,000 registered Democrats, 90,000 independents, and just 68,000 Republicans. Still, with strong support from women voters, Heckler won 51.1 percent of the vote to become the first Massachusetts woman to be elected to Congress on her own merits. In 1967 she went to Capitol Hill owing no political favors.

Once in Congress, Heckler became a spokeperson for the Equal Rights Amendment and other women's issues, and she often found herself doing battle with Republicans, even Republican presidents. She publicly condemned President Nixon's veto of a bill providing day-care facilities for children of working mothers. Heckler urged the House to override Nixon's veto, and then confronted the White House directly in an attempt to change the GOP platform plank. Eventually, the Platform Committee endorsed a plank for child care, and Heckler received a promise from Education

Committee chairman John Rhodes to cosponsor a day-care bill with her in the 93rd Congress. In 1978, Heckler cosponsored a resolution extending the deadline for ratification of the ERA, and in 1980 she unsuccessfully urged the conservative wing of the Republican Party to endorse the ERA.

Heckler was also a leader of congressional reform. She advocated discarding the seniority system in favor of electing committee chairmen by secret ballots cast by senior members of each committee. She proposed that House terms be lengthened from two years to four years, and that the franking privilege be suspended during the month prior to an election.

In 1982, redistricting removed Heckler's district from the electoral map, forcing her to run against the 4th District's Rep. Barney Frank (D). After losing a hard-fought campaign to Frank, she was appointed as secretary for the Department of Health and Human Services by President Reagan. In December 1985, Reagan named her as ambassador to Ireland.

The 1968 congressional elections brought only one woman to Capitol Hill, and she happened to be the first black woman ever elected to Congress. Shirley Chisholm (D-N.Y.) had earlier served in the New York State Assembly, where she gained a reputation as a maverick and a troublemaker. She decided to run for Congress after a black welfare mother came to her house with a campaign donation consisting of $9.62 in change. Chisholm defeated the Democratic organization candidate in the primary, but she was faced with a difficult battle against James Farmer, founder of CORE, in the general election. Her absence from the campaign for three weeks due to major surgery made things even worse.

Farmer denigrated her candidacy on the basis of gender, referring to her as a "mere" woman. His campaign claimed that women had been in control of black communities for too long, and he warned that this matriarchal dominance needed to be balanced by "a strong male image" and a man's voice in Washington. Chisholm had always said that she suffered worse discrimination as a woman than as a black, and in her campaign she sought out women leaders of social groups, civic clubs, and the PTA to counteract Farmer's focus on her gender. She won the election with 67 percent of the vote, and after her victory she said that if others tried to use her sex against her, she would once more turn the tables on them.

Chisholm later reflected: "When I decided to run for Congress, I knew I would encounter both antiblack and antifeminist sentiments. What surprised me was the much greater virulence of the sex discrimination. . . . I was constantly bombarded by both men and women exclaiming that I should return to teaching, a woman's vocation, and leave politics to the men."[37]

Chisholm's first speech in Congress challenged the Nixon administration and reinforced her image as an independent and uncontrollable woman. She told the House that our failure to fight and defeat the great enemies within our nation, poverty and racism, exposed American leaders as hypocrites in the eyes of the world when they talked of making people free.

Chisholm advocated abortion reform, and critics in her district accused her of emphasizing "women's lib" over "black lib" and spending too much time in Washington. Among her legislative legacy were two bills that bore her name. One was a comprehensive bill establishing day-care facilities, and the other established a memorial to Mary McLeod Bethune, founder and first president of Bethune-Cookman College. President Nixon vetoed the day-care bill, and the other bill was tabled. She cosponsored legislation to create a Martin Luther King holiday, to abolish the House Un-American Activities Committee, to establish a Department of Consumer Affairs, and measures concerning tax reform.

She was reelected in 1970 by 82 percent.

In 1971, speaking primarily for women and all disgruntled minorities, Chisholm declared her candidacy for the presidency and ran in a series of Democratic primaries. In her campaign she attacked President Nixon, accusing him of the "big lie" in general and of particular deception concerning the Vietnam War. Of herself she said, "I am the only fresh new voice. I am the only unique candidate, and the only dark horse, literally and figuratively." Initially, the black male members of Congress ignored Chisholm's candidacy. Characterizing their behavior as male chauvinism, she declared, "Black male politicians were no different from white male politicians. . . . This 'woman thing' is so deep. I've found it out in this campaign if I never knew it before."[38]

At the 1972 Democratic Convention she received 151.95 delegate votes for the presidency, and it might have been more. Walter Fauntroy, the congressional delegate from the District of Columbia, prevented her from entering the primary in the nation's capitol because he planned to enter as a favorite-son candidate. He promised to deliver the votes to Chisholm on the second ballot, but instead delivered them to the eventual Democratic nominee, Sen. George McGovern. For the next decade, Chisholm supported congressional programs to increase the minimum wage, with particular emphasis on domestic workers who were disproportionately female. She advocated increased funding for Medicare and Medicaid and served as honorary president of the National Association for the Repeal of Abortion Laws, a vanguard feminist organization.

In 1982, Chisholm announced that she would not be a candidate for reelection to an eighth term to the House. She had earlier expressed doubts about her ability to continue serving productively in an increasingly conservative Congress. "I did not come to Congress to behave myself and stay away from explosive issues so I can keep coming back. Under the circumstances, it's hard for me to imagine I will stay here long. There isn't much that I can do inside Congress in a legislative way. . . . I can work to be a major force for change outside the House, even if I cannot be one within it."[39]

A SECOND WIND

After the severe electoral dry spell in the 1960s, women's fortunes on Capitol Hill took a turn for the better that has maintained its momentum to this day. From 1970 through 1988, 52 nonincumbent women won election to Congress, more than had joined Congress in the previous 30 years. Many of these women have since departed Congress but have left a legacy that has indelibly established the agenda of the modern political woman.

Among the more charismatic women politicians of the 1970s was Bella Abzug (D-N.Y.), who rode the anti–Vietnam War movement to Capitol Hill in 1971. She was a founder of Women Strike for Peace, and organized New York Democrats to oppose President Johnson's Vietnam policies. In the process, she decided to run for Congress. She campaigned throughout the entire length of West Side Manhattan, wearing a variety of wide-brimmed hats that came to be her calling card. She won the primary against incumbent Leonard Farbstein and won 52 percent of the vote in the general election against Barry Farber, the candidate endorsed by both the Republican and Liberal parties.

Abzug's radical credentials were immediately on display. On the opening day of the 92nd Congress, after her official swearing in, she took a second oath on the Capitol steps. This "people's oath" was administered by her colleague and friend from Brooklyn, Shirley Chisholm, while a crowd of her constituents cheered. On that first day in Congress she also introduced her first bill, a measure requiring the withdrawal of American troops from Vietnam within six months. At the first meeting of the Government Operations Committee, to which Abzug had been assigned, she angered the chairman by opposing his proposal to exclude the press. When the chairman's proposal was enforced, she defied it by giving reporters a subsequent detailed description of the proceedings.

During her three terms in the House, she served her district by forcing the roll-back of New York rent increases, preventing the destruction of housing, providing greater police protection, and initiating a mobile food-stamp registration service. But she was most proud of the sex-discrimination amendment she added to the Public Works Acceleration Act and her work to help found the National Women's Political Caucus.

In 1972, the Republican-controlled New York State Legislature imposed a reapportionment plan that abolished Abzug's district, splitting it among three congressmen. She made a difficult choice to run in the primary against Rep. Bill Fitts Ryan, a liberal Democrat like herself. Bella told the voters that they had the opportunity to choose the "greater of two goods," but, in a bitter race, Ryan won by almost 2 to 1. Eight weeks before the general election, Ryan died, and the Democratic County Committee nominated Abzug to replace him. She ran against Ryan's widow, Priscilla, and won another bitter and personal race.

In 1976, Abzug left the House to run for New York's open Senate seat, but lost to Daniel Patrick Moynihan (D). She was also unsuccessful in a bid for the New York City mayoral nomination in 1977 and failed in two subsequent attempts to return to Congress.

Elizabeth Holtzman (D-N.Y.) was only 31 years of age in 1972 when she defeated 84-year-old incumbent Emanuel Celler, to become the youngest woman ever elected to Congress. Celler had represented Brooklyn's 16th District for 50 years, but Holtzman criticised him in her primary campaign for his poor attendance record, his opposition to cost of living increases for Social Security, and his support for the Vietnam War. She also pointed out that Celler had blocked the Equal Rights Amendment in the Judiciary Committee. Her startling upset victory over Celler caused *Time* to call her "Liz the Lion Killer," and she went on to easily defeat her Republican opponent in the general election.

This former civil-rights worker and assistant to New York Mayor John Lindsey spent less than $50,000 on her eight-month campaign, only a fraction of what her opponent spent. During her first term she gained a seat on the Judiciary Committee and participated in the hearings on the im- peachment of President Nixon. As a member of that committee she contrib- uted to the formulation of new rules of evidence in federal courts and revised immigration laws. In 1978 she helped win an extension of the ratification deadline for the ERA, and helped secure a prohibition on sex discrimination in federal programs. She also filed suit to halt American military action in Cambodia, leading a district court to rule the Cambodian invasion unconstitutional, though the court of appeals later reversed that decision.

In 1980, Holtzman chose to run for the Senate, and lost to Republican Alfonse D'Amato. She subsequently served as New York city comptroller, and in 1992 failed in a second try for the U.S. Senate, losing a bitter four-way New York primary race that included Geraldine Ferraro. Many believe that the awkwardness of that nasty campaign has ended Holtzman's political career. (See chapter 2).

Barbara Jordan (D-Tex.) was the first woman elected to the Texas senate and the first woman to serve there as president pro tem. The creation of a new 18th District in Texas eliminated her state Senate seat, leading her to Capitol Hill. In 1972, Jordan and Andrew Young became the first blacks elected to Congress from the South since 1898. In just three terms in the House, she earned national recognition as a defender of constitutional rights and champion of the needs of the underprivileged. She served on the Judiciary Committee, and, like Elizabeth Holtzman, participated in the Nixon impeachment hearings. She defended her vote for all five articles of impeachment as an act of constitutional responsibility, but expressed both relief and disappointment when President Nixon resigned before due process could take place. "The country definitely got short-changed," she wrote. "I don't know whether it would have been the long, agonizing nightmare which Gerald Ford said it would be for the country if we had gone through the trial. But I do know that it would have been done with finality."[40] She offered civil-rights amendments to various legislation and joined seven other members of the Judiciary Committee in opposition to Gerald Ford's nomination as vice president based on his weak civil-rights record.

In 1976, Jordan became the first woman as well as the first black to serve as keynote speaker at a Democratic National Convention, and she made a spectacular impression. The next day, a front-page story in the *Washington Star* proclaimed: "She was there to bear witness to a dream they yearn to claim, and the congregation responded with an 'Amen' chorus that would do credit to the Second Coming. The Democratic Party, which has been at this convention business for 144 years, never had an opening night like this before, and never will again." The *Star* concluded: "Barbara Jordan, descended at least spiritually from the slaves of yesteryear, was the unquestioned master of the 1976 Democratic National Convention."[41]

Jordan declined to run for reelection to the House in 1978, and has taught at the Lyndon B. Johnson School of Public Affairs at the University of Texas since then, and is currently chair of the U.S. Commission on Immigration Reform.

Geraldine Ferraro (D-N.Y.) had a relatively brief congressional career, but her accomplishments provided a new foundation for women's participation in American politics. Ferraro began her political life in 1974 as an assistant district attorney for Queens County, New York, prosecuting cases involving rape, child and spouse abuse, and domestic violence. She became head of a new unit, the Special Victim's Bureau, within which she became a forceful advocate for abused children. In 1978, Ferraro ran successfully for the U.S. House of Representatives, representing New York's 9th District.

While in the House, Ferraro focused much of her attention on the issues of wage, pension, and retirement equity for women and was a cosponsor of the 1981 Economic Equity Act. As a member of the Select Committee on Aging, she championed the cause of elderly women. Her pro-choice position on abortion conflicted with the views of the Catholic Church and many of her constituents, but she had popular support in her district on broader social and foreign-policy issues.

Ferraro quickly established a close working relationship with House Speaker Tip O'Neil (D-Mass.) and other members of the House leadership. During the 97th Congress she became secretary of the House Democratic Caucus, entitling her to a seat on the influential House Steering and Policy Committee. In the 98th Congress, Ferraro accepted appointment to the important Budget Committee.

On July 19, 1984, Ferraro became the first woman in American history to run for vice president of the United States on the ticket of a major political party. She accepted Walter Mondale's offer to join his presidential ticket, and was nominated by acclimation at the Democratic National Convention. In her subsequent campaign, Ferraro spoke before many women's groups and visited college and university campuses in an attempt to win the vote of younger Americans. The Mondale-Ferraro ticket lost to a Reagan-Bush landslide, but Ferraro had set a precedent and a standard that women throughout the nation would aspire to.

In 1992, Ferraro lost the New York primary for the U.S. Senate to state attorney general Robert Abrams in a four-way race that included former representative Elizabeth Holtzman. The bitterness of that failed campaign seems to have exiled both Ferraro and Holtzman from politics. Ferraro is currently a managing partner in a powerful New York law firm.

Rep. Lynn Martin (R-Ill.) spent a decade in the House of Representatives, during which she established herself as a Republican Party leader on and off Capitol Hill. During her first term in the House, she was appointed to the influential Budget Committee, where she served for three congresses. She soon came to function regularly as a floor manager for the Republicans. In 1984 and 1986 she was elected vice chair of the Republican Conference in the House, marking the first time a woman had held a position in the party's congressional hierarchy. Martin had been an early supporter and confidant of George Bush. When the Reagan-Bush team was preparing for the 1984 TV debates with the Mondale-Ferraro challengers, it was Congresswoman Martin who effectively trained Vice President Bush on how to handle a tough woman like Ferraro and at the 1984 Republican convention in Dallas she seconded Bush's nomination. In 1990 Martin left the House for an unsuccessful run at the Senate seat of Democrat Paul Simon. President Bush quickly appointed her as his secretary of labor, despite the fact that she differed with him on an important issue: abortion. Martin saw no problem in being an abortion-rights advocate in an administration that opposed abortion. "I can't imagine that the only people who should work for a president are those who sycophantically agree on everything," she said. "It would be the most boring Cabinet in the world and it would be of no use to the President."[42]

Martin had established her political independence as a congresswoman when she defied the Reagan administration by voting for economic sanctions against South Africa, and she later defied the Bush administration by voting to override the president's veto of family-leave legislation. But Martin was proud of the vision she brought to the Labor Department, and after the defeat of the Bush administration in 1992, she reflected: "My regrets are that the vision of the department didn't get integrated into the overall economic policy. Had that been the case, we might not be leaving now. . . . When you lose touch with how most Americans spend their days, you lose elections."[43]

After leaving government service, Martin remained active as a political analyst and television commentator, with particular emphasis on women's issues. She has been a powerful voice for workplace reform and pay equity for women on Capitol Hill, characterizing the current system on the Hill as "the Divine Right of Kings."

In 1993, Martin, a lifelong baseball fan, was on the short list of candidates for the job of commissioner of major league baseball. She did not get the job, in part because of the attitude expressed by one ball club owner, who said the owners would never allow a woman to tell them what to do. But during that same year, Martin indicated her interest in another job that would be available in 1996: the presidency of the United States. Republican pollster Linda Duvall commented: "It seems to me from the reception she is receiving that there is serious interest and people like her style of candidacy."[44] In February 1995, Martin was in New Hampshire battling five Republican men for the presidency, though she subsequently withdrew from the race.

THE EMERGING FEMALE LEADERSHIP

All but one of the women currently aspiring to congressional leadership have come from the group of women elected during the 1970s and 1980s. As the result of the 1994 Republican takeover of Congress, the Democratic women are being forced to adjust to the loss of majority power, but the legacy of their leadership experience remains.

Rep. Pat Schroeder (D-Colo.) first joined the House in 1972. Running on an anti–Vietnam War platform, she won a come-from-behind victory over her conservative Republican opponent. She left a promising career as counsel for Planned Parenthood of Colorado and as hearing officer with the state personnel board in order to pursue "honesty in government," something she said women could do best. In Congress, she quickly won a seat on the Armed Services Committee and became chair of its Subcommittee on Military Installations. She also has served on the Committee on the Judiciary and the Select Committee on Children, Youth, and Families. Among her legislative achievements have been the Family and Medical Leave Act and funding for day-care centers, and she helped to found the Congressional Caucus for Women's Issues, on which she served as cochair until 1994.

"When I think about my own goals in Congress," wrote Schroeder in her 1989 book, "I realize that I have always tried to create opportunities by correcting inequalities. . . . [I]f we get rid of the inequalities that hinder women, we strengthen the family at the same time. For me, building a family policy has meant finding a way to bridge a gap between public policy and the reality of women's lives."[45]

In addition to her continuing support for women's causes, Schroeder has remained an advocate of arms control, responsible defense spending, and improved benefits and working conditions for military personnel. She is currently the longest-serving woman in Congress, and one of the few women to chair a full committee, the Select Committee on Children, Youth, and Families. She was in line to chair the Post Office and Civil Service Committee until the Republicans gained control of Congress in 1994.

Sen. Barbara Ann Mikulski (D-Md.) has risen from the working-class neighborhoods of Baltimore to become one of the most influential women on Capitol Hill. She served on the Baltimore City Council for five years prior to her successful run for the U.S. House of Representatives in 1976, in which she won 75 percent of the vote. She ran uncontested in 1978, and in the next three elections she won 76 percent, 74 percent, and 89 percent of the vote respectively. Mikulski risked her safe House seat to run for the Senate in 1986, winning 61 percent of the vote to become the first woman ever elected to the Senate on her own, rather than succeeding a husband or father. "Some poor guy didn't have to die for me to get the job," she said.

The *Baltimore Magazine* wrote, "When you think of Barbara Mikulski you think of Chicago Boss Richard Daley on estrogen. . . . Known for angry jeremiads on women's rights, she quickly became a burr under the saddle of a Congress drunk on testosterone. But she also championed the forgotten ethnic middle class and the powerless poor, and her constituents adored her."

In 1989, Mikulski was the only woman chairing a powerful Appropriations subcommittee. She was described as "the most powerful woman in the U.S. Congress" because she controlled the subcommittee's $89 *billion* discretionary fund.[46]

During her House career, Mikulski served on the Committee on Merchant Marine and Fisheries, the Committee on Interstate and Foreign Commerce, and the Committee on Energy and Commerce. As a senator in the Republican-controlled 104th Congress, Mikulski sits on the Appropriations Committee, the Labor and Human Resources Committee, the Select Committee on Ethics, and seven subcommittees. In all of her committee work she has supported legislation dealing with women's rights, child care, national health insurance, and consumer protection. These assignments have allowed her to exercise important legislative influence on social issues.

Mikulski has been an outspoken feminist, active in the Congressional Caucus on Women's Issues. During the 1980s, she was a consistent critic of the Reagan and Bush administrations, accusing Reagan of waging war against the underdogs, women, children, and old people. In the 104th Congress, Mikulski serves as the secretary of the Democratic Conference, the third-ranking position in her party's leadership.

Rep. Barbara Kennelly (D-Conn.) came to the U.S. House of Representatives through a special election in 1982, following the death of Rep.

William R. Cotter. As the daughter of John Bailey, long-time Democratic leader in Connecticut and chairman of the Democratic National Committee in the 1960s, she grew up surrounded by the world of politics. Her late husband, James J. Kennelly, was a speaker of the Connecticut House. "Her father must have injected her and her mother must have fed her political milk," said Geraldine Ferraro, "because she really has this sixth sense. Obviously, she's going to be concerned about how something affects her district, but she looks at the bigger picture."[47]

Before coming to Congress, Kennelly had been a member of the Hartford City Council and had served as secretary of state for Connecticut. In her second term in the House she gained a seat on the powerful Ways and Means Committee, and in the 99th Congress she was appointed to the Democratic Steering and Policy Committee. These assignments gave her early legislative influence, allowing her to pursue issues of housing credits, welfare reform, tax reform, and child support. In 1983 Kennelly introduced the Child Support Enforcement Amendment, requiring states to establish a system for mandatory wage withholding if child-support payments were 30 days overdue. The following year the Senate and House unanimously passed the bill. In the 100th Congress she became the first woman to serve on the Permanent Select Committee on Intelligence. In 1991 she was appointed as a chief deputy whip in the Democratic leadership, and in 1994 she won the vice chairmanship of the Democratic Caucus.

Rep. Louise M. Slaughter (D-N.Y.) first came to Congress in 1986, when she was the only woman to defeat a sitting candidate. A native of Kentucky, she has spent most of her adult life in upstate New York, but her melifluous accent still seems inappropriate for a New Yorker. "I was viewed by my male colleagues as a remarkable piece of work that I could, with this accent, be elected in a Republican district in upstate New York," says Slaughter. "I never would have thought it possible, living in a district that has never elected Democrats, much less women with southern accents."

Jane Danowitz, executive director of the Women's Campaign Fund, says of Slaughter: "She's sort of a combination of Southern charm and back-room politics, a Southern belle with a cigar in her mouth." Lobbyist Amy Millman says, "She's a Kentucky woman in a New York politician's clothing. Therefore, she has all the skills to be a success in this town."[48]

Slaughter entered politics in the early 1970s, serving in the county legislature and state assembly as a proponent of local environmental issues. Between 1979 and 1982 she directed then Lieutenant Governor Mario Cuomo's regional office. In her second term in the U.S. Congress she was appointed by the house speaker to the powerful Rules Committee to fill the vacancy left by the death of committee chairman Claude Pepper. That appointment alone marked her as a rising star among Democrats. In late 1994, Slaughter and Barbara Kennelly ran for the position of vice chairman of the Democratic Caucus, with Kennelly edging out Slaughter in the vote,

93 to 90. The two women never felt that they were running "against" each other.

"I didn't look at it that way," says Slaughter. "It wasn't because Barbara was running that I ran. There was an open slot there and we both ran for it. I think she's wonderful. We've had a very close relationship and we still do."

With the Republican takeover of Congress in 1994, Slaughter was removed from the Rules Committee and stepped down after four years as chair of the Democratic Caucus's subcommittee on Reorganization, Study, and Review (OSR), which drafts caucus and House rules. During her service in Congress, she wrote legislation to ensure that homeless children could attend public school and fought to protect senior citizens from insurance fraud and to fund preventive-medicine programs for the elderly.

Slaughter is a leading legislator on "women's issues," particularly in the area of women's health, but she has a practical view of how to get the job done. "This is the third legislature I've served in, and in each of them the bills that have affected women most have almost always been voted in by men, because there were never enough women to pass them. So I came here [Congress] with the knowledge and assumption that there were a lot of men here who had the same sense that I did on women's rights and women's health, particularly on areas of choice. But those are still issues that we *live*, and it's critical that we take the lead on them."[49]

Rep. Rosa De Lauro (D-Conn.) is the only woman in the Democratic congressional leadership who entered Congress in the 1990s. She won election in 1990 by just over 7,000 votes in a rough campaign that saw her called "Walter Mondale in drag" by the Republican state chairman. De Lauro came to Congress with loads of behind-the-scenes political experience. She had served as chief of staff for Sen. Chris Dodd (D-Conn.) for seven years, managing his election campaigns in 1980 and 1986. Before that she had been a community organizer in the War on Poverty program, the first female executive assistant to the mayor of New Haven, and his campaign manager in 1978. Just before running for Congress she served as executive director for EMILY's List, the important political action committee that raises money for pro-choice female candidates. She is the daughter of two Democratic New Haven aldermen, and her mother, at 80 years of age, continues as the longest-serving alderman in city history.

During her first term in Congress she served on the Public Works and Transportation, Government Operations, and Aging Committees, focusing almost exclusively on district-oriented activities. Throughout her congressional career she has called herself "an advocate for the working middle-class," and among her primary concerns are jobs, taxes, and health care. In 1991 she successfully persuaded Democratic leaders to drop their plan for a nickle-a-gallon gasoline tax increase and proposed middle-class tax relief through increased personal exemptions. In the 104th Congress she serves on the National Security Committee and two subcommittees, and has joined the Democratic leadership as a deputy whip.

Rep. Cardiss Collins (D-Ill.) is the longest serving black woman in the history of Congress. After gaining her political experience as a committee-woman in the Democratic Party organization in Chicago, she joined Congress in 1973 through a special election to fill the vacancy left by the death of her husband. During her long service in the House, she has chaired the subcommittees on Manpower and Housing and on Government Activities and Transportation. Her longest committee service has been with the Committee on Government Operations, which, during the Republican-controlled 104th Congress, was renamed the Government Reform and Oversight Committee. Today, Collins is the ranking Democrat on that committee.

Collins has served as chair of the Congressional Black Caucus and is the first black and the first woman to serve as a Democratic whip-at-large. She was one of the cosponsors of the Clinton administration's health-care reform bill, but she has not been afraid to oppose the Democratic power structure. In 1994, she was a vocal opponent of the North American Free Trade Agreement (NAFTA), despite aggressive political arm-twisting by President Clinton and the Chicago political machine. Citing the loss of Chicago jobs to Mexico, Collins said the voters in her largely black district were more concerned about urban decay and layoffs than global economics.

In 1993, Collins was involved in a bitter and highly publicized exchange on the House floor with Rep. Henry Hyde (R-Ill.). During debate on the Hyde Amendment, which prohibits Medicaid funding for abortions (see chapter 3), Hyde said abortions for poor women were used to "refine the breed," and told Collins she ought to learn what was really happening in her district. Collins leapt to her feet, characterized Hyde's remarks as offensive and inappropriate, and demanded that Hyde apologize and that his remarks be stricken from the record. Both of her demands were met. "I don't think Mr. Hyde is in a position to know about what poor women need," said Collins later. "He's never been a poor woman, and on top of that, I don't imagine he knows many poor women."[50]

In November 1994, despite the Republican landslide nationally, Collins won 80 percent of the vote in her district to begin her 11th full term in Congress. In 1995, however, she announced that she would retire at the end of that term.

The Republican takeover of both houses of Congress in the 104th Congress allowed Republican women to bask in the majority power owned by Democrats for 40 years. A number of Republican women with years of leadership experience within their party had been overlooked by the media. Now they were seen in a new light: the limelight.

Two of these emerging Republican stars, Sen. Olympia Snowe (R-Maine) and Sen. Nancy Kassebaum (R-Kans.), first came to Capitol Hill in the elections of 1978. Kassebaum and Snowe have much in common, including a background as congressional staffers. Snowe's election to the House in

1978 filled a seat previously held by Rep. William Cohen (R), for whom she had worked as a staff assistant. During her eight terms in the House, Snowe served on the Committee on Government Operations, the Committee on Small Business, and the Committee on Foreign Affairs, and was the ranking Republican on the Subcommittee on International Operations. She was a cofounder of the '92 Group of Republicans seeking a majority in the House, a goal which was quickly realized in the Republican landslide of 1994. Throughout her career in Congress, Snowe has been the most prominent Republican spokesperson on women's issues, serving as cochair of the Congressional Caucus on Women's Issues. She has voted to support abortion rights and fetal-tissue research, positions which have not endeared her to the dominant right wing of her party.

Snowe continued to represent Maine's 2nd District, the largest district east of the Mississippi, until 1994, when she won the Senate seat of retiring Democratic Majority Leader George Mitchell (D). During her successful run for the Senate, Snowe campaigned on the promise: "I will worry about America's place in the world, but I will also worry about Maine's place in America." In 1995, her first year in the Senate, she was assigned to the powerful Budget Committee as well as the committees on Small Business, Foreign Relations, and Commerce. In addition, she assumed chairmanship of the Subcommittee on International Operations. Snowe is married to retiring two-term governor John McKernan Jr., her former House colleague.

Nancy Kassebaum had little experience in public life before her election to the Senate in 1978. At that time she became only the fourth woman ever to win election to a full six-year term, and the first woman elected to fill a full Senate term without having been a widow of a member of Congress. Her only previous elected position was on the school board of a small Kansas town, but as the daughter of former Republican senator and presidential candidate Alf Landon, she was well known in Kansas. Kassebaum had served as a staff assistant for Kansas Sen. James Pearson in 1975, and when Pearson retired in 1978, she ran for his seat, winning the GOP nomination against another woman, Jan Meyers, who would herself later join the House. In the general election Kassebaum was attacked by critics within her own party for her pro-choice position on abortion. The media, on the other hand, focused on her mild manner and diminutive size, with one commentator calling her a "wounded wren." The press also hounded her to release the tax returns of her estranged husband, leading Kassebaum to complain of a double standard imposed on women running for office. She expressed sympathy with Democrat Geraldine Ferraro's plight under similar circumstances.

Kassebaum nonetheless proved to be an effective campaigner, easily winning the general election in 1978 and reelection in 1984 and 1990. Her politics defy pigeonholing. She is fiscally conservative, though liberal on some social issues. On foreign policy, she sometimes opposed President

Ronald Reagan, refusing to support tyranny in the name of anticommunism. "There is a basic principle here that our party and our nation should take to heart," she advised conservative Republicans. "For too long, we have judged our friends only by their rhetoric on Marxism. If we want to protect our own interests, then we must also protect the basic values on which those interests are founded. In short, we should expect our friends not merely to oppose Communism, but to actively promote democracy within their own borders—for their good and ours."[51]

Kassebaum's most public breach of party discipline came in 1994, when she voted for President Clinton's crime bill. There was actually an effort to strip her of her seniority, but she survived the storm.

Despite her support for the ERA and her pro-choice position, Kassebaum has never received strong support from women's groups, perhaps because she defines women's issues broadly in terms of the general good. She joined the Women's Congressional Caucus during her first term, but has not been active in recent years. Indeed, her doubts about the appropriateness of the many congressional caucuses became common wisdom in 1995, when the new Republican leadership in Congress abolished such groups, including the Women's Caucus.

During her 17 years in the Senate, Kassebaum has served on a host of committees, including the powerful Budget Committee and Foreign Relations Committee. In 1995 she became only the second woman to ever chair a full Senate committee, taking over as head of the Labor and Human Resources Committee, where she has set forth a surprisingly activist conservative agenda, ranging from radical welfare reform to reduction of job-training programs. More than ever before, she seems destined for leadership in the new Republican Congress.

Fellow Kansan Jan Meyers (R) joined Kassebaum in the spotlight previously reserved for Democratic women when the Republican Party took control of the Senate and House in 1994. For the first time ever, two Republican women, both from Kansas, became chairmen of full committees, Kassebaum chairing the Senate Committee on Labor and Human Resources, and Rep. Jan Meyers chairing the House Committee on Small Business. Ironically, Meyers had lost the Republican senatorial primary to Nancy Kassebaum in 1978, but in 1984, when Rep. Larry Winn (R-Kans.) retired, Meyers won the party nomination and the general election for the 3rd District seat in Congress.

Before coming to Congress, Meyers had served in city government and the Kansas state legislature for more than 15 years. After joining Congress, she was chosen by her Republican colleagues to serve as both president and vice president of her class. At the request of House Republican Leader Bob Michel (Ill.), she was also named chairman of the Task Force to Rewrite the Rules of the House Republican Conference. Meyers was reelected in 1986 without opposition from either party, and she has won her four subsequent elections with 74 percent, 60 percent, 61 percent, and, most recently, with 57 percent of the vote.

Meyers has served on the Committee on Science and Technology, the Committee on Foreign Affairs, the Select Committee on Aging, and the Committee on Small Business. She later became vice chair of the Energy and Environment Study Conference, and in 1994, with the Republican takeover of Congress, she became chair of the Committee on Small Business, on which she had been the ranking Republican. Meyers thus became the first Republican woman to chair a House legislative committee since 1954, and the first woman in either party since 1976. She was named a Guardian of Small Business during the 99th, 100th, 101st, and 102nd congresses by the National Federation of Independent Businesses. She received the Spirit of Enterprise Award from the U.S. Chamber of Commerce in 1988, 1989, 1991, 1992, and 1993. No wonder that she was eventually chosen to chair the Small Business Committee.

As to the importance of having a woman head that full committee, Meyers says simply, "I don't know if there's any significance to a woman leading this committee. Women make up 52% of the population. I'm not into quotas, but it's important that they be represented."[52]

Rep. Barbara Vucanovich (R-Nev.) came to Congress in 1982 as the first Nevada woman ever elected to federal office. She represents Nevada's 2nd District, which encompasses the entire state except for the heart of Las Vegas. Although she had never before held elective office, she had long been active in state Republican politics, managing the senatorial and gubernatorial campaigns of politicians like Paul Laxalt. She was appointed to run Sen. Laxalt's northern Nevada office in 1974, a post she held until she herself ran for Congress.

Once in the House, Vucanovich became a respected member of the powerful Appropriations Committee, and in 1994, when the Republicans gained control of Congress, she assumed the chairmanship of the Appropriations Subcommittee on Military Construction. She also joined the Republican leadership as secretary of the Republican Conference, the seventh highest ranking position in the GOP leadership structure, which makes her a sitting member of the Republican Policy and Steering Committee. "This is a good day for Nevada," she said upon joining the leadership. "As a small state we've never had anyone in leadership before. I'm truly honored that my Republican colleagues have placed their trust in me."

Vucanovich's personal battle with breast cancer in 1983 led her to make preventive care and affordable mammograms a legislative priority. She is also the primary sponsor of the Family Reinforcement Act, which was a prominent part of the Republicans' Contract with America, initiated in the 104th Congress. "I look forward to being involved with the shaping of our party's legislative agenda," said Vucanovich. "I've also talked with Mr. Gingrich about taking a more active role in reaching out to women for support of our party's policies. I think we can make great strides for the women of our country."[53]

Rep. Susan Molinari (R-N.Y.) followed her father to Congress. She won a special election in 1990 to fill the vacancy left in New York's 14th District when her father, Guy Molinari, resigned to become Staten Island borough president. She had previously worked in Washington for the Republican Governor's Association and the Republican National Committee. She returned to New York City where she won election to the city council in 1985, serving there as minority leader until she joined Congress in 1990.

During her campaign for Congress, Molinari spoke out on environmental issues like water pollution, ocean dumping, and the protection of wetlands. Since joining the House, she has taken positions that are "tough-on-crime," fiscally conservative, and pro-defense. She has also been an executive member of the Congressional Women's Caucus, and a leader in the fight for the rights of crime victims, particularly women and children. In 1994 she was named chair of the New York City Commission on the Status of Women, and during the summer of 1994 she organized hearings to combat domestic violence. "The Surgeon General estimates that 30 percent of all emergency visits by women result from domestic violence," said Molinari. "That is unacceptable. Wife or girlfriend beating is unacceptable. We have to develop a zero tolerance when it comes to this type of behavior."[54]

In July 1994, Molinari married Rep. Bill Paxon (R-N.Y.), forming the first husband-wife team in the Congressional leadership. "There's no romance involved in setting a [wedding] date when you're both in Congress," said Molinari. "We chose a recess." Appropriately, Paxon had proposed to Molinari on the House floor.[55]

In 1994, when the GOP took control of Congress, Molinari was elected vice chairwoman of the Republican Conference, making her the youngest member of the Republican leadership. She serves on the important Budget Committee and chairs the Transportation and Infrastructure Subcommittee on Railroads.

NOTES

1. Hope Chamberlain, *A Minority of Members: Women in the U.S. Congress*, New York: Praeger, 1973, p. 6.

2. Hannah Josephson, *Jeannette Rankin: First Lady in Congress*, New York: Bobbs-Merrill Co., 1974, pp. 73, 76.

3. "The Lady from Montana," *The Nation*, May 31, 1917, p. 667.

4. "The Suffragists," *New York Times*, October 27, 1917, p. 16.

5. Josephson, *Jeannette Rankin: First Lady in Congress*, pp. 66, 162.

6. "Miss Rankin, War Opponent in 1917, Hasn't Changed Mind," *Washington Post*, December 9, 1941, p. 4A.

7. Josephson, *Jeannette Rankin: First Lady in Congress*, pp. 66, 162–4.

8. Josephson, *Jeannette Rankin: First Lady in Congress*, p. 182.

9. "Mrs. Catt on the Election," *New York Times*, November 21, 1920, p. 2.

10. "Miss Robertson of Oklahoma," *New York Times*, November 13, 1920, p. 10.

11. *Congressional Record*, 67th Congress, 3rd Session, or *Congressional Record—Senate*, February 26, 1985, pp. 3647–8.

12. Chamberlain, *A Minority of Members: Women in the U.S. Congress*, p. 50.

13. Annabel Paxton, *Women in Congress*, Richmond, Va.: Dietz Press, Inc., 1945, p. 35.

14. Kincaid, Diane, ed., *Silent Hattie Speaks: The Personal Journal of Senator Hattie Caraway*, Westport, Conn.: Greenwood Press, 1979, p. 44.

15. David Loth, *A Long Way Forward*, New York: Longman, Green and Co., 1957, pp. 194, 203.

16. Ibid., p. 252.

17. Chamberlain, *A Minority of Members: Women in the U.S. Congress*, p. 136.

18. Richard Pearson, "Margaret Chase Smith Dies," *Washington Post*, May 30, 1995, p. B6.

19. *Women in Congress*, Joint Committee on Arrangements for the Commemoration of the Bicentenial, Washington, U.S. Government Printing Office, 1976, p. 76.

20. Margaret Chase Smith, *Declaration of Conscience*, edited by William C. Lewis, Jr., New York: Doubleday and Co., 1972, pp. 12–14, 85.

21. Stephen Shadegg, *Clare Boothe Luce: A Biography*, New York: Simon and Schuster, 1970, pp. 76, 174–7.

22. Ingrid Winther Scobie, *Center Stage: Helen Gahagan Douglas, a Life*, New York: Oxford University Press, 1992, p. 123.

23. Ibid., pp. 182, 188.

24. The New York Times Oral History Program, Former Members of Congress Oral History Collection, No. 64, Katharine Price Collier St. George, Sanford, N.C.: Microfilming Corp. of America, 1981.

25. Emily George, *Martha W. Griffiths*, Washington, D.C.: University Press of America, 1982, pp. 83, 111, 149.

26. Chamberlain, *A Minority of Members: Women in the U.S. Congress*, p. 260.

27. "Out of Andy's Inn," *Time*, May 19, 1958, p. 18.

28. Chamberlain, *A Minority of Members: Women in the U.S. Congress*, p. 265.

29. Ibid., p. 237.

30. Marybeth Weston, "Ladies Day on the Hustings," *New York Times Magazine*, October 19, 1958, p. 93.

31. Richard L. Neuberger, "My Wife Put Me in the Senate," *Harpers*, June 1955, pp. 44–45.

32. Maurine Neuberger, "Footnotes on Politics by a Lady Legislator," *New York Times Magazine*, May 27, 1951, p. 18.

33. Chamberlain, *A Minority of Members: Women in the U.S. Congress*, p. 301.

34. Ibid., pp. 301, 306–7.

35. "Hormones in the White House," *Time*, August 10, 1970, p. 13.

36. Chamberlain, *A Minority of Members: Women in the U.S. Congress*, p. 313.

37. Salley Columbus, *The Black 100: A Ranking of the Most Influential African-Americans Past and Present*, New York: Citadel Press, 1993, p. 248.

38. Stephan Lesher, "The Short Unhappy Life of Black Presidential Politics, 1972," *New York Times Magazine*, June 25, 1972, p. 12.

39. Shirley Chisholm, *Unbought and Unbossed*, Boston: Houghton Mifflin and Co., 1970, p. 111.

40. Barbara Jordan and Shelby Hearon, *Barbara Jordan: A Self-Portrait*, Garden City, N.Y.: Doubleday and Co., 1979, p. 202.

41. Martha Angle, "Democratic Spark: Barbara Jordan," *Washington Star*, July 13, 1976, p. A1.

42. Charles Trueheart, "Lynn Martin, No Yes Woman," *Washington Post*, August 19, 1992, p. B7.

43. Judy Mann, "Republican Regrets, Regrouping," *Washington Post*, January 22, 1993, p. E3.

44. Judy Mann, "Martin in '96?" *Washington Post*, July 14, 1993, p. E15.

45. Patricia Schroeder, *Champion of the Great American Family*, New York: Random House, 1989, p. 114.

46. Alicia Mundy, "Babs in Boyland," *Baltimore Magazine*, October 1993, pp. 46–49.

47. Todd Purdum, "Choices Painful for Hartford Politician," *New York Times*, July 1, 1994, p. A13.

48. David Finkel, "Women on the Verge of a Power Breakthrough," *Washington Post Magazine*, May 10, 1992, p. 5.

49. Authors' interview with Rep. Louise Slaughter (D-N.Y.), April 12, 1994.

50. Steve Daley, "Snarls and Hisses Mark House Abortion Debate," *Chicago Tribune*, July 1, 1993, p. 1.

51. Nancy Kassebaum, "The Future of the Republican Party" (A speech given to the National Federation of Republican Women, Phoenix, Ariz., September 21, 1985).

52. Authors' interview with Rep. Jan Meyers (R-Kans.), January 6, 1995.

53. Press release by Rep. Barbara Vucanovich (R-Nev.), December 6, 1994.

54. Susan Molinari, "New York Holds Domestic Violence Hearings," *New York Times*, June 29, 1994, p. A22.

55. "Traveling Delegation," *Washington Post*, June 7, 1994, p. B3.

Chapter 2

The Decade of the Woman: An Uncertain Promise

BUILDING THE FOUNDATION

The 1980s was a decade of slow but steady increase in the number of women in Congress. The elections for the 97th through 101st Congresses (1980 through 1988) produced 19 newly elected women. After adjusting those electoral victories against the corresponding losses of incumbent women, there was an average increase of just over two women in Congress per election.

The current decade began with the promise of dramatic improvement in the representation of women in Congress. In 1990, 70 women won major-party nominations to the House, an all-time high. There were eight female candidates for the Senate alone, leading some journalists to predict that 1990 would be the "Year of the Woman." Such hopes, however, were short lived. Only one woman, incumbent Nancy Kassebaum (R-Kans.), was elected to the Senate. Former representative Claudine Schneider (R-R.I.), who lost her 1990 challenge to Sen. Claiborne Pell (D-R.I.), says she was sure that at least half of the eight women running for the Senate in 1990 would be elected. "When I lost, I was disappointed," she says. "When all the other women [except incumbent Kassebaum] lost, I was devastated." Schneider concluded that, for the first time, women's future in Congress seemed "foggy."[1]

Things were slightly better in the House, where 29 of the 70 women who ran for office in 1990 were victorious. But 24 of those 29 were incumbents, only five being newly elected women. When winners were balanced against losers, the 1990 elections brought a net gain of just three women in the entire Congress, only a marginally higher success rate than had been maintained throughout the 1980s. These modest gains led no one to anticipate the spectacular success of women in the 1992 elections.

The elections of 1992 brought more women to Congress than ever before. The number of women in the House nearly doubled, jumping from 29 to 48. In the Senate, women tripled their numbers from two to six. The huge increase prompted analysts to indeed dub 1992 the "Year of the Woman" and led many to believe women would continue their exponential growth on Capitol Hill throughout the decade. Once more, those hopes were quickly shattered when the 1994 elections produced no gains for women in the House and only one additional seat in the Senate—the lowest net increase for women in Congress since 1986. These disappointing results came despite a record number of women running for the House—a total of 112 women won major-party nominations for House office—and the second highest number of women in history, nine, running for the Senate.

Female political analysts were quick to play down the significance of the low congressional gains in 1994. During a conference organized by women's political organizations the day after the elections, Harriett Woods, president of the National Women's Political Caucus, pointed out that while there was a zero net gain for women in the House, 11 *new* women were elected to that chamber, the second highest number in history. Those 11 balanced out the three female retirees and eight incumbent losers. "It was not about women," said Amy Conroy, executive director of the Women's Campaign Fund. "It's about partisan politics and women merely got caught in the fury. The voters did not reject women."

The 1994 elections handed congressional Democrats their biggest defeat in half a century, and gave Republicans control of both the House and Senate for the first time since 1954. Because most congressional women were and are Democrats, they too felt the wrath of the American voter during the 1994 conservative landslide. Seven of the 11 new women elected to the House were Republicans. The lone female addition to the Senate was also a Republican. Female Democrats did not fare well, but compared to Democratic males they seemed relatively fortunate. "Democratic women only lost a net of five House seats," said Ellen Malcolm, the president and founder of EMILY's List—which stands for Early Money Is Like Yeast—an organization that helps raise campaign funds for pro-choice Democratic women. "That's incredible in a year when Democrats overall had much greater losses." The five losses represented a 14 percent cut in the ranks of Democratic women. Democratic men, on the other hand, lost a net of 50 seats, or a 22 percent drop in their numbers.

Even before the election results were tallied, many pundits were predicting that 1994 would be the "Year of the Republican Woman." The 1994 increase in the ranks of GOP women in Congress from 12 to 17 may not have justified such a grand characterization, but it certainly showed that Republican women had captured the momentum.

"The reason more women are involved in politics this time in the Republican Party is we reached out, we made a concentrated effort to get more women involved, and to change the mind set that you too can be the candidate. And we had record numbers come forth to be candidates this time," said Jeanie Austin, cochair of the Republican National Committee.

Though the results became evident in 1994, the efforts by the Republican Party to bring more women into its fold had actually begun several years earlier. President George Bush had asked Austin to launch a national program, "Women Who Win," that would identify and train Republican women to run for elective office and teach them to manage all aspects of a campaign. More than 1,500 women have attended these seminars since the program's inception. In 1994 alone, ten seminars were held in various cities throughout the country.

"Five years ago we started Women Who Win to encourage more Republican women to run for office," Austin said the day after the 1994 elections. "Today we see the results of that effort."

Bonnie Erbe, moderator of the women's talk show, "To the Contrary," said: "I do see a change in the Republican Party, quite frankly, because I covered the now-famous 1992 Houston convention and went to the WISH List breakfast, which is the fund-raising PAC for Republican women, and there was a room full of about 400 very bright, very accomplished, very wealthy Republican women who were furious about what was going on in the Republican party."[2]

In 1994, Republican women ran in record numbers for political office. More than $800,000 was donated to female candidates by the Republican National Committee and the National Republican Congressional Committee. A total of 113 Republican women filed for the House and Senate, just 12 less than the Democrats. In 1992, by comparison, only 90 Republican women had filed for candidacy, compared with 163 Democratic women. Following the 1994 primary balloting, 45 GOP women won their party's nomination to appear on the November ballots.

No incumbent Republican women in Congress were defeated in 1994, while eight Democratic female incumbents were turned out of office. Of those Democratic losers, six were members of the class of 1992—one quarter of those elected in the "Year of the Woman."

What went wrong for the idealistic, ambitious women from the class of 1992? Few political pundits expected female congressional candidates in 1994 to repeat the dramatic successes of two years earlier, but no one was prepared for the significant reverses and the paltry gain of just one seat in all of Congress. In the months preceeding the 1994 elections the National Women's Political Caucus predicted that women would increase their numbers in the House by about three seats and pick up one or two seats in the Senate. "We expect a continuation of the perhaps slow but steady progress of the past 20 years," caucus chair Harriett Woods said two weeks before the 1994 elections.[3] After all, a record number of women were running for office, and over the past 20 years an average of about four women were added to Congress each year.

Regardless of how one calculated the norms of the past, the 1994 elections were a disappointment for women. The day after the elections, the *Washington Post* wrote: "Two years ago, it was the Year of the Woman. This time around, the elections may be known as the Year of the Man, or the Year of the Angry Man." Indeed, the 1994 elections revealed, in mirror image, the largest gender gap since those figures were first reported in 1982. Fifty-four percent of male voters supported Republican candidates, while 54 percent of female voters supported Democratic candidates.

Along with a national political swing to the right, social changes across the country have had a significant impact on women candidates. The 1992 "Year of the Woman" was marked by public disgust with Washington and a strong anti-incumbent movement sparked by the House bank and post office scandals. The Cold War was over, and the emphasis on national defense, which had always worked to the advantage of male candidates, had virtually disappeared. For the first time, the congressional elections focused on stereotypically "women's issues." Health care, education, and, of course, the economy were now the major concerns of the electorate. There was a qualitative change in political style as well. In 1992, both male and female candidates represented themselves as compassionate and caring. The macho sabre-rattling that male politicians used during the Gulf War had been effective in 1990, but it would not sell in 1992. Polls showed that voters wanted change, new faces, new political ideas. High profile events like the Clarence Thomas-Anita Hill hearings and the navy Tailhook scandal brought women's issues to the forefront. Ross Perot's third-party presidential bid highlighted the appeal of "independent" candidates, and women fit the bill precisely. A poll in California before the primaries showed that Democratic voters favored a woman candidate over a male by 5 to 1, and Democratic women favored a woman candidate by 7 to 1.

"In 1992 we had the tremendous publicity of the rejection of women's objections to the Supreme Court nomination [Clarence Thomas]," said Rep. Patsy Mink (D-Hawaii). "It stimulated people's awareness of the few number of women in Congress. It forced more women to run and we had a wonderful issue. In 1994, we didn't have any easy issues. We were talking about health care and crime. In 1992, it was so obvious that voters wanted to give women a chance. If they had any doubt at the polls, they went and voted for a woman."[4]

Ellen Malcolm, president of EMILY's List, agrees. "In 1992, Democratic women were in an ideal environment of change and domestic issues. Nineteen-ninety-four was an era of crime and anti-incumbency."

The dominance of crime as an issue in the 1994 policy debate particularly worked against women's advantage. Public-opinion polls repeatedly showed crime topping the list of voter concerns, and women were viewed as being soft on crime. "Women are definitely hurt by the fact that crime is the number one issue," said Democratic pollster Celinda Lake, who has worked for many female congressional and gubernatorial candidates. "It's very hard for women to show toughness. . . . I think women can get over that barrier but it's one of the biggest barriers facing them." Sen. Dianne Feinstein (D-Calif.) agreed with Lake. "Women are always subjected to a different test: Were we tough enough? Particularly on the litmus-test issues like crime and the economy."

Lake advises her candidates to counter the "soft on crime" attacks by emphasizing "tough love" measures such as boot camps for juveniles and prosecuting teenagers as adults for violent crime.[5]

Some Republican women were able to escape such "soft on crime" characterizations in 1994 by linking themselves to the far right agenda. Idaho Republican representative Helen Chenoweth, for example, was originally thought to be too extreme in her conservative views to win her challenge against two-term incumbent Rep. Larry LaRocco (D). In fact, during the campaign, the head of the Democratic Congressional Campaign Committee, Rep. Vic Fazio (D-Calif.), called Chenoweth's ties to the religious right a "God send" for Democratic chances. In the end, however, Chenoweth defeated LaRocco 55 to 45 percent, the worst defeat for an Idaho incumbent since 1932. Other GOP women also featured their conservative message in their campaigns. During her successful run for the House, state senator Barbara Cubin (R-Wyo.) played up the fact that she was the prime sponsor of a "tough on crime" measure that appeared on the Wyoming ballot in November, allowing judges to impose life sentences without the possibility of parole.

Journalist and commentator Julianne Malveaux acknowledged that Republican women such as Sen. Olympia Snowe (Maine) and New Jersey governor Christine Todd Whitman were stars in the party because they were fiscally conservative but moderate on social issues. "At the same time," said Malveaux, "you have these Republican women who, quite frankly, I have to wonder if they have ever had to raise children, if they've ever been faced with fiscal challenges, because their rhetoric is ridiculous." Such rhetoric, however, clearly proved popular with the voters in 1994.[6]

Malcolm of EMILY's List predicted before the 1994 elections that GOP women would not be big winners because the Contract with America was silent on women's issues. The lack of concern with such issues, however, was again clearly inconsequential to the voters.

Another factor that generally worked against women during the 1994 elections was the lack of open-seat races—contests where no incumbent is running for reelection. Such races provide all newcomers, male or female, their best chances of coming to Capitol Hill. During the 1992 "Year of the Woman" there was an unusually high number of seats vacated by incumbents due to redistricting, retirements, and resignations. Women that year ran for 35 of those 91 open House seats. Of the 24 new women elected to the House that year, 22 were open-seat victors. In 1994, however, there were only 52 open House seats, and women ran for just 16 of them. Still, of the 11 new House women in the 104th Congress, nine came there by way of open-seat victories. The one female addition to the Senate was also the winner of an open seat. Women, in fact, faired better in open-seat races in 1994 than men. Fifty-six percent of the women running for open seats won, while only 49 percent of the men nominated for open seats won their elections.

Political analysts, ironically, point to the historic gains for women in the 1992 elections as a contributing factor to the minimal success they acheived two years later. In 1992, women ran as political outsiders, crusaders against big government, and catalysts for change. Many of the Democratic women who won that year took over districts that leaned Republican in registration or were at best marginally Democratic. Those women immediately became Republican targets.

"The wins of 1992 set up the losses of 1994," said Malcolm. "We learned how difficult it is to hang onto House seats that have a majority of the electorate in the other party."

The unprecendented numbers of women joining the House and Senate in 1992 also pushed the woman's image closer to the mainstream, diminishing their "outsider" status. A Democratic president with ever-falling popularity ratings also made the Democratic women in Congress appear to be part of the problem rather than the solution.

"In 1994, people focused on issues," said Enid Greene Waldholtz (R-Utah), one of two challengers to defeat women incumbents that year. "They were looking for candidates who would change the direction of Washington. It didn't bode well for women who supported the President. Republicans were seen as the agents of change."[7]

THE LOSERS

Ten incumbent women departed Congress in 1994. Marilyn Lloyd (D-Tenn.) retired after 20 years in the House. Rep. Helen Bentley (R-Md.) resigned to run in the Maryland gubernatorial primary, which she lost to newcomer Ellen Sauerbray. And eight incumbent women, *all Democrats*, were defeated at the polls, six of them from the historic class of 1992.

The political downswing for many of the women from the class of 1992 began just months after they were sworn into office. Those who had won by narrow margins that year may have sealed their doom in 1994 by casting a single vote in favor of President Clinton's budget package. In fact, all six of the defeated freshmen women voted in favor of the budget package when it hit the floor on August 5, 1993, and only one of the two defeated veteran women legislators voted against it.

"Democrats went down like dominoes," wrote Tony Kornheiser in the *Washington Post* shortly after the 1994 Republican landslide. "Marjorie Margolies-Mezvinsky was gone in less time than it takes to say 'Marjorie Margolies-Mezvinsky.' "[8]

In 1992 Margolies-Mezvinsky (D-Pa.) had won her race by just 1,373 votes, and had actually composed a concession speech in which she simply changed the word "defeat" to "victory" throughout the text. Later, she virtually predicted her defeat for a second term in her book, ironically titled *They Came to Stay*. In her final chapter, "The Vote," she describes in agonizing detail the process by which she was pressured to cast the deciding vote for President Clinton's Budget Plan, a vote which probably guaranteed her defeat in the 1994 elections.

Margolies-Mezvinsky actually cast three preliminary votes on the House floor *against* the Clinton budget proposal. First to be considered was the Budget Resolution, followed by the stimulus package, and Margolies-Mezvinsky was the only freshman Democrat to vote against both. Then came the president's full budget, called an "economic plan" because it contained new tax policies, and Margolies-Mezvinsky once more voted against it. She believed that the budget should have contained more spending cuts and less taxes. The president's economic plan was nonetheless passed by the House, 219 to 213, and subsequently by the Senate, through the use of a tie-breaking vote from the vice president. A conference committee then ironed out the differences in wording between the House and Senate bills, preparing the way for the dramatic final vote on August 5. Just hours before that vote, Margolies-Mezvinsky had appeared on local television in her district to tell her constituents that she remained opposed to the bill. She knew that changing her vote to support the president would be tantamount to political suicide, and she assumed she would not be asked to do so. All indications were that the Democrats had sufficient votes for passage, and Margolies-Mezvinsky was sure that if the president did need a last-minute vote, he would call upon other Democrats in safer districts, members who were not so new to this political game.

When Margolies-Mezvinsky entered the House floor for the final vote, she overheard Republicans confidently stating that the Democrats did not have the votes needed for passage. At this point she was notified that the president was on the phone asking for her. President Clinton asked her what it would take to get her vote. She told him frankly that such a vote might mean that she would not be returned to the House. She said a bipartisan conference, including members of the cabinet, should be held to review entitlement spending. She also said she would change her vote only if it were the deciding vote. As it turned out, she was forced to do just that, despite the fact that 41 other Democrats cast their votes against the final budget.

As she walked down the aisle after casting her vote for the president's budget, Republicans mocked and taunted her, shouting, "Bye-bye Margie" and telling her that her days in Congress were numbered. Indeed, on November 8, 1994, Rep. Marjorie Margolies-Mezvinsky lost to Republican Jon Fox by a margin of about 10,000 votes.

Rep. Karan English (D-Ariz.) was another bright and principled member of the class of 1992 whose support for the Clinton administration's agenda contributed directly to her ouster two years later. English first won election in a Republican-leaning district because of her reform-minded politics and an unexpected endorsement by conservative icon Barry Goldwater. But her votes for Clinton's budget package, the Brady Bill, the ban on assault weapons, and mining reform all became sensitive issues during her reelection bid, and when Goldwater said he could no longer support her, her fate was sealed. She spent $700,000 on her campaign and yet lost by 20,000 votes. "I think I was an example of the new trend [in 1992]," she said. "Now I am an example of getting rid of the new trend. . . . I lost to the Christian Coalition. And they didn't beat me, they beat this image that had been created over the past two years and I couldn't turn it around."

During the lame-duck session following the 1994 Republican landslide, English attended a Democratic Caucus meeting at which her dispirited colleagues suggested that freshmen like English might have avoided defeat at the polls if they had cast politically safer votes. English was offended by such talk. "I am angry," she said, "not that I lost the election, but that some of you are taking away the very things that made my service valuable to me. I am proud that I voted for the Brady Bill and the assault-weapon ban. I am proud of my vote for the budget bill. Many of us in the Women's Caucus have a slogan: We didn't come here to be somebody, we came here to do something." She was given a standing ovation by the assembled Democrats.[9]

Rep. Lynn Schenk (D-Calif.) had her congressional career ended after one term when she was defeated by local county supervisor Brian Bilbray, a surfer and former lifeguard, who declared, "She came in on the Clinton tide and will go out with the Clinton tide. We're going to wrap him around her neck like a millstone and toss them into the San Diego Bay." In reality, Schenk's TV ads had boasted that "she stood up to the President" by voting for a balanced-budget amendment. Schenk had always been known as a "pro-business Democrat," but like other women in the class of 1992, Schenk was hurt most by her vote for the 1993 Clinton budget package. Her opponent ran ads accompanied by the sound of a cash register, claiming that Schenk's budget vote cost local taxpayers more than $500,000. Despite Schenk's attempts to explain that only the wealthier Californians, like herself, would pay any additional taxes, her district, with an overwhelming Republican edge in registered voters, rejected her at the polls. After defeating Schenk by about 5,000 votes, Bilbray promised, "I'll come home every weekend to surf. I'll need to refuel my mind on the surfline."[10]

Rep. Leslie Byrne (D-Va.) was another prominent congresswomen from the class of 1992 whose career was ended after just one term. Like many of her defeated colleagues, she was elected by a district that would have been difficult to retain even if she hadn't voted in favor of the president's budget. Late in Byrne's 1994 reelection campaign, Vice President Al Gore came to her northern Virginia district to stump for her, but despite—or possibly because of—such visible help from the White House, she lost her bid for a second term, 46-to-54 percent, to the conservative Republican Tom Davis.

Though Byrne became a Republican target almost immediately after she won office in 1992, she was considered a rising star within Congress. She was elected whip of her freshmen class and worked closely with the House leadership in helping push forward the Democratic agenda. Colleague Carolyn Maloney (D-N.Y.)—who easily won a second term in 1994—believed Byrne would have a long and illustrious congressional career. Maloney recalled her early days on Capitol Hill, when she noticed that the rooms she toured were filled with pictures of former committee chairmen, *all men.* "So I started thinking," Maloney said, "who out of our terrific class would be the first one to make it to the wall, to be the first woman on that wall. And I chose Leslie, because of her determination, her strength, her commitment, her deep understanding of the legislative process and how to get things done."

Other members of Byrne's class agreed. During a fundraising event organized by Byrne in 1994, eight of her female colleagues joined her to speak about the importance of increasing the number of women in Congress and to garner support and dollars for the Byrne reelection campaign. "Leslie Byrne is a dynamic leader," said Lucille Roybal-Allard (D-Calif.). "She has tremendous energy and is really able to get things done. If we are going to accomplish our goal of making this country a better place for everyone, particularly for women and children, it's going to be very difficult to do it without Leslie Byrne."[11]

Rep. Karen Shepherd (D-Utah) was another of the women of 1992 who came to Congress on a shaky political foundation. She represented a district that gave Bill Clinton only 32 percent of the vote, and she herself won election with a bare 51 percent. This former magazine publisher and English teacher knew she was facing an uphill battle in 1994. Shepherd says her district is the kind of place where people confide to her in whispers that they voted for her in 1992. "Life is short; why not take your best shot," she said shortly before the 1994 elections. "If it's not good enough, I'm prepared to take my medicine."

Her medicine was a ten-percentage point loss to Enid Greene Waldholtz in 1994. Like five other women from the class of 1992, Shepherd became a one-termer in large part due to her willingness to vote for controversial

Clinton administration legislation like the "deficit-reduction package" and the crime bill. In her 1992 campaign she had pledged to support deficit reduction, but she also said she would oppose any tax increase. "I was wrong when I said it, and I wish I hadn't," she says. When forced to choose between the two campaign pledges, she says she chose to vote for the Clinton deficit-reduction package, "even if it cost me the election."[12]

The fact that Shepherd frequently opposed the president on other matters was overlooked. She was the first House Democrat to call for an independent prosecutor to investigate Clinton's Whitewater affair. She joined the conservatives in supporting term limits and won House passage of her bill banning gifts from lobbyists to members of Congress. She even voluntarily returned her own cost-of-living salary increase back to the treasury. But it didn't help. In a three-way race in 1994, she was defeated by Waldholtz.

Rep. Maria Cantwell (D-Wash.) was another political casualty from the class of 1992. She describes herself as a "pro-business Democrat," and in 1992 she relied on that image to become the first Democrat to win her district seat in 40 years. The 34-year-old Cantwell campaigned against traditional politicians who had "lost touch with reality." She says, "We didn't campaign to 'throw the bums out.' We campaigned on the idea of getting things done."[13]

She had previously served in the Washington state legislature, where she chaired the Committee on Trade and Economic Development. Her business focus continued in Congress, where she spoke for the computer-software industry in challenging the Clinton administration's export restrictions on cryptographic software. When Vice President Gore wrote a conciliatory letter to Cantwell agreeing to a review of existing export controls, a spokesman for the Microsoft Corporation, located in Cantwell's district, exulted: "Maria Cantwell has gone head-to-head with the powers-that-be and they blinked."[14]

During her single term in Congress, Cantwell worked with a freshman task force that recommended a variety of reforms, including a proposal to limit the terms of committee chairmen. They also pressured the White House to increase the budget cuts in the Clinton stimulus package. The White House subsequently agreed to additional cuts, though not as much as Cantwell would have liked. In addition to her budget battles with the White House, Cantwell voted against funding the $11 billion superconducting supercollider project and the space station. But all of this fiscal conservatism was politically erased by her vote in favor of the overall Clinton budget. In November 1994 she lost a tight race to Republican Rick White, a corporate lawyer who had never held elective office.

Rep. Jill Long (D-Ind.) and Rep. Jolene Unsoeld (D-Wash.) served three terms in the House before their 1994 defeats, but, like the losers from the class of 1992, they were vulnerable from the start. Long was only 36 years old in 1989 when she won an upset victory by less than 2,000 votes in a special election against Republican Dan Heath, who had soundly defeated her just a year earlier. Many considered her victory a fluke. After all, the Republicans had carried her district for 12 years, and the seat had previously been held by none other than Dan Quayle, who had left to become vice president. Lee Atwater, chairman of the Republican National Committee, admitted, "What happened is she ran a good Republican-style campaign. She used good cutting issues, like taxes. It's the kind of campaign I would have been proud of."[15]

In her successful 1990 reelection campaign, Long continued her strong antitax position, stating, "I'm cautious and moderate by nature. I was raised not to like taxes, to save money, to darn socks and refinish furniture—all the 4–H Club stuff." The local GOP chairman in her county said, "Tell the truth, she sometimes sounds more conservative than I do."[16]

In 1992, Long rode the Democratic tide to another reelection victory, accompanying the largest group of new women in congressional history. But in 1994, the odds finally caught up with her. Long attempted to project a conservative political image, even to the point of admitting, "I would be comfortable being a moderate Republican." But she was brought down by the old cliche, "When the voters are offered a choice between a Republican and a Republican, they'll always choose the Republican." Her attempts to outdo the Republicans by projecting her conservative antitax image faded under the relentless claims of her critics that she was a "big spender." Despite the fact that Long voted *against* the Clinton budget proposal, she was unable to overcome the attacks by her Republican opponent, Mark Souder, who defeated Long by 10 percentage points.

Rep. Unsoeld's political fate followed a similar path to that of Long, but there were a few significant differences. Unsoeld entered politics as a consumer advocate and campaign reformer. As a member of the Washington state legislature, she made a name for herself as an opponent of the powerful industrial polluters. Unsoeld joined the U.S. House of Representatives in 1988 by winning an open seat in a southwest Washington district that had long been controlled by the Democrats. Nonetheless, she had to squeak by in one of the closest elections in the country, winning by just 618 votes out of more than 200,000 votes cast.

In 1990, she was characterized by her critics as more "liberal" than her constituents, and therefore vulnerable. She was known throughout the state as an outspoken environmentalist, bringing her into occasional conflict with the local logging industry. She defended herself by citing her family's historic involvment with the industry. "My father and grandfather were timbermen. My father started out as a kid working a donkey engine on Larch Mountain. My brother is the third generation in this proud industry and today owns a wood treatment plant. My family has long been supported by timber dollars."[17] Unsoeld's husband, renowned as one of the first Americans to climb Mount Everest, had earlier been killed in a mountain avalanche. Jolene Unsoeld made her own reputation as the first woman to climb the north face of Wyoming's Mount Teton. Many in her district admired her guts, but constituent support was gradually eroded by the "jobs versus environment" issue.

Like Long, Unsoeld survived the 1992 elections during the Year of the Woman. Unlike Long, she voted for the Clinton budget proposal, and she was considered a long shot in 1994. Just a few months before the November elections she seemed to get a reprieve when her likely Republican opponent, Tim Moyer, pulled out of the GOP primary. But Linda Smith, a conservative Republican woman with strong support from the religious right, mounted a write-in campaign to win the GOP primary and went on to defeat Unsoeld by over 11,000 votes.

THE LEGACY OF 1992

The 1994 defeat of eight incumbent women, all Democrats and six of them from the record-breaking class of 1992, was big news, part of the media blitz on the conservative Republican landslide. Less noted was the fact that 23 women from the class of 1992, 19 of them Democrats, remained in the 104th Congress. Twenty of these women survived at the polls in 1994, and three women senators from that class did not face reelection that year. The legacy of this holdover from the Year of the Woman should not be underestimated.

The elections of 1992 proved historic not only in the numbers of women they brought to Congress, but also in the numerous precedents set by women in various races. The 1994 elections wiped out one of those "firsts," when it removed Rep. Byrne, who two years earlier had become the first woman elected to the House from Virginia. But most of the other groundbreaking victors in the Year of the Woman have managed to remain in office.

In 1992, California led the charge in setting several records, including becoming the first state in history to elect women to *both* its Senate seats. In addition, five new California women were elected to the House that year. The circumstances surrounding the California Senate elections in 1992 were ideal for the women candidates—there were no incumbents running for either seat. Sen. Allan Cranston's (D) retirement created one of the open seats and Sen. Pete Wilson's (R) 1990 gubernatorial victory created the other. As governor, Wilson quickly appointed Republican John Seymour to "hold" that seat until a special election in 1992 could select someone to fill the final two years of the term. Dianne Feinstein, the former mayor of San Francisco who had lost the governor's race to Wilson by a hair, declared her candidacy for the short-term seat. Barbara Boxer, with a decade of experience in the House, announced her candidacy for the other Senate seat.

In an interview in 1992, Feinstein seemed to acknowledge a negative stereotype of women politicians by claiming that "in the governor's race my being a woman was a disadvantage, not an advantage." She explained, "In the Senate race, I believe it is an advantage. I think people have doubts, still, about women in high executive offices, whether they can be the kind of managers that a man can be. . . . They don't doubt women in terms of their ability to advocate program change or public policy, which is, after all, the role of a legislator."[18]

In 1992, Feinstein campaigned as a feminist, something she had not done previously. Barbara Boxer had always been an outspoken feminist. The two women had never been political allies, and in past elections they had even endorsed each others' opponents. Both won their Senate primaries easily, and as the general elections approached they maintained commanding leads over their Republican opponents. But Boxer's adversary, Bruce Herschensohn, began to rise in the polls as he attacked Boxer as a "radical left wing" candidate who did not support "traditional family values."

As Boxer's lead all but vanished, Feinstein called a press conference to announce her formal endorsement of Boxer, something she had not done during the primaries. In her endorsement, Feinstein referred to Boxer and herself as the "new Cagney and Lacey." In the general elections, "Cagney" won an easy victory and "Lacey" won a close one. Boxer raised about $10 million in 1992, more than *any* other Senate candidate, while Feinstein was fourth among all Senate candidates. Exit polls showed that both women attracted voters on the basis of four issues: abortion rights, the need for more women in the Senate, the need for political change, and the environment.

In 1994, Feinstein won narrow reelection to her seat, but only after spending $14 million, the third most expensive campaign in the country. Her challenger, Rep. Michael Huffington (R), spent $28 million of his own money, along with an additional $1.5 million in contributions. He lost by just two points. Boxer's seat will not be contested again until 1998.

Boxer's victorious 1992 campaign for the Senate left her House seat open and provided the perfect opportunity for another woman to win a Congressional seat. Boxer assembled at her home a number of hand-picked potential candidates. Among them was Lynn Woolsey. With Boxer's support and encouragement, Woolsey decided to run for the House seat, and eventually became the first welfare mother ever elected to Congress. She had previously served for eight years on the local city council, but her earlier personal tribulations, including three years on public assistance, may have played a greater role in defining her political priorities. After a divorce, she had found herself on welfare and food stamps in order to feed her children, a problem faced by many women in her district.

"I am the only woman elected to the House [Congress] after having been on welfare," said Woolsey. "Twenty-five years ago I was left with three very small children. We were without a father, without a husband, and without any income whatsoever. I went immediately to work, but I wasn't making enough money to be able to keep my home or my car or to pay for child care or health care. I needed aid for dependent children. That was an experience that never leaves me, and I came to the House of Representatives knowing that my real job, and the job of government, is to make sure that people who are in need can be helped to become totally productive individuals in this society."[19] In the midst of the November 1994 Republican landslide, Democrat Woolsey won an easy reelection victory, defeating her Republican challenger by 20 percentage points.

In President Clinton's 1995 State of the Union address, he specifically singled out Woolsey. After declaring that "every one of us can change our tomorrows," Clinton said, "America's best example of that may be Lynn Woolsey, who worked her way off welfare to become a Congresswoman, from the state of California." Woolsey stood and received an ovation from Congress.

The California victories of 1992 also produced the first Mexican-American woman ever elected to Congress: Lucille Roybal-Allard (D). Roybal-Allard represents a heavily *Latino* district, which also includes portions of East Los Angeles such as Chinatown, Filipino Town, and Little Tokyo. Before coming to Congress, she served three terms in the state assembly where she led the fight for environmental protection in California. In Congress, she has been a trailblazer on women's issues, authoring laws on domestic violence, sexual assault, and other gender-based crimes. She declares, "The women members of Congress are saying we're not going to depend on the male leadership. We're going to start taking control of our own lives and our own destinies. We as women and members of Congress are going to pool our resources and work together to accomplish our goals, with the help and support of our male colleagues, but with the women taking a leadership role."[20] In 1994, with Democrats suffering defeat around the country, Roybal-Allard won reelection with an astounding 81 percent of the vote.

Rep. Jane Harman (D) is another Californian who won her seat in a 1992 upset victory in a district generally conceded to the Republicans. Though Harman's victory in 1992 was her first run for office, she had worked on Capitol Hill for 19 years as chief counsel to former California senator John Tunney and staff director to the Senate Judiciary Subcommittee on Constitutional Rights. She had also served as deputy secretary to the cabinet in the Carter White House and was deputy counsel to the Democratic Convention's platform committee. Harman attributed her success with the voters in 1992 to her "pro-choice, pro-change" message, but in 1994, running against a pro-choice Republican woman, Susan Brooks, Harman won reelection by barely 800 votes.

Rep. Anna Eshoo (D) is the sixth Californian woman from the class of 1992 to survive the elections of 1994. During her first race in 1992 she won election with 57 percent of the vote, and won a surprisingly easy reelection victory in 1994. Eshoo had previously served for ten years as a member of the San Mateo County Board of Supervisors, where she led the fight for expanded prenatal health care and medicaid reform. She says moving from a five-member board of supervisors to the largest legislative body in the country was a major adjustment. "Where once I spoke to department heads, I now speak to cabinet secretaries and the White House. It is at once exhilirating, serious, sobering and extraordinarily challenging."[21] Undeterred, she has taken the opportunity to distinguish herself on matters that go beyond what might be called "women's issues."

Florida added four new women to Congress in 1992, second only to California. Among those winners were Carrie Meek (D), the first African-American in 129 years to represent Florida in Congress. At 68, Meek was also the oldest woman to join the House in 1992. A granddaughter of slaves and the daughter of a sharecropper, Meek was raised in a family of 12 children. At the age of 11 she worked as a domestic servant. She also worked her way through school, paid her own college tuition, and eventually served more than a dozen years in the Florida legislature before winning national office. While serving on the state level, she became one of Florida's most powerful politicians, championing the poor and downtrodden and working to improve access to government services, education, and affordable housing. Because of her service on an appropriations subcommittee in the Florida senate, she succeeded in gaining appointment to the coveted Appropriations Committee in the U.S. House during her very first term in Congress. In 1994, Meek won reelection running *unopposed*.

Rep. Karen Thurman (D-Fla.) won election to the 103rd Congress in 1992 in a four-way race for a newly created seat. She had earlier served on the local city council and for three terms as a Florida state senator. She had been the first woman ever to chair the Florida Senate Agriculture Committee. In Congress she is described as "a man's woman," and her legislative experience has allowed her to establish ties beyond the group of women elected with her in 1992. Her moderate views helped her successful reelection campaign in 1994, when she defeated race car legend "Big Daddy" Don Garlits (R) by 14 percentage points.

Tillie Fowler (R-Fla.) had a long history of public and community service before coming to the House in 1992. She had served as a legislative assistant to former representative Robert Stephens, Jr. (R-Ga.) and was general counsel in the White House Office of Consumer Affairs during the Nixon administration. In 1989 she became the first woman ever elected as Jacksonville's city council president. She served as chair of the Florida Endowment for the Humanities and was a member of Jacksonville's Commission on the Status of Women. She ran unopposed in her 1992 congressional primary and won 56 percent of the vote in the general election. In her successful 1994 reelection bid she was unopposed in the general election.

Corrine Brown (D-Fla.) served ten years in the Florida House of Representatives before joining the 103rd Congress. Throughout her political career she has worked for better housing, better education, and better health care for her constituents. In winning her 1992 congressional primary, she emphasized her commitment to the poor, and in the November elections she won 59 percent of the vote. In 1994, she maintained virtually the same margin of victory in defeating Republican Marc Little.

The state of Washington also set new records in 1992, electing two new women to the House, a Republican and a Democrat, and, for the first time ever, sending a woman to the Senate. Of the two new congresswomen, only the Republican survived the 1994 elections. Rep. Jennifer Dunn (R-Wash.) was one of four Republican women elected to Congress in 1992, winning her race with over 60 percent of the vote. She brought with her a long record of state, national, and international experience, including service as Washington state Republican party chairman from 1981 through 1992. She was a delegate to the 1984 and 1990 meetings of the UN Commission on the Status of Women and has long been outspoken on women's health issues. She became the only member of her freshman class to hold a seat on the Joint Committee on the Organization of Congress, and was the first woman ever appointed to the Republican Committee on Committees. In 1994, she improved on her 1992 victory margin, defeating Democrat Jim Wyrick by 24 percentage points.

Patty Murray (D-Wash.) became Washington state's first female senator after being heralded in the press as the "mom in tennis shoes." She had been so characterized, disparagingly, when she first joined the state senate, but it soon became a badge of honor. Halfway through that term, she was named minority whip, and a newspaper poll of local "political insiders" ranked Murray fifth among 53 state senate and house members after her first year in office.

Murray says she was motivated to run for the U.S. Senate by the Thomas-Hill hearings, but her opportunity arose in 1992 when incumbent Senator Brock Adams (D-Wash.) was tainted by charges of sexual molestation. Murray was the first Democratic challenger to announce her candidacy, but when Adams withdrew from the race, other candidates quickly declared. In a state primary that allows all candidates, regardless of party, on the ballot, Murray ran against five major and six minor candidates and came out ahead with 29 percent of the vote. Women voters favored Murray 2 to 1 over her closest rival in the primary. In the general election, she won 55 percent of the vote, with women supporting her by a 58-to-42 percent margin. As she joined the 103rd Congress at age 42, Murray was at least ten years younger than any other woman senator, and she was the only one whose children still lived at home. Murray will have to test her popularity at the polls again in 1996.

New York State added two women to the 103rd Congress. Rep. Carolyn Maloney (D-N.Y.) was one of only two freshmen women to defeat an incumbent in the 1992 general elections, and Rep. Nydia Velazquez (D-N.Y.) was one of two freshmen women to defeat a Democratic incumbent in the primaries. Velazquez was recruited by her community to run for the House and represent a newly drawn Hispanic-majority district in Brooklyn. She had earlier been the first Hispanic woman to serve on the New York City Council. In 1992, she won the Democratic congressional primary, beating five contenders, including nine-term incumbent Stephen Solarz, who chose to run for the newly drawn district after his district had been dismantled. In the general election, her opponents made public the fact that she had once attempted suicide, but Velazquez nonetheless became the first Puerto Rican woman elected to Congress, winning 77 percent of the vote. She was reelected in 1994 in spectacular fashion, winning with an astounding 92 percent.

Maloney had difficulty raising money because the major funding organizations didn't like her chances to win. Even EMILY's List turned her down, saying, "You're not a terrible candidate; it's just that you can't win." Maloney did gain the enthusiastic support of organizations like the National Women's Political Caucus and the National Organization of Women (NOW). Only after some of the polls showed growing support for Maloney did EMILY's List decide to back her. In a major upset, she won by almost 5,000 votes against a candidate who outspent her $1.4 million to $277,000. She recalls, "It was absolutely thrilling on my first day in Congress, seeing 48 women walk down the aisle, not to get married, but to be sworn into the U.S. Congress. And we didn't beat down the doors to get here just to let the air in."[22] In her successful 1994 reelection bid, she improved on her 1992 performance, defeating Republican Charles Millard by 27 points.

The second woman to unseat an incumbent in 1992 was Rep. Pat Danner (D-Mo.) who defeated eight-term Rep. Tom Coleman (R) with 55 percent of the vote. Before coming to the Hill, Danner served for ten years in the Missouri State Senate. She had earlier been a district assistant on the staff of the late Rep. Jerry Litton. During the Carter administration, she had been appointed cochair of the Ozark Regional Commission, becoming the first and only woman to chair a regional commission. In 1994, she was one of 11 women running against another woman, and she defeated Republican Tina Tucker by 32 points.

Texas added a Democratic woman to the House and a Republican woman to the Senate in 1992, and both were trailblazers. Rep. Eddie Bernice Johnson (D-Tex.) had a varied background as businesswoman, nurse, health care administrator, and Texas lawmaker before her election to the 103rd Congress in 1992. She served three terms in the Texas legislature, was appointed by President Jimmy Carter as regional director of the Department of Health, Education, and Welfare, and in 1986 became the first woman and the first black to represent the Dallas area in the Texas senate since the period of Reconstruction. In 1992, she won election to the U.S. House of Representatives with 74 percent of the vote against a Republican woman, Lucy Cain. She was elected whip of the Congressional Black Caucus, and her legislative priorities were the economy, health care, education, the environment, and job opportunities for minorities. She won reelection in 1994 by the same margin of victory she had earned in 1992, once more defeating Republican Lucy Cain by almost 50,000 votes.

The state of Texas gained its first woman senator in history when Republican Kay Bailey Hutchison won a special election on June 5, 1993, to fill the vacancy created when Sen. Lloyd Bentsen (D-Tex.) became President Clinton's secretary of the Treasury. Huchison's victory gave the GOP both senators in the Lone Star State for the first time since Reconstruction, and she accomplished this feat by winning the highest percentage of votes of any Republican running in Texas since 1875. She drew 67.3 percent and swept 239 out of 254 counties.

Hutchison had made Texas history years earlier when, in 1972, she became the first female Republican elected to the state legislature. In 1982 she made an unsuccessful run for Congress, losing a close runoff after a brutal campaign. After a few years as a successful businesswoman, Hutchison returned to politics in 1990, winning the race for the state treasurer's post that Ann Richards gave up to run for governor.

During her successful 1992 campaign for the U.S. Senate, Hutchison represented herself as moderately prochoice, supporting *Roe v. Wade* but favoring some abortion restrictions and opposing federal funding for abortions. She had the support of the religious right, the defense industry, and the Perot crowd. She focused her campaign more on President Clinton than on her opponent, appointed Sen. Robert Krueger (D), and the strategy was enormously successful in a state where Clinton's unfavorable rating was an astronomical 74 percent. She opposed the Clinton administration's tax proposals and the BTU tax in particular. She repeatedly told voters that Clinton's proposed economic package could hang on one vote, and that, if elected, she would vote to defeat it. As we saw, a number of Democratic women were defeated in 1994 because they had voted *for* Clinton's budget package. Hutchison was elected in 1992 on the *promise* that she would vote against it.

In September 1993, a little more than a year after her election to the Senate, Hutchison made Texas history once more, becoming the first senator from the Lone Star State to be indicted while in office. She was charged with four felony counts of misusing state workers and computers for personal and political purposes while she was still Texas treasurer, and of trying to cover up the crime. When a legal technicality forced the district attorney to dismiss the grand-jury indictments, new indictments were sought. Early in 1994, Hutchison was acquitted in court, paving the way for her triumphant reelection bid in which she defeated Democrat Richard Fisher, 61-to-38 percent.

When Carol Moseley-Braun (D) won a stunning upset in the 1992 Illinois senatorial primary, she became the first black woman ever nominated for the Senate by a major party. When she defeated Republican Richard Williamson in the November general election, she became the first black woman to serve in the Senate and only the fourth black ever to serve in the chamber. Moseley-Braun had first drawn national attention in 1990, when, while serving as recorder of deeds in Cook County, she was named cochair of Sen. Paul Simon's (D-Ill.) reelection campaign. She was particularly effective in her criticism of Rep. Lynn Martin (R-Ill.), the Republican woman who ran against Simon.

In late 1991, Moseley-Braun set her own sights on the senate, declaring herself a primary challenger to incumbent Sen. Alan Dixon (D-Ill.). She publicly denounced Dixon's support for Clarence Thomas in the recently concluded battle with Anita Hill and expressed her intention to run him out of office. Indeed, her ultimate victory over Dixon was the first tangible political fallout from the Thomas-Hill conflict. During her primary campaign, she won the endorsement of Cook County Illinois Democratic Women—a group that supports women candidates and feminist causes—and feminist author Gloria Steinem, who spoke at a news conference at Moseley-Braun's Chicago headquarters. Moseley-Braun also visited the United Auto Workers headquarters in Aurora, Illinois, where workers at Caterpillar Inc. had been locked out of their jobs, and stressed her 93 percent pro-labor voting record while she was a state representative. With broad grass-roots support, she swept to an upset primary victory.

In the general election campaign Moseley-Braun received support from groups like EMILY's List and the National Organization for Women, and she eventually raised more than three times as much money as her Republican challenger, Richard Williamson. But she ran against President Bush as much as she did against Williamson. In criticizing the administration's antiabortion policy, she accused the Bush administration of reaching into private bedrooms to determine whether women should be pregnant. Her campaign suffered a temporary setback when she was accused of providing taxpayer-supported care for her mother, and in a replay of the stereotypes faced by Jeannette Rankin 65 years earlier, she was faulted for crying during intense media questioning about her mother's finances. Still, she won the November election by eight points, winning 48 percent of the white vote and 58 percent of the female vote.

Moseley-Braun has never run away from a fight in the Senate, and one of her most frequent opponents has been Sen. Jesse Helms (R-N.C.). In May 1993 she roused Helms's anger by asking the Senate to deny the United Daughters of the Confederacy a patent renewal for an insignia that features the Confederate flag. In a symbolic battle against the old south, she won the victory in the Judiciary Committee, and the Senate voted not to extend the patent, which had first been granted in 1884. "[F]or those of us who are African American, honoring our ancestors meant that we would not renew the design patent for the Confederate flag," she said.

Many women and blacks said Moseley-Braun had shamed the old boy's club into doing what was right, but Jesse Helms never forgave her. She tells of an incident that occurred shortly after the Senate rejected the Confederate symbol. She was on a Senate elevator with Sen. Orrin Hatch (R-Utah) when the doors opened and Jesse Helms stepped in. "He saw me standing there," she recalls, "and he started to sing, 'I wish I was in the land of cotton. . . .' And he looked at Senator Hatch and said, 'I'm going to sing Dixie until she cries.' And I looked at him and said, 'Senator Helms, your singing would make me cry if you sang Rock of Ages.' "[23]

Moseley-Braun has recently declared that she "absolutely" will run for a second Senate term in 1998.

When Rep. Blanche Lambert (D-Ark.) joined the 103rd Congress, she became the youngest woman serving in the House. Her opponent in the 1992 primary was Rep. Bill Alexander (D-Ark.), in whose Washington office she had earlier worked answering phones and writing letters. Even after her election to the House, many on Capitol Hill still recognized her as a staff member, not a congresswoman. She tells the story of two aquaintances who approached her on Capitol Hill and asked, "Who do you work for now, Blanche?" She answered, "For the folks back home." In 1994, she defeated Republican Warren Dupwe, 54-to-46 percent.

Rep. Cynthia McKinney (D-Ga.) came to the 103rd Congress with a background of civil-rights activism. She also had experience in academia, having taught at three Atlanta-area universities. She subsequently served in the Georgia State Assembly, where her father had previously served. The congressional district that she now represents is largely black, and was created in part through her own local efforts. She won the 1992 primary election runoff after leading a field of five candidates, and then gained 73 percent of the vote in the general election. In 1994, she defeated Republican Woodrow Lovett by a whopping 32 percentage points.

When Rep. Eva Clayton (D-N.C.) joined the 103rd Congress she became the first African-American to represent North Carolina since Reconstruction. This 58-year-old mother of four was quickly named president of her freshman class, the first woman ever to hold that office. She didn't bear much resemblance to the typical old boy on Capitol Hill, but she was unintimidated. "I do not have to run away from difference," she said, "nor do I have to become like a man in order to feel that I am equal."[24] Before joining Congress Clayton had been North Carolina's assistant secretary for community development, and in 1990 was named the state's outstanding county commissioner. In 1992 she won election to the U.S. House of Representatives by a margin of 36 points over her Republican opponent. In her 1994 reelection victory, she defeated Republican Ted Tyler by 22 points.

Deborah Pryce (R-Ohio) was one of four Republican women elected to the 103rd Congress. She had resigned a judgeship to run for the open seat created when Rep. Chalmers Wylie (R-Ohio) withdrew from the race just ten days before the filing deadline. Wylie, who had served in Congress for 26 years, had been named in the House bank scandal that tainted a number of incumbents. Pryce had little time to deliberate, and today she says that what finally convinced her to run was her belief that, once in Congress, she could really raise the consciousness level of her community about women, their involvement in politics, and their contribution to the broader society. In 1994, Pryce easily won reelection, defeating Democrat Bill Buckel by 36 points.

Elizabeth Furse (D-Ore.) had never run for elected office before her 1992 campaign for Congress. Born in Kenya and raised in South Africa, she spent her youth organizing women's anti-apartheid groups. When she moved to the United States, she worked as a community organizer in California and for northwestern Indian tribes. In 1992, Les AuCoin, an 18-year incumbent in the House, decided to run for the Senate seat of Bob Packwood, leaving an open seat in Furse's district. Her opposition to the Gulf War was a motivating factor in her decision to run. She admits that, in the beginning, she didn't think she could be elected because she was branded as a "way-out liberal," but she won by 6 points over Republican Tony Meeker. In her 1994 bid for a second term, Furse narrowly defeated her Republican opponent by just 319 votes.

FUNDRAISING: CHANGES OVER THE YEARS

While women made historic gains in 1992, they did not take their success for granted. They quickly realized that their congressional service would be short lived if they did not work jointly to help maintain their numbers in office. As they approached the 1994 elections, Democratic women of the House joined forces and hit the campaign trail together. In one example, nine women organized a series of fundraising events in which they traveled across the country as a group. Such events were a new and highly personal way for the women to join forces in an attempt to protect their gains in Congress.

"A lot of us have male campaign managers," said Rep. Lynn Woolsey (D-Calif.) during one of the events in Virginia. "And we're doing this show all over the country trying to raise money for each other, and it is so hard to explain to these guys that this is all the show has to be. We don't have to bring on anybody else because this is the show."

Former representative Leslie Byrne (D-Va.) admitted that the role of political candidate and fundraiser was new to most women, but it was a role in which they could easily succeed. Byrne described the first time she met Karen Shepherd (D-Utah), a fellow member of the class of 1992 who, like herself, would eventually lose her bid for a second term.

"We were at a women's campaign fundraiser, and we found out that not only did we both come from Utah but we had the same pollster," Byrne said. "We talked about the pollster we had and how he returned our phone calls and how he was a good guy. I started to laugh and she said what are you laughing at. I said, do you realize that we're talking about our pollster the same way our mothers used to talk about their gynecologists?"

Rep. Cynthia McKinney (D-Ga.), one of the 1992 women to survive the 1994 elections, explained the difficulties that are unique to women when trying to finance a campaign. McKinney said she had a very difficult time funding her first race for the House, especially when she tried to approach male donors.

"I was given a list of movers and shakers in Atlanta and these were people that I had to contact if I was going to be able to launch a credible campaign. So I began to go down the list. All of them were men, by the way. There were CEOs of Fortune 500 companies, and these were really people that I had never had access to in my entire life. I kept getting 'no' after 'no' after 'no,' though all I was asking for was 15 minutes of their time. And finally it dawned on me. Every one of these men had a woman who answered the phone for him. And so I began to ask the secretaries, 'Wouldn't you like to have a woman representing you in Congress?' And the secretary would say, 'Yes, I would.' And I would say, 'Well, you know, I'm that woman.' And sure enough, we were able to utilize the woman's network to get inside some of those old doors that never would have been open to us."[25]

Fundraising has traditionally been a difficult task for female politicians. Former Rep. Bella Abzug (D-N.Y.) says, "Women lose because they don't have enough support; they don't have enough support because they don't have enough money to conduct effective campaigns; they have trouble raising money because people think they're losers." She calls this the "Catch-22" of women's politics.[26]

Successful 1994 challenger Enid Greene Waldholtz (R-Utah), who defeated first-term representative, Karen Shepherd (D), views the difficulties women face when fundraising not as a gender bias, but as an incumbent bias.

"It's not so much the problems of being a woman, but problems of running against an incumbent," Waldholtz said. "When I ran, they said, 'She's not going to win because she's challenging an incumbent.' When you take on an incumbent, people are not interested in supporting you. They don't think you can win. Women have also not been at the top echelons of politics for the past twenty years. The old bulls have been here for twenty years, and their connectons are extensive. That's a tremendous help. Until women have been in the upper levels of politics for a long time, they won't have the connections. You've got to have an established relationship. Women are also not in the upper echelons of the business world. That can make it difficult for women politicians to raise money, too. As the business world improves its numbers in terms of women, so will the political world."[27]

In 1982, the Women's Campaign Fund documented that the average male challenger spent $170,000 on his campaign as compared to $133,000 for the average female challenger. Indeed, in congressional elections between 1972–1982, women, on average, raised less money than men, but when the figures are adjusted for whether the candidate was an incumbent or challenger, there is no significant difference between male and female candidates. In short, incumbents, regardless of gender, usually raise much more money than their challengers.

In 1992, redistricting forced many incumbents to campaign in areas where they were not well known or where their party was not dominant. Some incumbents were weakened by the bank scandal or by the appearance of a self-serving vote to raise congressional pay. For a variety of reasons, there was a strongly anti-incumbent mood among voters, and who would better personify the congressional outsider than women candidates. As a result, in 1992, both political parties were willing to aggressively recruit women, and women's PACs provided increased amounts of essential seed money.

In 1983 there were 16 women's PACs. By 1992 there were 42 PACs that either gave money predominantly to women or received donations primarily from women. The total financial support for female congressional candidates from these PACs in 1992 was $11.5 million, a 400 percent increase over the $2.7 million raised by women's PACs in 1990, which in turn was a 150 percent increase over the $1.1 million raised for women candidates in 1988. In the 1992 House elections, 48 percent of the 108 women candidates raised more money than their opponents. The two successful female challengers actually raised more money than their incumbent opponents.

EMILY's List was the most powerful of the 42 PACs devoted to raising money for female candidates. In 1992, the PAC supported 55 women candidates, 8 for the Senate and 47 for the House. All of the 19 successful Democratic female candidates for open seats were funded by EMILY's List, as were 11 unsuccessful candidates for open seats. EMILY's List candidates for open seats had a 63 percent success rate compared to a 56 percent success rate overall for women seeking open seats.

EMILY's List raised four times as much money in 1992 than it had in previous years, holding fundraisers and asking its members to contribute to women candidates for Congress. In this way, this PAC alone channeled more than $6 million of early money to women congressional candidates in 1992. Barbara Boxer's campaign is said to have received more than

$300,000 from EMILY's List members, who formed the core of her early donor's list. Other PACs, like the National Organization for Women (NOW) and the Women's Campaign Fund, also raised record amounts of money for women candidates in 1992. A pro-choice Republican PAC called WISH List contributed more than $450,000 to women candidates.

In 1992, officials in both parties felt that many women candidates for Congress had a real chance to win, and they were therefore more willing to make party resources available to them than they had been in the past. Research indicates that this party support did not represent a conscious effort to increase the number of women in Congress, but was more or less typical party support for competitive candidates. Still, the nature of that support differed by party. During the 1992 campaigns, the Democratic Party demonstrated the will to promote women, but it claimed that it lacked the means. Don Foley of the Democratic Senatorial Campaign Committee complained that the Republicans have a recruitment budget, but the Democrats do not.

Democratic political consultant Ann Lewis explained that the Republicans had an organizational advantage when it came to promoting women. The Republican Party, she claimed, was a top-down hierarchy with centralized fundraising, while the Democratic Party was more like a federation of state parties. For that reason, Lewis said, the presidential selection process was the only truly national Democratic operation. Everything else, she claimed, was run state by state, with some states richer and more effective than others.

Lewis, who used to recruit for the Democrats, says, "My Republican counterpart would go to candidates and say, 'We'll get the nomination. We'll max on funding.' I'd say, 'Look, it's going to be a lot of fun, but you're going to have to fight for the nomination, and maybe I can get you a dollar.' " Lewis concludes, "Democrats think of politics as organizing. Republicans think of politics as marketing."[28]

Political money has always gone to likely winners. In the past, women candidates have lacked political experience and incumbency and thus have attracted less private money and party support. But today there is a sizable and growing pool of women politicians who can raise as much money as men.

In 1992, Dianne Feinstein raised $1 million more than her opponent, an appointed incumbent, and Carol Moseley-Braun raised more than three times what her Republican opponent raised in the general election. Barbara Boxer actually raised more money than *any* other candidate in 1992, including incumbents. In 1994, Feinstein again broke records in fundraising against millionaire challenger Rep. Michael Huffington (R). In the most expensive Senate race in history, Huffington spent $29 million to Feinstein's $14 million, but Feinstein actually *raised* more money than Huffington, $10 million to $1.5 million. Almost $28 million of Huffington's campaign expenses were paid from his own pocket.

CHANGING ATTITUDES

The difficulty in recruiting female politicians is an even larger obstacle than fundraising, blocking women's path to Congress. A survey conducted in the summer of 1994 by Democratic pollster Celinda Lake for the National Women's Political Caucus (NWPC) showed that women were much less likely to run for political office than men. The survey polled 1,000 voters across the country and found that 18 percent of men had considered or would consider running for political office, while only 8 percent of women ever thought of launching a campaign. A second survey of male and female executives and lawyers—a likely pool for recruiting candidates—found that 38 percent of the men but only 25 percent of the female lawyers and executives had considered running for office. During the 1994 November elections, women made up just 14 percent of candidates for the House, and 13 percent for the Senate.[29]

NWPC President Harriett Woods complains, "Women win as often as men, [yet] this survey shows that women still aren't convinced."[30] But the survey did find that younger women felt more confident and qualified to run for political office. Slightly less than half of the younger women polled expressed fears of political inadequacy, while 61 percent of older women did.

Freshman representative Sue Myrick (R-N.C.) says the fears women have in running for office are deeply ingrained from childhood. "Women are afraid to take risks," she said. "Men are raised to play football, to bash their heads and come back for more. Women are raised to stand back. We aren't raised to be risk takers."[31]

National polls of voters show that sexual biases are slowly disappearing in American politics. In 1970, 1975, and 1984, the Gallup Poll asked: "If your party nominated a woman to run for Congress in your district, would you vote for her if she were qualified for the job?" In 1970, 13 percent of those polled said they would not vote for a qualified woman. In 1975, that number had fallen to 9 percent, and by 1984 it had fallen to 6 percent. A 1987 study found no significant differences between voter reactions to Democratic male and female congressional candidates.

Another study conducted by the National Women's Political Caucus in the fall of 1994 showed that women, in general, win elective office as often as men. The survey looked at congressional races between 1972 and 1992. During those 20 years, only 7 percent of candidates for the House and Senate were women. A total of just 53 women ran for the Senate during that period, but when women did run, the survey showed, they won as often as their male counterparts. In House races, incumbent women won 96 percent of their races compared to 95 percent for men. About 48 percent of women running for open seats won, compared to 51 percent for men, and female challengers opposing incumbents won 4 percent of their races compared to 6 percent for male challengers.

"The research clearly shows that electoral success has nothing to do with sex, and everything to do with incumbency," the study concluded. "One reason for the common perception that women have a tougher time winning elections than men is that most incumbents are men, and incumbents win far more often than challengers and open seat candidates."[32]

The survey, in fact, suggested that women are treated more fairly in politics than they are in the business world. While there are 56 women serving in Congress, only one Fortune 500 company is headed by a woman. The survey projected huge increases in the ranks of House and Senate women *if only they would run*. If women made up half of all open-seat and challenger candidates in the general elections for the House beginning in 1996, assuming 50 open seats each cycle, women would hold one-third of all House seats by the year 2000, the survey found.

While the survey showed that men and women faired almost equally in winning elections, it also found that women incumbents running for reelection had opposition more frequently than their male counterparts. In House races, 95 percent of the women incumbents had general-election opponents compared to just 85 percent for men.

The survey also showed that while men and women, on average, fared almost equally well when running for open House seats, women's success rates in those contests fluctuated dramatically depending on the year. While men have kept a steady success rate of about 50 percent since 1972, women's numbers during the last two decades ranged from as high as 80 percent in 1974 to as low as 15 percent in 1980. The extraordinarily high percentages of open seats in one year and extremely low percentages in another clearly indicate that changing social and political climates across the country have a much greater impact on the campaigns of women than on those of men.

Despite continuing problems in recruitment, women have been running for congressional office more and more frequently over the years, with increases in female candidacies seen in nearly every year since the 1960s. In 1968, 19 women won major-party nomination for the House. Just one woman was nominated for the Senate that year. By 1976, that number had nearly tripled for House candidates, with a record 54 women being nominated. Again, just one woman was nominated for the Senate. In 1988, another record was set in House elections when 69 women won major-party nominations. Two women were nominated for the Senate that year. In 1990, another record was set when 70 women won nomination for the House and nine for the Senate. Next came the spectacular Year of the Woman, described earlier. Even 1994, disappointing because of overall negligible gains, saw a record 112 women nominated for House seats. Nine women were nominated for the Senate, just two short of the record set in 1992.

"Since the early 1970s, the year of the woman has happened nearly every election cycle," says Lucy Baruch of the Rutgers University Center for the American Woman and Politics. "The year of 1994 was a great year for woman because of the numbers of women running."

Baruch was not discouraged by the stagnant growth in the number of women in Congress. She pointed to the record number of women elected to statewide offices in 1994 as an important achievement that will affect congressional races in the future. More than 80 women were elected to posts ranging from governor to state treasurer to corporation commissioner, and more than 1,500 women serve in state legislatures, providing a huge pool of qualified and attractive candidates for future congressional races.

"We have a record number of women now serving in statewide offices. That's critical to us," said Amy Conroy, executive director of the Women's Campaign fund, following the 1994 elections. "We are in this for the long haul. We have already begun focusing on 1996."

States where term limits will soon go into effect for local legislatures will also afford women new opportunities to run for office. Eight states have passed local legislation imposing term limits on *their* federal representatives and senators beginning in 1998, but the U.S. Supreme Court ruled in May 1995 that such limits were unconstitutional. Efforts to pass a constitutional amendment imposing federal term limits on all members of Congress are now under way and could eventually open up more House and Senate seats to women candidates.

"We have no official position, but we plan to take full advantage of term limits," said Harriet Woods, president of the National Women's Political Caucus. "Term limits are the biggest bonanza of potential open seats one can imagine."[33]

In the meantime, term limits for state legislatures will kick into effect for 20 states in 1996, opening up hundreds of legislative seats that will afford women greater chances of winning state office than ever before. As more women enter state office, it is expected many of those same females will eventually turn their sights on national office.

State legislatures are not the only breeding grounds for strong and viable candidates. Women's groups have also begun looking into the business community for candidates.

Jody Newman of the National Women's Political Caucus said her organization was working with business women to try to show them the importance of politics in their lives. Newman said her organization has begun approaching large corporations offering two- and three-day seminars to train women for political campaigns. The group recently held such seminars with McDonnell-Douglas, Pfizer, and Anheuser-Busch.

The Democratic Congressional Campaign Committee has also acknowledged the need to recruit more women candidates. At the beginning of the 104th Congress, new DCCC chairman Rep. Martin Frost (D-Tex.) named Rep. Pat Schroeder (D-Colo.) as a cochair whose responsibilities would focus on recruiting women to run for the House in 1996. "There were a number of Republican women elected in 1994 to Congress," Frost said. "We need to bring more Democratic women to office. Traditionally, women have done well for the party."

Schroeder said women candidates have historically been ignored by the national political organizations. She referred to the campaign of Rep. Zoe Lofgren (D-Calif.) in 1994. Before winning her general-election race, Lofgren first had to defeat a number of male Democratic primary opponents.

"She had all these guys running against her in the primary," Schroeder said. "Basically, the DCCC just recruits guys."[34]

In addition to recruiting candidates, women's poltical groups are also trying to protect or target those freshman women who may be vulnerable in the next elections. Most of the Democratic women defeated in 1994 had served in Republican-leaning or marginal districts, and Democratic women's groups are now turning the tables, targeting Republicans elected in districts that are mostly Democratic in registration. Get-out-the-vote campaigns are also emerging as a useful tool to elect new women or protect incumbent women.

"As Congress continues to move to the right, we will see a strong move among women and minorities to vote," said Ellen Malcolm of EMILY's List. "We can more than hold our own. Democratic women are the future of the Democratic party."[35]

In 1995, EMILY's List launched a $10 million project, "Women Vote!" to mobilize women voters through the year 2000. The project is designed to build a political base to elect more Democratic women by bringing more women to the polls. Women voters across the country will be contacted through the mail and by phone. The project was launched in response to the drop in female participation during the 1994 elections. While women accounted for 54 percent of voters in 1992, they comprised only 51 percent in 1994.

WOMEN VERSUS WOMEN

As more and more women win national office, a relatively new phenomenon has emerged: women challenging women in primaries and general elections. In 1992, five general elections for Congress pitted women against women, with four of those races contesting open seats. In the 1994 general elections, 11 female incumbents, eight Democrats and three Republicans, were challenged by other women. Two of those incumbents—Democratic representatives Jolene Unsoeld (Wash.) and Karen Shepherd (Utah)—lost their seats to Republican women.

"If there ever was any notion that a woman didn't run against another woman, that's totally out the door," said Peter Fenn, a consultant to Unsoeld.

All contests involving women seem to receive special scrutiny by the press, but the sparks seem to fly particularly in primary battles. As previously mentioned (chapter 1) when two former congresswomen and Democratic stars, Geraldine Ferraro and Elizabeth Holtzman, squared off in New York's 1992 Democratic senatorial primary, it was treated as the "mother of all catfights." Adding to the drama was the irony that this battle was occurring during the Year of the Woman.

Women's groups were split. Ferraro, the Democratic vice-presidential nominee in 1984, was endorsed by EMILY's List. Holtzman, formerly the youngest woman ever to serve in Congress and now New York City's comptroller, was endorsed by Eleanor Smeal, president of the Fund for Feminist Majority, and by the New York State and City chapters of the National Organization for Women. The Women's Campaign Fund attempted to resolve the conflict by endorsing *both* Ferraro and Holtzman.

"In a way it's painful to have two women leaders running in New York," said NWPC's Harriett Woods. "It's painful because both of them can't win. Many of us wish these two particular women had not run against one another because we like both of them. On the other hand, if more and more women are running, this will happen again."

The New York primary also contained two male candidates, state attorney general Robert Abrams and civil rights activist Al Sharpton. Early polls showed Ferraro and Abrams as the frontrunners, with Holtzman third and Sharpton a distant last. By August 1992, the month before the primary elections, Ferraro had pulled out to a 13-point lead over Abrams, with Holtzman and Sharpton falling far back. Holtzman's campaign sounded increasingly desperate as it watched the women's vote shift to Ferraro. Holtzman acknowledged that "there are a number of women who feel uncomfortable about having to make a choice. But it's just like Solomon—you can't cut this baby in half. You have to go to the voting booth and choose."[36]

Ultimately, it was not the race itself between Ferraro and Holtzman that made women uncomfortable. It was the bitter and ugly campaign that disturbed them. The campaigns of the two women targeted each other almost exclusively. Holtzman, in particular, focused her attack on Ferraro, accusing her of mafia ties and ethics violations during her tenure in the House. There was even a TV ad accusing Ferraro of taking rent from a pornographer. Ferraro, who had been a prominent defender of Anita Hill, responded with a TV ad drawing a parallel between Hill's tribulations and her own. "Just a year ago," the voice-over began, "a woman with courage faced lies, innuendos and smears. Now another woman whose life has been a fight for change is being smeared. Geraldine Ferraro is being smeared by Al D'Amato [New York's incumbent Republican senator], Bob Abrams, and even Liz Holtzman."

The *New York Times* was as disturbed by Ferraro's response as it was by Holtzman's attacks. "Is Ms. Ferraro implying that she expects more of Ms. Holtzman purely and simply because she's a woman?" asked the *Times*. "If so, the remark is as exclusionary as if she'd said it about someone who shares her faith or her ethnicity."[37]

Holtzman's sharp attacks on Ferraro had a clear and measurable effect on potential voters. Ferraro's lead over Abrams dropped to eight points in early September, and by the time voters went to the polls in mid-September, Ferraro's lead over Abrams had disappeared. But Holtzman had gained nothing from her attack strategy. The final vote count showed Ferraro losing to Abrams by a hair, while Holtzman came in dead last, behind Al Sharpton. Voters said they had been bothered by the nasty charges and countercharges during the final days of the campaign, and many complained of the ferocity of Holtzman's attacks on Ferraro.

"It was the ugliness of the battle that the public really responded to," said Tracy A. Essoglou, a member of the Woman's Action Coalition. "You saw people instinctively turn to Abrams. . . . When both Abrams and Holtzman started challenging Ferraro, rather than believing her and standing with her, some went with Abrams, who was just as much a part of the mud-slinging."

Women's groups were desolate over the outcome. "It's a terrible disappointment because New York is a state that was ready to and would elect a woman to the United States Senate," said NWPC's Woods. "It's a great missed opportunity." Letty Cottin Pogrebin, a founding editor of *Ms* magazine, was candid in her denunciation of Holtzman's nasty campaign. "In my view and the view of many other people with whom I have spoken, I will never support her for anything again," she said. "Her turn would have come. It was clear she never would have won this race. It was hubris that kept her in."

But some women, including feminist author Betty Friedan, decried the double standard that would blame Holtzman for Ferraro's defeat. An aide to a prominent New York politician explained: "Liz's gambit was to try to take Gerry out. When it didn't succeed, there was the perception that this was some kind of horror. But she tried to deliver a death blow and that is an option that any politician has at their disposal, though many people have taken it as some kind of betrayal of feminist idealogy."

Holtzman herself put the best face on her last-place finish, and insisted that she had no regrets about the tone of her campaign. "I think that to apply a standard to women who run—saying that they have to be treated differently and treat others differently—it's just wrong," she said. "We have to have the same expectations of candor from all of the candidates."[38]

The final disappointment and irony came in the November general elections, when Robert Abrams, victor over Ferraro and Holtzman, was vanquished by their common enemy, Republican Alfonse D'Amato.

The Ferraro-Holtzman battle had all the elements to make it a media spectacle: two female political stars letting their hair down in the Big Apple, a town known for its rowdy political campaigns and its uninhibited press coverage. Given the increasing number of women competing for office, would this kind of personalized feminine conflict be repeated across the country, and would it ultimately discourage female candidates from running against women, or running at all? This has not proved to be the case. The agony of the Ferraro-Holtzman conflict came not so much from the fact that two women were competing, but that they were from the same party and eminently electable, yet both were defeated. They were both broadly popular, and it was common knowledge that they were destined for higher office. Yet their political careers were apparently ended, though both are still young as politicians go. Running such candidates against each other was a colossal blunder that both parties will probably avoid in the future.

The 1992 California primaries, both Republican and Democrat, for Los Angeles County's 36th District bore some resemblance to New York's Ferraro-Holtzman battle. The GOP primary had 11 competitors, but the two heavy-hitters were Maureen Reagan, daughter of former President Ronald Reagan, and Joan Milke Flores, 11-year Los Angeles city councilwoman. Reagan had lost badly in California's 1982 GOP primary for the U.S. Senate, when her campaign was undermined by reports that her father, then in the White House, opposed her candidacy. Her support for abortion rights and the Equal Rights Amendment had always clashed with her father's conservative views, but in 1992 the Great Communicator publicly endorsed her early in the primary campaign and helped her to raise more money than any other candidate in the race.

Republican Flores, a veteran in Los Angeles politics, attacked Reagan as a carpetbagger—Reagan had recently moved to the district from nearby West Los Angeles—and recruited some big names from the GOP's far right to attack Reagan. Flores made effective use of a campaign mailing, titled "What's in a Name," in which arch-conservative Rep. Dana Rohrabacher described Flores as the "real Reagan Republican." Of Maureen Reagan, Rohrabacher said, "There is nothing in her background to indicate that she has the skills, experience or commitment to carry on President Reagan's legacy." Rohrabacher claimed, "The Reaganites in the White House always knew she was in the enemy camp."

Maureen Reagan clearly represented the moderate views within the Republican Party, while Flores was regarded as "Madonna to the GOP's conservative wing." H. Eric Shockman, a USC political science professor, concluded: "I'm looking at the thirty-sixth as a bellwether that will help tell where the heart and soul of the California GOP will be going." Indeed, Flores won the primary, Reagan sank into obscurity, and the California Republican Party has been racing to the right ever since.

A similar primary struggle emerged in the same district between two Democratic women. The best financed candidate was Jane Harman, a Washington attorney and former official in the Jimmy Carter White House. Challenging Harman was Ada Unruh, daughter-in-law of the late state treasurer, Jesse M. Unruh. Though Harman had lived in California since 1970, she, like Reagan in the GOP race, was accused of carpetbagging because of her recent move to the district. Harman's motto was, "Pro-Choice, Pro-Change," but Unruh charged that her loyalties would lie inside the Washington Beltway, not in the district. "If that's the worst they can say about me, then fine," responded Harman. "My focus is on November. I want to beat a Republican."[39]

Harman earned that chance by defeating Unruh in the Democratic primary.

Now, following two "woman-against-woman" primaries, California's 36th District approached a "woman-against-woman" general election. Party registration in the district was 46 percent Republican and 42 percent Democratic, an advantage that had been magnified in the past by the ability of Republicans to turn out the vote. The common wisdom locally was, "Whoever wins the Republican primary will be our next representative to Congress," and that made Joan Milke Flores the clear front runner in the general election. But California's South Bay voters had long tended to send conservative men like Robert Dornan and Dana Rohrabacher to Congress. Would they be willing to elect a conservative *woman*?

Flores initially received strong backing from Los Angeles business and harbor interests, as well as support from anti-abortion groups, while Democrat Harman, running for office for the first time, had the support of pro-choice women's groups. Flores painted Harman as a carpetbagger from inside the Washington Beltway, just as she had successfully characterized Maureen Reagan in the Republican primary. Harman attacked Flores as an entrenched, old-style politician who had accomplished little for the district and whose anti-abortion views were out of step with the voters. Flores responded, "I have gone through all the rigors of a single mother trying to make a living. I've been through it. . . . And abortion is not the only issue that women are interested in. They're interested in jobs and the economy and taxes. . . ."

Early polls showed Flores with a double-digit lead over Harman, but the gap began to close as voters discovered the candidates' positions on abortion. "In this 'Year of the Political Woman,' it's not just any woman," declared Harman. "I think this district more than any other in the country offers a very stark choice between women, and marks . . . the next level of women in politics."

When the voters went to the polls in November 1992, they gave Harman a decisive victory over Flores, but two years later Harman would have a more difficult battle against still another Republican woman, Councilwoman Susan Brooks. This time, the nationwide conservative and anti-incumbent tide made Harman even more vulnerable in her Republican-leaning district. In addition, her new female opponent was pro-choice, removing one of Harman's strongest campaign issues from 1992. Also, like so many other Democratic women from the class of 1992, Harman had acquired the political albatross of her vote for the Clinton budget plan. "My budget vote, which is controversial, will prove to be a wise vote," argued Harman. "[The] $500 million in deficit reduction, some of which has already occurred, I think is spurring the economy." She nonetheless claimed independence from the Clinton White House, citing her votes against NAFTA and for a balanced-budget amendment. Harman concluded, "I am a representative, and I have fought for people who happen to be Democrats, Republicans and independents, with good results."[40]

As election day approached, both women increased their attacks. Each charged the other with violations of federal election laws. Both denied the charges. Senate minority leader Bob Dole (R-Kans.), campaigning for Brooks, held up a *Time* magazine photo of Harman smiling at President Clinton and remarked, "It's bad enough you had to vote for [the Clinton Budget], but don't look happy about it." Brooks added, "She comes to the district and acts like a Reagan Republican. But she goes back to Washington and votes like a Clinton liberal."

Harman responded, "If [Brooks] wants to run against Bill Clinton, there's a presidential election coming up in 1996. This is a local campaign. . . . It's about my record of coming through for local voters."[41]

As bitter as the 1994 campaign had been, the election results turned out to be a confusing burlesque. On the day after the election, the vote count showed Brooks winning by just 93 votes, and she was immediately whisked off to Capitol Hill by House Speaker-to-be Newt Gingrich to join the seven other new Republican congresswomen. But by the time Brooks arrived in Washington, a revised vote count showed Harman ahead by 260 votes. No matter. Brooks appeared on CNN where she was referred to as one of the "new members" of Congress. On the "MacNeil/Lehrer News Hour" she was introduced as a "newly elected Republican." The Capitol Hill newspaper *Roll Call* actually ran a story about Brooks as the likely freshman class president. In the real world, shortly before Thanksgiving, Harman declared victory when the official vote count gave her an 800-vote edge.

Undaunted Republicans invited Brooks back to Washington for freshman orientation, but she sensibly declined. Nonetheless, Brooks and her lawyers continued to maintain that Harman won with votes cast illegally by nonresidents. Harman asked the House Oversight Committee to dismiss Brooks's complaint, noting that the challenger did not meet deadlines for filing papers and failed to follow other required procedures, such as pursuing a recount or state-court challenge, but the Republican-controlled Congress postponed action on Harman's request. Finally, on May 9, 1995, a three-member task force of the House Oversight Committee voted along party lines to give Brooks until May 19 to document her charges. "What we're doing is saying, 'Put up or shut up,' " said House Oversight Chairman Bill Thomas (R-Calif.). But even when Brooks was unable to "put up," the Republican-controlled Oversight Committee decided to send a three-member task force to Harman's Los Angeles district for a June 26 "field hearing."

Harman responded: "The taxpayers of this district—now required to pay the considerable costs of a special hearing in California which could have been held without expense in Washington—should not have to put up with this any longer. With her refusal to accept the decision of the voters in November, Susan Brooks is imposing a 'sore loser' tax on all the citizens of the district."[42]

Brooks eventually dropped her challenge, but Democrats have accused her of using the challenge to gain name recognition for a rematch in 1996.

Harman's reelection victory is attributed at least in part to California's statewide "Women Vote!" project, aimed at mobilizing "occasional" Democratic women voters. In 1994, more than 16,000 women voters were targeted in Harman's district. These women had voted in the 1992 presidential election, but not in the midterm elections. All indications were that they would sit out the 1994 midterm elections as well, unless they were motivated to do otherwise. The "Women Vote!" project began by sending these women a letter from Hillary Rodham Clinton, which was followed up by phone calls and a vote-by-mail application. Ultimately, 1,749 of the targeted women applied to vote by absentee ballot—more than enough to put Harman over the top.

Harman's series of primary and general-election battles against women showed no signs of the political fratricide that resulted from the 1992 New York primary. Ideology, not gender, was where the battle was joined. Perhaps the most important aspect of the women-versus-women elections in California's 36th District is that women won them all. Republicans, Democrats, primaries, general elections—a woman was the ultimate victor at every stage. In such circumstances, gender guilt and recriminatory postmortems are inappropriate, no matter how fierce the campaign rhetoric may have been.

Rep. Ileana Ros-Lehtinen (R-Fla.) was the only sitting congresswoman to be challenged by another woman in 1992, and that race was fought over an issue so explosive that the challenger, Magda Montiel Davis, was the target of repeated bomb threats. The issue on which this election turned was

Fidel Castro, and though both women were anti–Castro Cuban exiles, Davis favored easing the embargo against Cuba. In Miami, that was cause for her to be pilloried in the Spanish-language press as a *Castrista* and *comunista*, making her a target of right-wing Cuban terrorist groups. While all of these fireworks were occurring, the incumbent Ros-Lehtinen virtually ignored Davis in her campaign rhetoric, concentrating instead on her own strong anticommunist credentials.

The press did all the dirty work, and in that regard the Florida election bore some resemblance to the New York primary of just a few months earlier. But the press coverage and postelection analysis showed little interest in the "cat fight" angle, and women's groups had no cause for handwringing. Two women won their party's nomination, and one of them went to Congress. In a two-party system, you can't do better than that. Still, it appears that Davis had seen enough of Miami's violent politics. In 1994, Ros-Lehtinen ran unopposed.

In 1994, 11 incumbent women were challenged by women, and only two incumbents, Rep. Karen Shepherd (D-Utah) and Rep. Jolene Unsoeld (D-Wash.), lost. Shepherd actually ran against the same woman in 1992 and 1994, first defeating Enid Greene, 53-to-47 percent, and then losing by almost 20,000 votes in 1994 to the new and improved Enid Greene Waldholtz (now married and sporting a longer name).

Texas Democrat Eddie Bernice Johnson defeated Republican Lucy Cain in 1992 by a whopping 74-to-26 percent, and, for good measure, she did it all over again in 1994 by a virtually identical margin. Also in 1992, Lynn Schenk (D) beat Judy Jarvis (R) by ten points in California. In 1994, Rep. Nancy Pelosi (D-Calif.) defeated Elsa Cheung, Rep. Rosa De Lauro (D-Conn.) defeated Susan Johnson, Rep. Nancy Johnson (R-Conn.) defeated Charlotte Koskoff, Rep. Jan Meyers (R-Kans.) defeated Judy Hancock, Rep. Pat Danner (D-Mo.) defeated Tina Tucker, Rep. Barbara Vucanovich (R-Nev.) defeated Janet Greeson, and Rep. Nydia Velazquez (D-N.Y.) defeated Genevive Brennan.

Ideology, religion, and race were the major factors in these races, and gender was not an issue. It should also be mentioned that virtually none of the recent general-election races between women have been tightly contested. Of the 16 general election races between women in 1992 and 1994, only one was decided by less than 6 percentage points. The average margin of victory in such races during 1992 was about 21 percentage points, and the average margin in 1994 was more than 32 points. This may help to explain the lack of drama associated with those contests.

Another reason for the relative absence of significant gender conflict in general elections between two women is the Republican party line on gender. The "official" conservative view, parroted by women politicians themselves, is that they are not congresswomen, they are congresspersons, there are no women's issues, there are only constituent issues. Even the

universal desire to increase the number of women in Congress is down-
played because it smacks of "quotas." Given this "gender-blind" approach
by one of the two parties involved in every general election, it is no surprise
that the campaigns tend to submerge feminine conflict.

THE NEW CONGRESSIONAL WOMAN

The 1994 Republican landslide, and particularly the victories of the seven
Republican women in the House, may have shattered the idea of a homo-
geneous "woman's agenda." For one thing, it widened the crack in the
staunchly pro-choice position of most congresswomen. Of the 11 women
elected to Congress in 1994, six are pro life. Only one of the seven new
Republican women are pro choice. Pro-choice representatives Jolene Unsoeld (D-Wash.) and Karen Shepherd (D-Utah) both lost to antichoice
Republican women: Linda Smith and Enid Greene Waldholtz.

Women in Congress have traditionally been more liberal than their male
counterparts, but the views and priorities of the newly elected congressional women are as varied as among the male members. "As we move
closer to parity it stands to reason the issues the women choose to advance
would be as diverse as the group we are electing," said Pat Reilley of the
National Women's Political Caucus.[43]

Narrowly defeated Republican challenger Susan Brooks put it more
bluntly: "We can share tampons, but we don't necessarily share political
views."

Within the increasingly partisan atmosphere on Capitol Hill, party alle-
giance is dividing women as never before. One vivid example of the
conflicting political agendas of today's congressional women came on the
1994 campaign trail when Rep. Susan Molinari (R-N.Y.) flew across the
country to Oregon to campaign against her Democratic colleague, Rep.
Elizabeth Furse (D-Ore.), in support of her ultra-conservative opponent,
Republican Bill Witt. Witt's base of support included the Oregon Citizens
Alliance (OCA), a group led by Christian conservative activists who opposed abortion and sponsored the notorious "Measure 13" in Oregon,
which would prevent local governments from protecting the civil rights of
homosexuals. Molinari, as a moderate Republican, would never have endorsed such positions, yet she made a television ad attacking Furse as soft
on crime and endorsing Witt. Furse won the race with just 50 percent of the
vote against Witt and two independent candidates, but she still remains
bitter about the carpetbagging incident.

Enid Greene Waldholtz, who successfully challenged incumbent Rep.
Karen Shepherd (D-Utah) in 1994, was careful not to run on a so-called
"women's platform." She, in fact, denies that there are such things as
women's issues and feels that no political candidate, male or female, should
use gender as a campaign issue.

"I think, frankly, that women who try to use gender as an issue should not be suprised when men bring it up and women don't like it. I tried to make a point in my campaign not to stigmatize issues as women's issues. I think it's important that we look at issues as how they impact all of us, men and women. I set my own agenda. Nobody can set that for me. What you're seeing now is women in both parties with different views across the spectrum. Nobody can stand up and speak for all women."[44]

One of Waldholtz's colleagues from the record-breaking 1994 class of Republican women, Rep. Sue Myrick (N.C.), says Republicans are less likely than Democrats to view issues as male or female. "We approach it on the Republican side much more as issues of concern to the general population, not just women," she said.[45]

On the other side, Democratic women seem less willing to scuttle the "woman's agenda," which brought many of them to Congress and is still featured in their campaigns. In 1992, Patty Murray (D-Wash.) successfully used her nickname, "mother in tennis shoes," to help her win a Senate seat, while Lynn Woolsey (D-Calif.) touted her former status as a welfare mother to help win a House seat. In 1994, motherhood again became a campaign issue when Zoe Lofgren (D-Calif.), in filling out her declaration of candidacy, included "mother" in the blank where candidates describe their occupation. Election officials balked, citing California law that prohibits such descriptions under the heading "occupation."

"They're telling me motherhood is not a job," Lofgren said after being told she could not describe herself as a mother on the ballot. "As any mother will tell you, it is a job, 24 hours a day. It seems to me that being a parent is probably the most important job to the future of our country. If the law says that doesn't count, the law is wrong."[46]

Lofgren, who at the time of the election was also a full-time politician—a Santa Clara supervisor—said her decision to use the term "mother" along with "county supervisor" stemmed from her belief that children and their needs are not receiving sufficient attention from the federal government. Lofgren won her race for the House, defeating her male challenger with 65 percent of the vote.

Lofgren was one of just four new Democratic women elected to the House in 1994, as Republicans generally dominated the ranks of congressional winners. The seven new GOP women were immediately and prominently embraced by incoming House Speaker Newt Gingrich (R-Ga.), who doled out prime committee and leadership posts to several of the women. Sue Myrick (R-N.C.) was quickly named to the Republican Transition Team, the group responsible for easing the new Republican majority into place and pinpointing congressional operations that needed to be reformed, upgraded, or eliminated. Myrick, 54, came to Congress after serving two years on the Charlotte City Council and four years as Charlotte mayor. Two years before winning her House seat in 1994, she ran unsuccessfully for the

Republican nomination for U.S. Senate. That run, coupled with her previous experience in local politics, gave Myrick wide name recognition going into the five-way primary. She eventually won the nomination and easily defeated her heavily outspent Democratic challenger. On the campaign trail and in office, Myrick has focused on tougher sentences for criminals. She supports the death penalty and believes that those who commit crimes against children and the elderly should have their sentences doubled. On health care, Myrick says many people are uninsured by their own choice, and government therefore has no responsibility to guarantee coverage to every American.

Like many of her Republican female colleagues, Myrick says gender did not play a role in her campaign.

"In 1994, we didn't run as women," she says. "We ran as the best candidate. We were accepted across the board as the best candidates. We weren't differentiating between men and women."

But while she says Republicans focus more on issues rather than gender, she predicts more and more women will run for office in the future. "There isn't any question that the Republican party is changing," she says. "We've [women] been accepted into the Republican leadership. It's just that the Republican party has come to realize they've got a wealth of talent out there. In the past, there have not been as many Republican women running as Democratic women. That's why there were more Democratic women in office."[47]

Another Republican freshman embraced by the House leadership in 1995 was Enid Greene Waldholtz (R-Utah). In the opening days of the 104th Congress, Waldholtz was appointed by Speaker Gingrich to the Rules Committee, the first Republican newcomer to be named to the panel in 70 years. Waldholtz had begun lobbying for the committee assignment within days of her election. While she had never before held elective office, she was not new to politics. She is the former national chairperson of the Young Republicans and previously served as deputy chief of staff to Utah's Republican governor, Norman Bangerter.

Waldholtz, 37, came to office in 1994 after spending $2 million of her own money on the race. She campaigned extensively on the GOP's Contract with America, advocating a balanced budget and pledging to serve no more than 12 years in the House.

Waldholtz, one of the two women to defeat female incumbents in 1994, denies that the elections were a step backward for women in congressional politics. "We have more Republican women freshmen now than we have ever had in any class. We have as many women as we did before, only the partisanship changed among freshmen." She adds: "It will be the Year of the Woman when nobody brings it up. In 1994 we took a big step in that direction. Only when the shock wears off can it really be called the year of the woman. It will mean we've come further when it's no longer a surprise to people."[48]

The second woman to turn a female incumbent out of office in 1994 was Linda Smith (R-Wash.), who defeated three-term representative Jolene Unsoeld (D). Smith, a state senator and Christian activist, came to Congress after becoming the first person in Washington state to receive her party's nomination as a write-in candidate. Smith's grass-roots network of Christian activists, along with her efforts to spearhead two successful citizen initiatives on campaign ethics and tax reform, gave her strong name recognition in the 1994 campaign and helped energize her all-volunteer organization. That organization mailed write-in instructions to 150,000 homes and called 40,000 households. The write-in campaign was launched after the Republican's frontrunner, millionaire businessman Timothy Moyer, dropped out of the race one month before the primary. Smith benefited greatly from the $2 million Moyer had spent against Unsoeld before quitting the race.

Once coming to the Hill, Smith, 45, was named as the chair of the Small Business Subcommittee on Tax and Finance, making her one of only three freshmen to be named as panel chairmen.

During Helen Chenoweth's (R-Idaho) campaign against two-term Rep. Larry LaRocco (D), she was called an "extremist" and a mouthpiece for the radical right. The name-calling was sparked in part by statements such as Chenoweth's claim that state civil rights laws have protected "everyone but the white Anglo-Saxon male." After coming under criticism for the remark, Chenoweth refused to apologize, saying, "I think it speaks for itself."[49] In a state where Clinton's popularity ratings are among the lowest in the nation, LaRocco's shaky position as the only Democrat in the Idaho delegation proved more damaging than Chenoweth's "extreme" views. She won with 55 percent of the vote and handed LaRocco the worst defeat for an Idaho incumbent in 62 years.

Chenoweth, 57, describes herself as "Mr. Smith goes to Washington in a skirt." She says she had never before seriously thought of entering politics. Though she had never previously run for office, she had served as a congressional aide. Before facing LaRocco in the general election, she became the upset winner in a four-way Republican primary. Her close ties with social and religious conservatives helped her overwhelmingly defeat her Republican primary opponents, including former lieutenant governor David Leroy. A staunch opponent of abortion, Chenoweth was also the only major political figure in Idaho to support an unsuccessful state ballot initiative that would have restricted civil-rights protections for gays.

Another strong opponent of abortion and gay rights is Andres Seastrand (R-Calif.), who succeeded one-term republican Michael Huffington (R) after he lost a bid for the Senate. Like many of her freshman Republican colleagues, Seastrand drew heavy support from the Christian coalition and the Eagle Forum. Like Chenoweth, she successfully fought charges that she was too far to the political right, winning her seat with fewer than 2,000 votes against religion professor Walter Holden Capps.

Religion was a major issue in Seastrand's campaign. When a local newspaper reported that Seastrand gave a church sermon blaming Southern California's earthquakes, floods, and fires on "God's wrath," Seastrand decried the report as an assault on her religious beliefs.

The only female Republican freshman who is pro choice is Rep. Sue Kelly (R-N.Y.). A former rape crisis counselor, Kelly's victory came only after defeating six conservative men, including former representative Joe DioGuardi, in the primary. In the general election, she defeated Hamilton Fish Jr., the son of the retiring incumbent who had held the seat for 26 years. Fish was, in fact, the latest in a long line of congressmen named Hamilton Fish, going as far back as 1843. It was expected that his prominent name would carry him to victory, but Kelly ended a political dynasty and became the first woman to ever represent that New York district.

Kelly, 58, credits her victory to "a lot of hard work—ringing door bells, visiting shops, phoning people—and the fact that the people of this district were very ready to hear something besides politics as usual." Kelly describes herself as "a hard-working Republican woman who has been active in the party for 35 years."

"I've been getting Republicans elected for decades until this year when I decided 'Why not me?' "[50]

Kelly's strong pro-choice stance is balanced by her conservative positions on crime and fiscal policy. She supports capital punishment and the balanced-budget amendment. During her general election campaign, the Westchester Coalition for Legal Abortion withdrew its earlier endorsement of Kelly, citing her support for the Contract with America, which contained some positions objectionable to the abortion-rights coalition.

Freshman representative Barbara Cubin (R-Wyo.) gained notoriety during her 1994 campaign when it was reported that she had distributed penis-shaped cookies to her colleagues in the Wyoming state legislature. She denied making the cookies, but admitted to distributing them. Ironically, the incident did not seem to harm Cubin during an election year that was dominated by the call for greater "family values."

Cubin, 49, won the open seat vacated by Rep. Craig Thomas (R), who was running for the Senate, to become the first woman elected to Congress from Wyoming. A chemist by training, Cubin first became involved in politics through community grass-roots organizations. She was elected to the state house in 1986 and to the state senate six years later. In winning her Republican nomination for the U.S. House, she bested a wide field of candidates, which included a state house speaker and a former congressional aide.

Once on Capitol Hill, Cubin was elected by her 72 fellow Republican colleagues to serve as the secretary of her freshman class.

On the Democratic side, Sheila Jackson Lee (Tex.) was the only new black woman elected to Congress in 1994 and one of only four challengers to defeat incumbents during the primary elections. The man Lee brought down in the primary was a giant in Texas politics. Craig Washington (D) had served for 22 years in state politics before coming to the Hill in 1989 to fill the seat of Rep. Mickey Leland (D), who had been killed in a plane crash during a relief mission to Africa. After her 63-to-37 percent primary victory over Washington, Lee easily won the general election in her overwhelmingly Democratic district.

Lee, 45, a mother of two children, nine and 15 years old, was elected by the 13 House Democratic freshmen to serve as their class president. She says she has a strong commitment to child care and health care reform, but says any welfare reform must provide health and child care along with job training. As Democratic freshman class president, Lee acknowledges that while her class may be small, she hopes they will leave a mark on Congress. "The attitude of the freshman class, the Democrats, has been that we collaborate and we collectively serve and so we have come here through the storm of 1994, the bold, the brave, and the few."[51]

One Democratic freshman who, like her Republican colleagues, says gender did not play a role in her campaign was Karen McCarthy (Mo.). McCarthy won her primary race by defeating ten other candidates, including four women. In the general election to succeed Rep. Alan Wheat (D), who was black, McCarthy defeated a black Republican, Ron Freeman. Freeman, a former professional football player, received backing from former HUD Secretary Jack Kemp, but his conservative views proved unpopular in his Democratic district.

"Frankly, I wanted to run on my talent, skills, abilities, and positions on the issues, not on my being a woman," McCarthy said. "Gender was not an issue in my campaign, and that was a great relief to me. Out there in America, gender, race are not what's important to the voters at the time of election."

Still, McCarthy says women do bring a "unique perspective" to the legislative table. The former chair of the state House Ways and Means Committee, McCarthy says women's views are needed on such "nonfeminist" issues such as taxes. For example, McCarthy says tax laws have historically not been favorable toward single women.

"It's important that our voices are heard," she says. "Men would give it some notice and then proceed. Having women at the table improves legislation."[52]

While McCarthy says gender did not play a major role in the 1994 elections, "motherhood" became a prominent issue in several races. Rep. Lynn Rivers (D-Mich.) says she entered politics as a "mom who got mad at the system." A central theme of Rivers's campaign was her life story, which she says voters could identify with. Rivers got married the day after her high school graduation and had her first child when she was 18. Still, she worked her way through the University of Michigan and then law school.

Rivers, 39, won the seat being vacated by 15-term Rep. Bill Ford (D). Before coming to the Hill, she served for eight years on the Ann Arbor Board of Education and for two years in the Michigan State House. Like her predecessor, who chaired the Education and Labor Committee, Rivers says education and jobs will be the focus of her agenda. She says education is the key to improving the economy by preparing students for a changing job market.

Like Rivers, Rep. Zoe Lofgren (D-Calif.) used motherhood to her advantage in the 1994 elections. She launched her campaign while standing on a kitchen breadbox in the living room of her house, stressing her middle-class roots and her motherly concerns about violence in the schools and streets.

"I think the voters . . . sent me here to stand up for working people and their children," she said shortly after her election. "That's what we talked about for nearly a year, to focus on our future, to make sure that we invest especially in young people from a very early age on to college, to make sure that we have a generation that is adequately prepared and focused to be productive as a work force and reputable as citizens. If we do that we will avoid all kinds of problems in crime and dependency."

Lofgren, 48, succeeded 16-term Rep. Don Edwards (D). Her toughest race was in the primary, but after winning the Democratic nomination against a number of men, she easily defeated her Republican opponent.

Like Rivers, Lofgren says she is concerned about education in America and has attacked the Republican's Contract with America for its lack of attention to the issue. "I do agree that the election was a rejection of business as usual," she said. "There's no question that that was true. I ran not to protect the status quo. But I don't think that necessarily translates to the Contract with America."[53]

NOTES

1. Wendy Kaminer, "Crashing the Locker Room," *Atlantic Monthly*, July 1992, p. 65.

2. Interviews on "To the Contrary," Maryland Public Television, November 13, 1994.

3. "Caucus Predicts More Women Will Be Elected to Congress," *Washington Post*, October 27, 1994, p. A26.

4. Authors' interview with Rep. Patsy Mink (D-Hawaii), December 2, 1994.

5. Kevin Merida, "'Insiders' Now, Women on Hill Work to Preserve Gains of '92," *Washington Post*, September 6, 1994, p. 1.

6. Interview on "To the Contrary," November 13, 1994.

7. Authors' interview with Rep. Enid Greene Waldholtz (R-Utah), January 10, 1995.

8. Tony Kornheiser, "How the Gingrich Stole Christmas," *Washington Post*, November 13, 1994, p. F8.

9. Kevin Merida, "Hill Reformers of '92 Bow to Class of '94," *Washington Post*, December 1, 1994, p. A1.

10. *USA Today*, December 1, 1994, p. A2.

11. Fundraising panel featuring Democratic representatives Leslie Byrne (Va.), Cynthia McKinney (Ga.), Anna Eshoo (Calif.), Lynn Woolsey (Calif.), Lucille Roybal-Allard (Calif.), Karen Shepherd (Utah), and Carolyn Maloney (N.Y.), June 21, 1994.

12. Dennis Farney, "Utah's Shepherd Guards a Democratic Outpost as Party's Support Sags, GOP Challenge Grows," *Wall Street Journal*, September 19, 1994, p. A16.

13. "Maria Cantwell Goes to Washington," *Washington Post*, March 24, 1993, p. B3.

14. John Markoff, "An Administration Reversal on Wiretapping Technology," *New York Times*, July 21, 1994, p. D7.

15. Robin Toner, "Loss of Seat Dims GOP Hopes," *New York Times*, March 30, 1989, p. A16.

16. "Indiana House Race Shows Incumbency Is Still of Value," *New York Times*, November 3, 1990, p. 32.

17. Timothy Egan, "Debate over Logging Means Trouble for Incumbent in Washington State," *New York Times*, September 25, 1990, p. A18.

18. *Los Angeles Times*, April 28, 1992, p. A1.

19. Fundraising panel featuring Rep. Lynn Woolsey (D-Calif.) and other Democratic congresswomen, June 21, 1994.

20. Ibid.

21. "Postcards from the Capitol," *Los Angeles Times*, June 3, 1993, p. A5.

22. Fundraising panel featuring Rep. Carolyn Maloney (D-N.Y.) and other Democratic congresswomen, June 21, 1994.

23. Roxanne Roberts, "In a League of Her Own," *Washington Post*, August 15, 1993, p. C1.

24. Clara Bingham, "The Women on the Hill," *Vogue*, August 1993, p. 267.

25. Fundraising panel featuring Democratic congresswomen, June 21, 1994.

26. Carole Chaney and Barbara Sinclair, "Women and the 1992 House Elections," in *The Year of the Woman*, ed. by Elizabeth Adell Cook, et al., Boulder, Colo: Westview Press, 1994, p. 127.

27. Authors' interview with Rep. Enid Greene Waldholtz (R-Utah), January 10, 1995.

28. Kaminer, "Crashing the Locker Room," p. 63.

29. Alan McConagha, "Inside Politics," *Washington Times*, December 16, 1994, p. A5.

30. Ann O'Hanlon, "Politics," *Washington Post*, December 18, 1994, p. A27.

31. Authors' interview with Rep. Sue Myrick (R-N.C.), February 2, 1995.

32. Jody Newman, "Perception and Reality: Chapter II, A Study Comparing the Success of Men and Women in the 1994 Primaries, Executive Summary," *National Women's Political Caucus*, September 1994, p. 1.

33. Benjamin Sheffner, "What If Court Upholds Term Limits," *Roll Call*, May 4, 1995, p. 1.

34. Authors' interview with representatives Martin Frost (D-Tex.) and Pat Schroeder (D-Colo.), January 12, 1995.

35. Postelection press conference on women and politics, Washington, D.C., National Education Association, November 10, 1994.

36. George Curry, "2 N.Y. Senate Hopefuls Split Women's Groups," *Chicago Tribune*, March 29, 1992, p. 5.

37. "Unfair Standard," *New York Times*, August 30, 1992, Sect. 4, p. 14.

38. Catherine Manegold, "Holtzman and Ferraro Fought Double Standards as Well as Each Other," *New York Times*, September 16, 1992, p. B6.

39. George Hatch, "GOP Heavy-Hitters," *Los Angeles Times*, May 25, 1992, p. B1, B4.

40. Ted Johnson, "GOP Efforts to Unseat Harman Move into High Gear," *Los Angeles Times*, March 20, 1994, p. J4.

41. Ted Johnson, "Brooks Hammers at Harman's Ties to Clinton," *Los Angeles Times*, October 20, 1994, p. B3.

42. Tim Curran, "House Oversight Task Force Will Go on the Road to California, Too," *Roll Call*, June 8, 1995, p. 10.

43. Diane Duston, "Now Women Are Challenging Women in Congress," *Associated Press*, October 24, 1994.

44. Authors' interview with Rep. Enid Greene Waldholtz (R-Utah), January 10, 1995.

45. Authors' interview with Rep. Sue Myrick (R-N.C.), February 2, 1995.

46. Jennifer Warren, "It's a Vote Against Motherhood, Says Rebuffed Candidate," *Los Angeles Times*, April 8, 1994, p. 3A.

47. Authors' interview with Rep. Sue Myrick (R-N.C.), February 2, 1995.

48. Authors' interview with Rep. Enid Greene Waldholtz (R-Utah), January 10, 1995.

49. "Politics," *Washington Post*, September 11, 1994, p. A21.

50. James Feron, "In the 19th, A Family Seat Vs. First Woman," *The New York Times (Westchester Weekly)*, September 18, 1994, p. 1.

51. Interview on Charlie Rose's "This Is America," Maryland Public Television, December 22, 1994.

52. Authors' interview with Rep. Karen McCarthy (D-Mo.), February 15, 1995.

53. Interview on the "McNeil-Lehrer News Hour," Maryland Public Television, November 16, 1994.

Chapter 3

Aspiring to Power

COMMITTEE POWER

Though women came to the House and Senate in unprecedented numbers during the 1990s, their power within Congress has grown only minimally. One factor in women's slow ascension to congressional power has been their meager representation in the committee structure, within which all major business on Capitol Hill is accomplished. Ironically, it was not 1992, the Year of the Woman, that gave women their greatest boost within the congressional power structure. The Year of the Woman led to the 103rd Congress, during which no woman was able to attain a full committee chairmanship within the House or the Senate. During that same Congress, only six of the 117 subcommittees in the House and only two of the 86 subcommittees in the Senate were chaired by women. It was, in fact, the 1994 Republican landslide that pushed a record number of women into the upper echelons of the congressional leadership.

The 1994 elections, which brought Republican control over both houses of Congress, were expected to make things worse for women, but despite the net gain of just one congressional seat for women, the committee picture brightened in the 104th Congress. The Republican-controlled 104th Congress produced two full committee chairmanships for women in the House and one in the Senate. Seven House subcommittees and two Senate subcommittees were handed over to women. Sen. Nancy Kassebaum (R-Kans.) became the chair of the Education and Labor Committee—the first woman since 1945 to head a Senate committee and only the second in history. In the House, the new Republican leadership thrust Rep. Nancy Johnson (R-Conn.) to the top of the ethics committee—formally known as the Committee on Standards of Official Conduct—and Rep. Jan Meyers (R-Kans.)

into the chair of the Small Business Committee. Meyers and Johnson, who under Democratic contol had been the ranking members of their panels, became the first female chairs of full committees in that chamber since 1976. Rep. Barbara Vucanovich (R-Nev.) became one of the 13 new "Cardinals," as the chairmen of the powerful House Appropriations subcommittees are called. Vucanovich now chairs the subcommittee on Military Construction, which will oversee $9 billion of expenditures in fiscal 1995. Vucanovich also made history in the 104th Congress when she and Rep. Susan Molinari (R-N.Y.) became the first women in history to serve simultaneously in the Republican leadership.

But while the Republican takeover improved the numbers of women in top committee and leadership positions it did not alleviate the gross under-representation of women as rank and file members of the most powerful committees in the House. On the Appropriations Committee, responsible for doling out all federal funds, women make up just three of the 24 Democrats on the panel. Only one of the 32 Republican appropriators are women. On the Commerce Committee, one of the Hill's true power bases with extensive jurisdiction over such things as telecommunications, health care, energy policy, and foreign commerce, there are no women among the 25 Republicans, and only three women among the 21 Democrats who sit on the panel. Those three were all part of the record-breaking class of women elected to office in 1992.

The most dramatic public display of women's exclusion from committee power came in late 1991, when the Senate Judiciary Committee held confirmation hearings on Clarence Thomas, President Bush's nominee to the Supreme Court. Those hearings became the year's hottest Capitol Hill story when Anita Hill, a distinguished law professor, accused Thomas, a district court judge and former head of the Equal Employment Opportunity Commission (EEOC), of sexual harassment during the period when she worked under him at the EEOC. Hill's charges were initially kept out of the public eye by the all-male Senate Judiciary Committee, which chose not to pursue them.

Over in the House, many women rose to the floor to protest the Senate committee's inaction, and seven congresswomen actually marched to the Senate to meet with the majority leader and demand that the Juduciary Committee fully investigate Hill's sexual harassment charges. Challenged at the door by a Senate staffer, they were denied access as "strangers." Only after pointing out the television cameras documenting the confrontation were the congresswomen able to convince the guardians of the Senate that a brief meeting with the majority leader was the best way to avoid an awkward incident. The humiliating encounter is described in detail in Sen. Barbara Boxer's book, *Strangers in the Senate*.

Eventually, hearings were held, though many considered them to be a travesty. The personal lives and characters of Thomas and Hill were examined by the all-male committee and by millions of fascinated television viewers. Rep. Louise Slaughter (D-N.Y.) recalls, "[A]s I was watching those men on the Judiciary Committee peering down at Anita Hill, I became so filled with emotion. . . . I was so nervous for her. . . . I was like a hen on a hot egg."[1]

The public judgments rendered on Thomas and Hill would vary, predictably along ideological and gender lines, but one conclusion was virtually unanimous: something was very wrong with the committee process that staged this event. The *Atlantic Monthly* said, "The committee looked like an aging former football team from some segregated school. . . . In a post-literate age the video images of the Judiciary Committee were also powerfully persuasive; they dramatized the homogeneity of the Senate more than statistics and polemics ever could."

The image of the Senate Judiciary Committee, 18 white, middle-aged men, ignoring and trivializing Anita Hill's sexual harassment charges against a man who, if confirmed, would interpret the nation's sexual harassment laws for a generation, made men uneasy and women furious. Former New York congresswoman Bella Abzug said she was not surprised at the all-male committee's cavalier treatment of sexual harassment, because it was a way of life for them.

On the morning when Anita Hill was scheduled to testify before the committee, Sen. Barbara Mikulski (D-Md.) called chairman Joseph Biden to protest the proceedings. As a result, invitations were hastily issued to Mikulski and Sen. Nancy Kassebaum (R-Kans.) to attend the Judiciary Committee hearings as "guests." Both women declined.

Mikulski complained that their invitations were offered just 15 minutes before the hearing began. She wasn't even in Washington. Mikulski says bluntly, "I was not on the committee. It was not my job to give an imprimatur to the hearings. It was not my job to prop them up or do a whitewash." Sen. Kassebaum explained, "Barbara and I felt it would have been demeaning."[2]

Sen. Barbara Boxer (D-Calif.), then one of the House women who marched on the Senate to protest the conduct of the hearings, recalls: "[T]he Senate Judiciary Committee, looking like a relic from another time and place, struck a chord of irrelevancy. . . . America, and in particular, American women, were uncomfortable with the way the whole issue was handled, were uncomfortable with the way the Senate looked—and the Anita Hill incident became a catalyst for change. . . . Change became the political slogan of the 1992 elections, and who would personify change more than the people who *weren't* on the Senate Judiciary Committee."[3] Even behind the scenes, the all-male committee exercised questionable, perhaps biased, judgment in ways that are only now coming to public attention. Angela Wright, a former employee of Clarence Thomas who could have corroborated Anita Hill's charges, was never called to testify before the committee.

Like Hill, she told of being harassed by Thomas, and she believed that Hill's charges were credible because she had been subjected to similar treatment. Wright says, "Clarence Thomas did constantly pressure me to date him. At one point, Clarence Thomas made comments about my anatomy. Clarence Thomas made comments about women's anatomy quite often. At one point, Clarence Thomas came by my apartment at night, unannounced and uninvited."

Wright had been subpoened to appear and flown to Washington, where she waited for three days. Wright recalls that none of the men on the committee, Republican or Democrat, *wanted* her to testify. Sen. Paul Simon (D-Ill.) remembers a meeting of the Judiciary Committee members in Sen. Ted Kennedy's (D-Mass.) office at which time a consensus was reached *not* to call Wright as a witness. Simon recalls that the Republicans felt that Wright's story "confirmed the sexual harassment side of things," while the Democrats feared that the credibility of Wright's story might be compromised because she had been fired by Thomas. According to Simon, no senator at that meeting argued that Wright must be called.

In the end, the committee members agreed to limit their witness lists, and Wright didn't make the cut. She remembers one senator saying that Thomas's denial of Hill's charges was good enough for him. Another senator told her that if there was "no touching" there was "no offense." Charles Ogletree, one of Anita Hill's attorneys, called the committee's treatment of Wright "despicable and unforgivable." Sen. Simon says he was later "stunned" to learn that still another woman was available to corroborate Wright's account. Today he claims that if he had known that when the committee members met, he would have insisted that Wright be called.

Cynthia Hogan, counsel for Sen. Biden (D-Del.), the Judiciary Committee chair, says the Republicans were so anxious to prevent Angela Wright from testifying that they agreed to accept the transcript of her deposition *unrebutted*. Because this meant that they accepted it as basically true, Hogan regarded it as a tremendous victory at the time. But when Wright's deposition was essentially ignored by the Judiciary Committee and the press, it was clear that there was no victory here.[4]

In the wake of the controversial Thomas/Hill hearings, two women, Sen. Dianne Feinstein (D-Calif.) and Sen. Carol Moseley-Braun (D-Ill.), joined the Judiciary Committee, to sit alongside Anita Hill's former interrogators, men like Strom Thurmond (R-S.C.), Orrin Hatch (R-Utah), and Arlen Specter (R-Pa.). There is hope that the Anita Hill affair will allow a woman's voice to be heard on *all* congressional committees, but history suggests that major change will come grudgingly. In the 78 years since the first woman was elected to Congress, there have been only 12 women who have held full committee chairs—two in the Senate, ten in the House. Two of those women, representatives Yvonne Brathwaite Burke (D-Calif.) and Martha Griffiths (D-Mich.), headed the somewhat trivial Select Committee on the

House Beauty Shop. When Sen. Nancy Kassebaum (R-Kans.) was named to head the Committee on Labor and Human Resources in 1995, she became the first woman to head a Senate panel in 49 years. The only female who had previously headed a committee in that chamber was Sen. Hattie Caraway (D-Ark.), chair of the Committee on Enrolled Bills from 1935 to 1946.

The very first woman chair in Congress was Rep. May Ella Nolan (R-Calif.) who headed the Committee on Expenditures in the Post Office Department from 1923 to 1926. The woman who served most frequently as a committee chair was Rep. Mary Norton (D-N.J.), who headed the District of Columbia Committee from 1933 to 1938, followed by the Labor Committee from 1939 to 1948, and then the House Administration Committee from 1951 to 1952. From 1939 to 1944, Rep. Caroline O'Day (D-N.Y.) chaired the Committee on the Election of the President and Vice President. Rep. Edith Rogers (R-Mass.) chaired the Veterans Affairs Committee from 1949 to 1956, and Rep. Leonor Sullivan (D-Mo.) headed the Merchant Marine and Fisheries Committee from 1973 to 1976. More recently, Rep. Pat Schroeder (D-Colo.) headed the Select Committee on Children, Youth, and Families for two years before it was abolished in 1993 when the House eliminated all its "select" panels.

The lack of female representation among congressional leaders and committee heads cannot be rationalized simply by their small numbers in elected office. In 1993, blacks made up about 14 percent of the House Democrats, the majority party at the time, and held 14 percent of full committee and subcommittee chairs. Hispanics comprised 6 percent of the House Democrats, and held 5 percent of the chairmanships. Women, on the other hand, comprised a total of 14 percent of the House Democrats, yet held only 4 percent of the chairmanship positions. With the Republican takeover of the House, the parity between women's representation within the Republican party and their representation among committee chairs increased greatly, largely due to their relatively small numbers within the party overall. In 1995, women made up 7 percent of the new Republican House majority, and represented 8 percent of full and subcommittee chairs.

The obstacles today's congressional women face in winning prime-committee assignments have roots that run deep into the male-dominated culture of Capitol Hill. In 1949, when Rep. Reva Bosone (D-Utah) first came to Congress, she requested a seat on the Interior Committee. No woman had ever before served on that panel. Bosone told her administrative assistant to approach Rep. Jere Cooper (D-Tenn.), chair of the Ways and Means Committee and the man who had final say over committee assignments at the time.

Bosone later recalled her staffer's encounter with Cooper: "So she went to him and he said, 'Oh, my. Oh, no. She'd be embarrassed because it would be embarrassing to be on the committee and discuss the sex of animals.'

And she [the AA] called me back and said he [Cooper] didn't think it advisable. He wouldn't appoint me. And I said you go right back and tell him it would be refreshing to hear about animals' sex relationships compared with the perversions among human beings. She did and she came back and said to me, 'He laughed and said she can go on the committee.' "[5]

Rep. Julia Hansen (D-Wash.), the second woman in history to serve on the House Appropriations Committee and the first to head a subcommittee on that panel, described the difficulty she had in becoming the chair of the Appropriations Subcommittee on the Interior and related agencies in 1967.

"I had a little struggle to get it. The chairman, George Mahon [(D-Tex.)], was running around and asking the members if I would be a good chairman, because it was the first woman he confronted as a chairman. And finally one day I pounced on him and I said, 'Mr. Chairman, have you ever run around and asked the members of the committee if a man would make a good chairman?' He looked kind of sheepish. The Business and Professional Women's Clubs of his own native state of Texas sent him a very strong letter supporting me, so I was very grateful for that. No, no you don't get on the Appropriations Committee if you are a woman very easily. At least at the time I got on. And the second thing, you didn't get to be chairman either easily."[6]

Rep. Shirley Chisholm (D-N.Y.) also had a difficult time negotiating her committee assignments with the male power structure. In 1969, during her first term in the 91st Congress, she requested assignment to the Education and Labor Committee, which dealt with issues relevant to her urban constituency in Brooklyn, New York. In case her first choice was unavailable, she indicated a willingness to serve on Post Office and Civil Service or Foreign Affairs. Instead, this black congresswoman from the Brooklyn ghetto was assigned to the Agriculture Committee. She later recalled, "The Agriculture Committee sounded like a ridiculous assignment for a black member from one of the country's most deprived city neighborhoods. . . . Then I found out what my subcommittee assignments were to be: rural development and forestry. Forestry! That did it."

She called House Speaker McCormack (D-Mass.), saying she didn't know if she was following protocol, but she wanted to talk to him because her committee and subcommittee assignments did not make sense.

When the speaker told her that she would just have to be a good soldier, Chisholm responded: "All my forty-three years I have been a good soldier. The time is growing late, and I can't be a good soldier any longer. . . . If you do not assist me, I will have to do my own thing."

The speaker seemed confused. "Your what?" he asked.

"Doing your thing means that if you have strong feelings about something, you do it," she said.

McCormack said he would talk to Wilbur Mills (D-Ark.), chairman of the Ways and Means Committee that controlled Democratic committee assignments. Mills did not appreciate a freshman woman going over his head to complain about a committee assignment. The chairman of the Agriculture Committee was also furious.

When no action was taken on her request, Chisholm took the matter to the House floor. For some time she tried to speak, but was deliberately not recognized. Finally, she walked down the aisle to the "well," the space between the front row of seats and the speaker's dais, where she could not be ignored.

The perturbed Mills asked her why she was standing in the well.

"I've been trying to get recognized for half an hour, Mr. Chairman," Chisholm said, "but evidently you were unable to see me. . . . I would just like to tell the caucus why I vehemently reject my committee assignment."

Her speech eventually resulted in a reassignment to the Veterans Affairs Committee, prompting the delighted Chisholm to remark, "There are a lot more veterans in my district than there are trees." But a number of colleagues were quick to tell her that she had committed political suicide. "The leadership will have it in for you as long as you're here," she was told. Indeed, Chisholm's relationship with the Democratic leadership never recovered.[7]

When Rep. Pat Schroeder (D-Colo.) came to Congress in 1973, her desire to end the Vietnam War led her to request assignment to the Armed Services Committee. "My first fight in Congress therefore was a very tough one, for the committee was then a male bastion," she recalls. "It also didn't help that the chairman of the commitee, F. Edward Hebert (D-La.), a conservative Southern Democrat who boasted about his male chauvinism, did not consider me worthy of the seat. Women, he claimed, knew nothing of combat, since they had never been a part of it."

Schroeder researched the war records of all the committee members, and when a member who had never been in the armed services challenged her on the basis of her lack of combat experience, she replied, "Then you and I have a lot in common."

She concludes: "[I]t seemed to me the committee often justified its actions in the name of defending women and children and yet it never bothered to ask women and children what they wanted."[8] Schroeder finally succeeded in getting a place on the Armed Services Committee against the wishes of the chairman, but not without the kind of battle few of her male colleagues had to wage in their first few days in the Capitol.

After her appointment to the committee, Schroeder was summoned to the office of chairman Hebert. "He told me he had an adult room and an adultery room," Schroeder recalls. "I was offended by that, and then he said, 'The Lord givith, the Lord taketh away, and I am the Lord. You'll do just fine on this committee if you remember that.' "[9]

Even today, women requesting assignments to the committee of their choice may be told that the "woman's slot" on that committee has been filled.

"I think it's an unconscious discrimination," said former speaker of the House Jim Wright (D-Tex.). "A lot of guys my age fail to see the talents of some of these women. It will take time, but it will happen, believe me."[10]

Even when women attain top positions on committees, they cannot always expect to be treated with the same respect as their male counterparts. Rep. Lynn Woolsey (D-Calif.) recalls how a senior member of a committee on which she served responded to her first speech in the House. After he and a number of male colleagues had watched her speech on TV in a conference room, he told her, "We couldn't hear you. But one of the guys in the meeting said, 'Who's that good-looking broad?' and I said, 'That's Lynn Woolsey. She's on my committee.' " Woolsey told her male committee colleague, "I suppose you think that's a compliment."[11]

Rep. Patsy Mink (D-Hawaii), a member of the Education and Labor Committee, says, "I think some of the old fogies say things that might be offensive. Even on the Education and Labor Committee they say things like, 'Oh, there she goes again.' There are less of us so we're easier to dismiss. It's tough when you're in a room with seventy-two men and two women. It's tough to push your legislation through. Women's issues don't appear to men to be so important. But if you force a vote in committee, they'll be with you because fifty percent of the voters in their district are women. You always have to say, 'Mr. Chairman, a roll call vote please.' Everybody will grumble, but you have to ask for a roll-call vote so the men will be on the record for or against a women's issue. You have to take it to the limit. It's a battle of wits."[12]

During a health care hearing of the Ways and Means Subcommittee on Health in the spring of 1994, Rep. Nancy Johnson (R-Conn.), one of only two women on the powerful Ways and Means Committee, offered her opinion on President Clinton's proposed health reform package in opposition to the views of Rep. Jim McDermott, a Democrat from the state of Washington. Subcommittee chairman Rep. Pete Stark (D-Calif.) responded condescendingly to Johnson: "The gentlelady got her medical degree through pillow talk. The gentleman from Washington got his through going to school." Stark's remarks were meant to establish that Johnson's knowledge of health care issues was insufficient and came solely from "pillow talk" with her husband, who is a doctor.

Representatives Marge Roukema (R-N.J.) and Jennifer Dunn (R-Wash.) took to the House floor to lash back at what Roukema called Stark's "out of line" comments. "I, too, am the wife of a physician and I am deeply offended by this sexist slur," fumed Roukema. "Are you asserting that all wives are the victims of pillow talk brain washing?"

Dunn then rose to blast Stark, saying, "Let's try to keep the health care debate out of the gutter."

"I have never seen a male colleague make that kind of statement to another male," Johnson said. "There are many, many instances in which women are put in a position to fight far harder to be heard on a subject on which they are knowlegeable."

Thirty-five House members, all Republicans, signed a protest letter to Stark circulated by Rep. Deborah Pryce (R-Ohio). Stark eventually apologized to Johnson, who accepted the public apology, but said she still considered Stark's remarks demeaning. "At first I thought, 'Did I hear right?' " said Johnson. "I don't think it was intentional. But frankly, intention is no longer an excuse. It's a question of disrespect."[13]

Former representative Leslie Byrne (D-Va.) calls such comments by her male colleagues "grandpa talk," when the male member is not trying to be mean spirited or intimidating, but simply knows no better. Byrne related the story of one of the first times she went before the Rules Committee asking for permission to introduce an amendment on the floor.

"It was an amendment to the budget bill on intangible property, pretty esoteric stuff," Byrne said. "And so I was pitching this amendment, how important it was, and one of the gentlemen who had been sitting there quietly for a long time kind of looked up at me when it came time for the committee to ask questions and he said, 'I don't think I like your amendment, but you sure brighten the place up.' And my response was, 'I can't tell you how much that means to me.' "[14]

Other congressional women say they have had similar experiences with their male counterparts, but acknowledge that women may be treated more fairly in Congress than in many other careers. In commenting on the Stark incident, Louise Slaughter (D-N.Y.) pointed out: "Stark did say those things, but Nancy [Johnson] was able to snap right back and tell him exactly what she thought without fear of retribution of any sort. Women in, say, the Navy can't do that. That's a major difference, because the Constitution says who a Member of Congress is, and none of us are better or worse than the others. [In that regard] we really do have equality here."

Slaughter, however, did admit that she has experienced treatment similar to Johnson's. "I had something similar happen to me, something that every woman in America will recognize. I've never been in a group of women that does not acknowledge it," Slaughter told us. "It happened to me as recently as last week. You're in a room with three men. It takes at least three men for this phenomenon. You're all discussing a problem, and you, the woman, throw out an idea. You watch your male colleagues' eyes sort of glaze over, and as soon as your mouth is closed one of them jumps in with something that has no relation to what you said. But within ten minutes, one of those three men will put forth the idea that you had, and the other two will simply love it. Now you know you've experienced that."[15]

Such experiences may be particularly common for women who serve on the more powerful, male-dominated committees. Nancy Johnson was the only Republican woman on the powerful Ways and Means Committee at the time of the incident and Rep. Barbara Kennelly (D-Conn.) was the lone Democratic female on that 38-member panel.

The Republican women acquiring new committee power tend to talk their party's line on gender, downplaying its significance. Rep. Jan Meyers (R-Kans.), the new head of the House Small Business Committee, says, "As we have more women in Congress, it's obviously important that we move into roles as subcommittee chairs, full committee chairs, and into the leadership. But I don't know that I bring a particularly unique perspective to the committee or that there is any significance to a woman leading this committee. I rose in the same way as anyone else, through the seniority system. As we have more women in Congress, that will happen more and more frequently."[16]

Capitol Hill journalist Cokie Roberts, daughter of former Congresswoman Lindy Boggs (D-La.), put such rhetoric in perspective. "What happens to all women elected to Congress—including, much to their amazement, women who are extremely conservative—is that they find they are the advocates for women and children all over the country. Many women are on committees specifically so they can carry the water for women and families."[17]

Despite the appointment of three women as full committee chairs in 1995, most women are likely to continue to function on male-dominated committees under the power of male chairmen. The isolated position of women on such committees can produce awkwardness, even under the best of circumstances. Louise Slaughter recalls the difficulty she experienced when discussing women's health on the Rules Committee. "I was the only woman on the Democratic side when we first addressed the health care issue. And, yes, it was new to them, because nobody else had ever led the discussion into the arena of women's body parts. It had never been talked about. There was some blushing and I think some concern that we would talk about breasts, out loud, and the cervix. It might still not be something a lot of men would feel comfortable talking about. But they understand the health part of it, and that's what I wanted."[18]

CONGRESSIONAL LEADERSHIP

Along with their small numbers in top committee positions, women's power within Congress has also been stymied by their lack of representation in leadership positions. There are only five women among the 31 leadership positions in the House and Senate. Sen. Barbara Ann Mikulski (D-Md.) serves as the Democratic Conference secretary, while representatives Barbara Kennelly (D-Conn.) and Rosa De Lauro (D-Conn.) are the lone female representatives in the House Democratic leadership. Kennelly serves as caucus vice chair and De Lauro is a deputy whip. Representatives Susan Molinari (R-N.Y.) and Barbara Vucanovich (R-Nev.) are the only women in the Republican leadership in either chamber.

This meager presence in the leadership was embarrassingly obvious, for example, when only the top congressional leaders were invited to Bill Clinton's inauguration day luncheon on Capitol Hill in 1993, and no women received invitations. Only after Barbara Kennelly complained were the deputy whips invited, a position she held at the time. Female leadership was similarly absent in 1994 when President Clinton signed the Family and Medical Leave Act, a bill whose success depended on years of effort by women in Congress. No women, however, were invited to speak at the historic signing ceremony that took place on the White House lawn.

In the House, women have been able to maintain a fairly consistent, though barely audible, voice in the leadership of that chamber. For most of the 1980s, women Democrats were represented by the position of secretary of the caucus. Rep. Geraldine Ferraro (D-N.Y.) held that position from 1981 until she left Congress in 1985. Ferraro was succeeded by Rep. Mary Rose Oakar (D-Ohio), who, upon taking over as secretary, promptly changed the name of the post to vice chair of the Democratic Caucus.

Even in her leadership position in the caucus, Oakar, like most women in Congress, was given only grudging respect by her male colleagues. After finding herself frequently excluded from White House congressional leadership meetings, she demanded that then speaker Tip O'Neill (D-Mass.) arrange for her invitation to such meetings. When she was finally invited, she found herself seated on the periphery of the room, rather than at the table with the others. She walked out of the meeting, and returned only after a White House aide followed her to the parking lot and assured her of a seat at the table.

In 1991, when the post of chief deputy whip opened up, Speaker of the House Tom Foley (D-Wash.) split the post into three slots, giving one to a woman (Kennelly), one to a black, and one to a southerner, three groups that had not previously been represented in the top leadership ranks.

The 104th Congress paved the way for a head-to-head leadership match between two women. Kennelly and Rep. Louise Slaughter (D-N.Y.), two friends, both decided to run for the vice chairmanship of the Democratic Caucus, the fourth-ranking spot in the House Democratic leadership. Kennelly won the post by one vote. After Kennelly's victory, Rosa De Lauro (D-Conn.) was appointed by the Democratic leadership to fill the "woman's slot" among the deputy whips.

Republican women also took steps to enter their party's leadership during the 104th Congress. Rep. Susan Molinari (R-N.Y.) was voted in as the vice chairman of the Republican conference and Rep. Barbara Vucanovich (R-Nev.) won the post of conference secretary. They became the first women in the GOP leadership since Rep. Lynn Martin (R-Ill.) held the vice-chairmanship job from 1985 to 1989. It was also the first time ever that two women served simultaneously within Republican leadership ranks. Molinari would also become part of the first husband and wife team in the leadership of either party.

"I'm glad my colleagues didn't listen to the media who said only one woman would win," Vucanovich said after winning her leadership race. "Republicans traditionally have not done quotas."[19]

Vucanovich said her and Molinari's victory signaled a changing agenda for the Republican party. "I hope this says Republicans are trying to bring some balance to the party. I think women bring a lot more compassion. Rather than just looking at things from the point of view of the white male, we need to offer alternative views. We need to find ways that Republicans can offer an agenda for women and minorities. They have allowed the Democrats to set the agenda for women," she said. Vucanovich added that in her new leadership role, she would do her best to bring women and minorities across the country into the Republican party.

Democrat Patsy Mink plays down the significance of a female vice chair of the party caucuses. "They let you run for vice chair because it goes nowhere," says Mink. "Where there is a significance to a post, women can't get there." Mink attributes women's meager presence in the congressional leadership to their small numbers and limited seniority. "Everything is decided by numbers," she says. "Power is by numbers. Men don't want to give up their rightful numerical majority power. You'd have to have Congress made up half of women to get a female speaker. I think it's that bad." Still, Mink does not advocate the destruction of the [House] seniority system. "For women, if we lose the concept of seniority, we're even deeper in the hole of obscurity."[20]

Louise Slaughter agrees that the lack of seniority is an obstacle to attaining leadership positions, but she notes, "The Congress was here a hundred and some years before women [even] had the right to vote, so our limited seniority is understandable." In a system where seniority is the most powerful tool for advancement, shorter terms generally result in less powerful committee and leadership positions. On average, women have traditionally had shorter tenures in Congress than men. According to a 1993 study by Sally Friedman of the Political Science Department at the State University of New York Rockefeller College, women hold congressional office for an average of four terms compared to five terms for men. Blacks, on average, stayed in Congress for seven terms. Women often end their congressional careers early to run for higher office.

"Before I got here it was apparent to me that every time an incumbent woman approached a safe election, the people who supported her would try to convince her to try for something else when it came up," Louise Slaughter said. "When I was first elected I was the only woman in the New

York State Legislature, and I had followed probably the strongest delegation of women in this country. When you've got Bella Abzug and Shirley Chisholm and Geraldine Ferraro, these were strong women coming out of the New York delegation. Any one of them could have been Lord knows what by now [if they had remained in Congress], but they all decided to go foward and do something else. That's something that you really have to factor in as to why there aren't more women in the leadership. The men have just stayed around longer."[21]

Women also tend to enter congressional office at a much later age than their male colleagues, reducing the amount of time they have to accrue seniority. The 1993 Friedman study looked at members serving in Congress between 1965 and 1991. It showed that while 41 percent of the men were 40 years of age or younger when they first came to the Hill, only 19 percent of the women were 40 or younger when they first won congressional office. The largest percentage of women, 45 percent, were 50 or older. Only 18 percent of the men were 50 or older when they first came to Congress.

One reason women have tended to enter congressional office later in life than men may be their closer relationship to their children: many women decide to wait until after their children are grown to run for national office.

Also, according to the Friedman study, women have tended to have much less previous elected experience. The lack of such experience can easily make the difference between knowing how to rise up through the political pecking order or remaining bogged down at the lower end of the leadership ladder. The study showed that 75 percent of the congressmen studied had held previous elected office, while just 45 percent of the female representatives had such experience.

Regardless of how one explains women's low seniority in Congress, incumbent women are losing their tolerance for a seniority system that may require more than a decade of congressional experience before one may become a subcommittee chair and another decade to become a committee chair. Former representative Shirley Chisholm (D-N.Y.) has long complained that the only criterion that matters in picking members for committee vacancies is their length of service in Congress. "Congress calls it the seniority system," Chisholm says. "I call it the senility system. . . . The seniority system keeps a handful of old men, many of them southern whites hostile to every progressive trend, in control of the Congress. These old men stand implacably across the paths that could lead us toward a better future. But worse than they, I think, are the majority of members of both houses who continue to submit to the senility system."[22]

Gloria Steinem has written, "[C]ongresswomen need to make it clear that they won't wait 20 years to chair a committee. That means taking on the grandest dragon of them all—congressional rules." Steinem quotes an incumbent congresswoman who declares, "We have to change the process and challenge those glazed-over obstructionists who think that they're chairmen for life."[23]

Sen. Dianne Feinstein (D-Calif.) says, "The women in the Senate can't wait thirty years to accomplish our goals. We've done our apprenticeships in state politics and in the PTA and in county government. We have important voices and we should be heard."[24]

Some junior congresswomen are trying to change the system. After her election to Congress in 1992, former representative Maria Cantwell (D-Wash.) complained, "Here we elect a class [in the House] that is more reflective of what the American public looks like, but because of the seniority system they tell us you can't set the agenda for another thirty years." Another member of that freshman class, former representative Karen Shepherd (D-Utah), pushed a rules change within the Democratic Caucus that instructed the panel in charge of nominating committee chairs to "consider" the "diversity of the Caucus," in addition to seniority, when issuing nominations. Rep. Maxine Waters (D-Calif.) took an even more defiant approach. "If the leadership holds a meeting and says the only people who can come to these meetings are the [committee] chairs. . . . women have to say we're coming too. If we go along with their definition of who gets in a meeting, we'll never get in."[25]

THE WOMEN'S CAUCUS

While the Republican landslide of 1994 gave GOP women a numerical boost in their institutional power, it proved a major setback for bi-partisan cooperation on the women's legislative agenda. One of the first moves by the new Republican leadership was to disband all Legislative Service Organizations (LSOs), which included such groups as the black, Hispanic, and women's caucuses. The caucuses had occupied 16 offices, employed 96 staff members, and spent more than $4 million annually from members' office accounts. Claiming that such organizations were a waste of the taxpayer's money, Republicans removed the budgets, staffs, and Capitol Hill offices of 28 caucuses, including the women's caucus. Critics accused the Republicans of political motives, since the "joint" staffs and budgets of the caucuses simply reverted to the personal offices of the members involved, saving no money.

Leaders of the women's caucus saw the removal of office space and the prohibition of pooled staff and joint budgets as an attempt to silence minority voices within Congress.

"They can abolish our Caucus, but they cannot ignore our agenda," said Nita Lowey (D-N.Y.), the incoming caucus vice chair. "We remain determined to advance our interests and protect our priorities from assault. Republican and Democratic women will continue to work together on a whole range of issues—preserving the right to choose, fighting crime, reducing teen pregnancy, making child care more affordable to middle-class families, getting tough on deadbeat dads. We will continue to be a force for progress and change on behalf of women and their families."[26]

Still, concern over the Republican-led break up of the bi-partisan caucus sparked the creation of the Democratic Women's Members Organization, chaired by Patsy Mink (D-Hawaii). "Our members feel strongly that the bi-partisan Congressional Caucus on Women's Issues should continue and we intend to fully participate in that organization," Mink said. "However, we also believe that there is a strong need for the Democratic women Members to organize and advance our issues, help women candidates, and actively participate in our party's strategy for success in the 1996 elections."[27]

The reorganized women's caucus also established a separate nonprofit research arm, Women's Policy Inc., that attempts to provide the same information services that were available from the caucus during the 103rd Congress.

The incoming Republican vice chair of the Caucus, Rep. Connie Morella (R-Md.), had fought her party's leadership, writing letters and lobbying members in an unsuccessful attempt to retain the caucus. "It's very unfortunate," says Morella. "The Caucus accomplished so much." Outgoing vice chair Pat Schroeder (D-Colo.) called the abolition a Republican "gag rule for American women by seeking to silence the Members of Congress who work in their behalf."

Schroeder said she hoped women of both parties would continue to work together, even without a formal caucus. "The question is how many Republican women will stay on," Schroeder said. "It's really troubling whether they will stay on." Indeed, Schroeder claimed that some GOP women were facing pressure to declare themselves "Newtwits" and decline to join the new women's caucus. Republican Susan Molinari (N.Y.) denies feeling such pressure.[28]

To the surprise of many, and the chagrin of the conservative Republican leadership, seven of the Republican women in the House joined the newly constituted caucus. As of March 1995, the Republican members of the caucus included Nancy Johnson (Conn.), Sue Kelly (N.Y.), Deborah Pryce (Ohio), Connie Morella (Md.), Susan Molinari (N.Y.), Jan Meyers (Kans.), and Marge Roukema (N.J.). Prominent among the missing Republicans were six of the seven Republican freshmen women. Only freshman Republican Kelly had chosen to join.

All Democratic women except one, Elizabeth Furse (Ore.), joined the new caucus. Furse had complained that the new caucus watered down its pro-choice position in order to attract a broader membership, but it was also common knowledge that Furse found it difficult to work alongside Susan Molinari, who had campaigned aggressively for Furse's opponent in Oregon during 1994.

The caucus's reduced emphasis on abortion rights was evident in early 1995 when Nita Lowey called a news conference to support President Clinton's surgeon general nominee, who had admitted performing a number of abortions during his years as an obstetrician. Instead of speaking as cochair of the women's caucus, Lowey represented herself as cochair of the little-known House Pro-Choice Task Force. Lowey explained that she wanted to bring together a diverse group of lawmakers and not make the surgeon general's nomination "a women's issue."

Schroeder was one of the early organizers of the bi-partisan women's caucus. "The idea for the caucus grew out of an informal group I participated in from the time I arrived in 1973," recalled Schroeder. "The congresswomen used to reserve a table in the members' dining room and meet regularly during lunch to exchange information. In many ways it was an extension of the suburban 'coffee-klatsch'; but in this situation it not only kept us in touch with each other, it gave us a chance to develop strategies for getting our legislation through Congress. We decided to make the group a formal entity because we thought we would be more powerful as a unified body."

Formally organized in 1977 as the Congresswomen's Caucus, the group gave women a chance to discuss issues important to them and to bring their agenda to the attention of high-level cabinet staff. Because there were just 18 women in the House and two in the Senate at that time, the caucus was open to all congresswomen, some of whom were anxious to limit the group's activities in order to avoid rocking the congressional boat. "Conservative members were worried about being labeled feminists, and the feminists were afraid of being muzzled, so it was hard for us to agree on what to do," explains Schroeder. "The Congresswomen's Caucus in its early form was more an ongoing tea party than a convincing legislative caucus." There was an easy consensus among the women to support the Equal Rights Amendment, but other more controversial issues were avoided in order to ensure unanimous Caucus support before endorsing any position.[29]

The Reagan administration's hostility to the entire women's agenda created a crisis in the Congresswomen's Caucus. In 1981, the group reorganized as the Congressional Caucus for Women's Issues, at which time it broadened and strengthened its legislative focus, with particular emphasis on economic issues. Caucus dues were increased from $50 to $2,500, placing the group on a par with other LSOs. Congresswomen who had been caucus members in name only quickly dropped out, leaving a core of more dedicated members. At this time the "consensus process" was replaced by a more democratic process facilitated by cochairs. Membership was opened up to men, though congresswomen retained control of the caucus through an executive committee of women members. Finally, the caucus developed an omnibus legislative package called the Economic Equity Act (EEA), made up of a variety of bills aimed at creating economic equality for women. The components of the EEA would change from session to session, but the goal remained the same.

At their first meeting in 1993, the caucus's executive committee went on record for the first time as supporting abortion rights. While most women maintained their membership in the group following the adoption of the new platform, several women, both Democratic and Republican, left the caucus because of their anti-abortion positions. The caucus's broader legislative agenda for the 103rd Congress included a new version of the EEA, which would lift the ceiling on damages allowed for victims of sex discrimination; improved health care services and medical research for women; and a package of bills to increase prevention and punishment of rape and other crimes against women.

The flood of new women brought to the Hill by the 1992 elections also forced the women's caucus to further restructure itself to handle its increased membership. In 1994, for the first time in more than a decade, the caucus readied itself for two new cochairs. Rep. Pat Schroeder (D-Colo.) had served as the Democratic chair since 1981, while Rep. Olympia Snowe (R-Maine) had served as the Republican head of the group since 1983. Both chairs were leaving their posts because of the opportunity for higher responsibility. Schroeder was in line to take over the chair of the Post Office and Civil Service Committee while Snowe was making a run for the Senate. In 1994, the caucus also drafted new bylaws for the first time in more than a decade, including a provision for term limits for the group's officers and the creation of two new vice-chair positions. The changes were aimed at spreading the caucus's leadership power among the expanded female membership. Caucus elections had previously been informal to the point of being automatic.

"There have been so few women in Congress, [that] by acclamation in the past, people have just said, go ahead," said Del. Eleanor Holmes Norton (D-D.C.) of the caucus's tradition of reelecting the same cochairs each year. "Our bylaws were embarrassingly out of date. The process of not electing a chair was condoned by us because there were so few of us. By acclamation we said let's just continue this way. It was a tightly knit insurgent group that had very few members that had not a lot of incentive to change how it operated," continued Norton.

Norton meanwhile announced her campaign for the Democratic cochair of the women's group in early 1994. She was challenged by Rep. Nita Lowey (D-N.Y.), who called the new term limits adopted by the caucus a great way to bring more women into leadership roles. "Our numbers here have increased, our power has evolved and our influence has increased," Lowey said. "The Women's Caucus is becoming a power, a power that's evolving."[30]

The 1994 campaigns for new cochairs, as well as for the newly created posts of co-vice chairs, were the first truly contested elections the caucus had held since Snowe and Schroeder took over the group. Rep. Maxine Waters (D-Calif.) chaired the caucus task force charged with drafting the new bylaws.

Waters explained that the increased size of the caucus required bylaws that would allow for more competitive elections. She said that by allowing greater numbers of women a chance to lead the caucus, women could also broaden their opportunities for leadership roles outside the caucus.

"Increasingly, there will be more opportunities for women to serve as subcommittee and full committee chairs," said Waters. "We will be more in the leadership, and the Women's Caucus plays into that. Service in the Caucuses gives you the opportunity to work at providing leadership. It better prepares you for those roles."

While the women's caucus is often viewed as a Democratic organization, Rep. Connie Morella (R-Md.) said it is important for women of both parties to become active in the group's work. Morella was the only candidate for the Republican cochair of the caucus in 1994.

"You need to have a bipartisan Caucus," Morella said. "You need to show there's support among Republicans on these issues. We don't often think of Republicans as being as involved in the Caucus as they are." Morella pointed to economic equality, domestic violence, the environment, and reproductive rights as issues that women of both parties have addressed legislatively. "These are issues that transcend party lines and Republicans should be heard and should be involved," Morella said.[31]

As women of both parties have become more involved in the women's caucus, so have men. Ever since the caucus voted to allow men to join the group as associate members in 1981, men have learned the political advantage of aligning themselves with women's issues. In 1994, the women's caucus actually had more male members than female. Of the 165 total members, only 45 were women. No men, however, are allowed to serve on the caucus's executive committee, which drafts policy and elects the group's officers. Male members receive the caucus's weekly newsletters and policy briefings, and, perhaps most important, they gain the ability to tout their membership on the campaign trail. Aides close to the caucus say it is not uncommon for men to suddenly become caucus members during a tough reelection bid.

"When a Member has a woman challenger, often they'll call up and want to join," said a caucus aide. "But it varies. You have men who are very, very sincere and the issues are important to them and their constituents. Others, no doubt, have joined because staff have pushed them."

JOINING THE TEAM

During tough election campaigns, men in Congress recognize the political advantage of belonging to the women's caucus, but they have not returned the favor by granting women full access to the broader "men's team." The exclusive nature of the men's club called Congress will not be changed easily. It has a centuries-old tradition. Even the art works displayed around the Capitol suggest that women are invisible in government. Only seven of the approximately 190 statues and busts in our Capitol are of women. In and around the elegant buildings on Capitol Hill, the paintings and sculptures glorify the male history of our nation and its government.

The few statues that do honor women have been relegated to some of the more remote areas of the Capitol.

The debate over such artistic inequity came to the fore in 1995 as the 75th anniversary of suffrage approached. A marble statue honoring suffragettes Susan B. Anthony, Lucretia Mott, and Elizabeth Cady Stanton had been dedicated in the Capitol in 1921, but hours after its unveiling it was placed in the Capitol crypt, where it fell into obscurity. Most of the building's statues line the popular Statuary Hall or Rotunda, but the crypt is a little-visited area, a former repository for broken furniture and trash cans.

Shortly after its dedication, the inscription on the statue was painted over by order of a congressional committee, which complained that it "was so fulsome as to place the women above Christ." The inscription refers to the trio of figures as "the three great destiny characters of the world" who "guided the only fundamental universal uprising on our planet."[32]

Numerous times since its dedication, legislation calling for the statue's relocation was defeated, but in 1995 it appeared that the busts would finally be moved to a more appropriate area. In July of that year, Sen. Ted Stevens (R-Alaska) introduced a resolution calling for the relocation of the figures to the Rotunda in preparation for the August 26th celebration of the 75th anniversary of the ratification of the suffrage amendment. The resolution unanimously passed the upper chamber, but languished for weeks in the House. The House subsequently adjourned for the summer without acting on the measure, and the suffrage celebrations took place with the statue still consigned to the crypt.

Even fundamental recreational facilities have been denied to women because of a "men only" tradition. In the mid-1970s, it took the strong urging of Rep. Bella Abzug (D-N.Y.) to make the men's swimming pool available to women. Next came the challenge to one of the most sacred male sanctuaries on the Hill, the House gym, which, until recently, was closed to all women. The gym provided men with weight machines, bikes, a swimming pool, and other exercise equipment. When then-freshman representative Barbara Boxer (D-Calif.) complained about the all-male gym, she was told to use the "Ladies Gym," a facility which, in the words of Rep. Pat Schroeder (D-Colo.), consisted of "ten hair dryers and a ping-pong table."

Boxer had doubts about the "separate but equal" facilities, and during her second term she recruited some younger male members, like George Miller (D-Calif.), Marty Russo (D-Ill.), Tom Downey (D-N.Y.), and Dick

Durbin (D-Ill.) to lobby for the integration of the congresional gym. But the "gym committee," composed of older male members, was unwilling to alter tradition. In response, Boxer, along with Congresswomen Mary Rose Oakar (D-Ohio) and Marcy Kaptur (D-Ohio), wrote a song to dramatize the "gym problem." Set to the tune of "Has Anybody Seen My Girl," the lyrics were:

> Exercise, glamorize,
> Where to go, will you advise,
> Can't everybody use your gym?
> Equal rights, we'll wear tights,
> Let's avoid those macho fights,
> Can't everybody use your gym?
> We're not trim, we're not slim,
> Can't you make it hers and him?
> Can't everybody use your gym?[33]

The Boxer trio actually sang its song at a meeting of congressional whips, and as a result, the men's gym was soon opened to women.

Over the years, women members have had to fight for such mundane things as their own bathrooms. During the 103rd Congress, the Senate finally agreed to build a bathroom near the Senate floor specifically for women members. Previously, women had to walk down a level to reach the nearest facility, while men were within several feet of a bathroom. On the House side, women members are still forced to go to a lower floor and share the nearest ladies room with the general public. A private women's lounge is available to female House members, but that room is even more remote, located several hundred feet off the House floor. Male House members, on the other hand, need walk just ten feet from the House floor to their private facility, closed to the public and complete with a shoe-shine stand.

The female class of 1992 recently succeeded in crashing the previously all-male congressional basketball and baseball teams. In March 1993, fresh-man Rep. Lynn Woolsey (D-Calif.) became the first woman in history to shoot hoops for Congress. "[S]ince we've been rather outspoken about using the gym and playing basketball with the men," said Woolsey, "I decided I better put my body where my mouth is." Two-term delegate Eleanor Holmes Norton (D-D.C.) also joined the House basketball team as assistant coach, although she did not hit the court. During the team's first game of the 1993 season against the Georgetown University Law Center, Woolsey, who played guard, came off the bench twice, though she was held scoreless.

"I should have shot once," Woolsey said after her first game. "But I was being too much of a team player." Woolsey, 56, said she decided to sign up for the team after she received a letter from its head coach, Rep. Lane Evans (D-Ill.), saying: "In the past we have not had any women Members of

Congress join the team; this year we wanted to change that by having an all inclusive bipartisan, male/female team."[34]

Women also broke the gender barrier in 1993 when they participated in the 32nd annual congressional baseball game, which pits Republicans against Democrats. Representatives Maria Cantwell (D-Wash.), Blanche Lambert (D-Ark.), and Ileana Ros-Lehtinen (R-Fla.) participated in all of their teams' early morning practices leading up to the big night, and they stepped up to the plate once each during the actual game. Cantwell walked in the third inning to become the first woman ever to reach base in a congressional game. Most of the members participating in the game wore the full uniforms of their home-town teams, but Cantwell donned only a Seattle Mariners jersey and shorts, because "the team didn't have any pants that were small enough."

While none of the women got a chance to score during the game, they apparently enjoyed the experience enough to sign up again for the 1994 game. In that game, won by the Democrats 9–2, representatives Cantwell, Ros-Lehtinen, and Lambert represented congressional women for the second year in a row. Ros-Lehtinen walked in one time at bat, and Cantwell, who played right field, scored one run.

Despite their marginal success in integrating the Capitol Hill recreational activities and facilities, women continue to suffer a more serious exclusion that directly affects their legislative performance. The strong and entrenched male culture on Capitol Hill serves as a constant obstacle to female legislators, posing numerous social barriers that place women at a serious disadvantage with their male colleagues.

The lobbying process is so integrated into the male subculture that women on Capitol Hill are rendered, at best, irrelevant. Ellie Smeal, the founder of the Fund for a Feminist Majority, recalled what a male lobbyist told her about dealing with male legislators. "They fish together, they hunt together, they play cards together, and they whore together."[35] Rep. Patty Murray (D-Wash.) says, "The modus operandi is very different from what women do. We don't go to all the dinners and receptions and slap people in the hall. Lobbyists will have to find a different way to get to us."[36]

Many newly elected women in Congress are shocked when they first confront the biases of their male colleagues on the Hill and have difficultly deciding how to handle it.

"There's a constant balancing game that we all have to do, and it's not easy, it really isn't easy when you always have to determine [whether] now is the time to challenge an opponent or do you wait until another time," said Rep. Lucille Roybal-Allard (D-Calif.). "One of the things that we all deal with as women in Congress is constantly having to weigh and determine the reason that you're in a particular situation. For instance, why certain comments are being made and whether it really is intended to be offensive, if this is the right time to speak up. Or there may be instances, particularly with some of the more senior Members of Congress, when they make comments to you like, 'My don't you look lovely,' which is one we've all heard, and you have to think that maybe they're just tying to be courteous, and from the general direction they're coming from, that may be the only way that they can relate to us."[37]

Rep. Enid Greene Waldholtz (R-Utah), elected in 1994, says she tries not to become preoccupied with the male-dominated Hill culture. She described several incidents when Capitol police assumed her husband was the new member and that she was the spouse. "It's dangerous to get too caught up in that. We're still in a transitional period. I can't really blame them if they're playing the odds and assume the man is the Member."

Even women who have served on the Hill for years are frequently surprised by comments made by their male colleagues.

"It was amazing to see all these women getting sworn in," Rep. Pat Schroeder (D-Colo.) said of the opening day of the 103rd Congress. "And a lot of the old bulls came over to me and said this place looks like a shopping mall."

Indeed, in a televised debate, Rep. Henry Hyde (R-Ill.) echoed this image. When Harriett Woods, president of the National Women's Political Caucus, called for more women in Congress, Hyde responded, "There are some who say there are so many women now on the floor of Congress it looks like a mall."[38]

How could such a characterization be parroted by a member of an institution in which women represented only 10.8 percent of the total membership? The answer is that women are still regarded as strangers in Congress and are frequently treated with disrespect. A particularly disturbing example of disrespect occurred recently when a Republican colleague of Sen. Barbara Mikulski (D-Md.) gave a speech in which he used an unfortunate metaphor to describe Mikulski's behavior, saying she "just threw her panties at me." Mikulski's staff advised her not to make a public issue of the remark, but she said, "If I let it go now, then I will always have to be silent if something like this comes up again. If I speak now, this kind of thing will stop." Mikulski told the press, "I find his comments insulting and outrageous and I want an apology."

The Republican senator responded that he was just kidding and his comments were all in fun, but Mikulski asked, "If someone said that about your wife or daughter, wouldn't you be offended?" An apology was quickly offered and accepted, and the matter ended with a joint press release.[39]

Occasionally, women in Congress lose their cool, and they are made to pay for it. In late July 1994, when Hillary Clinton's chief of staff, Maggie Williams, testified at a Whitewater hearing before the House Banking Committee, Rep. Peter King (R-N.Y.) interrogated Williams aggressively, and in a long, accusatory speech, implied that she was lying. Rep. Maxine

Waters (D-Calif.), a member of the committee, felt that King had treated Williams disrespectfully.

"You are out of order," she told King.

"You are always out of order," King shot back.

"You are out of order," Waters repeated. "Shut up."

In a follow-up speech, King said, "She's not going to tell me to shut up. She's not going to tell the American people to shut up."

Waters followed with her own one-minute speech. "Madam Chairwoman," she began, "the day is over when men can badger and intimidate women."

Rep. James Sensenbrenner (R-Wis.) interrupted, claiming that Waters's words were offensive and must be "taken down."

"We won't allow men to intimidate us," Waters continued, causing the chairwoman to bang the gavel.

The GOP floor watchdog, Rep. Bob Walker (R-Pa.) shouted, "Have the Sergeant at Arms remove her!" Rep. Sensenbrenner repeated Walker's demand.

Pointing to Sensenbrenner, Waters said, "You see a man who [attempted to] shut up a woman."

The chairwoman continued to bang the gavel and Waters finally left the podium with the parting comment, "This is a perfect example of what they try to do to us."

Following this unruly floor dispute, the parliamentarians consulted at length with House Speaker Tom Foley (D-Wash.), after which Foley took the chair and announced that, though Waters's words were in themselves proper, her "demeanor" was "unparliamentary." Rep. Pat Schroeder (D-Colo.) rose to question Foley on what he meant by "demeanor." Other Democratic women and staffers felt that Waters was being disciplined for nothing more than displaying emotion, something congressmen do frequently with impunity.

Foley ordered that Waters be punished by permitting no further recognition of her on that day. However, as tradition dictates, Foley asked the House for unanimous consent to reinstate Waters's floor privileges immediately, and hearing no objection, it was done.[40]

FAMILY PROBLEMS

Women running for Congress have historically been placed in a "double bind" with respect to their families. If they are unmarried or have no children, the press treats them as somehow abnormal. If they have children, they are faulted for leaving them inadequately attended. Moms in Congress are criticized and scrutinized in ways that their male colleagues with children are not. Rep. Patsy Mink (D-Hawaii) recalls, "It's particularly difficult in your first campaign. When I ran in 1964, they used to say, 'Oh, she's going to abandon her children,' or 'Oh, I guess they'll be divorced because her husband will never leave Hawaii to go to Washington.' They said that all the time."[41]

Pat Schroeder (D-Colo.) faced the same criticism when she was first elected, as people asked how she dared come to Congress when she had two small children at home. When Schroeder ran for Congress in 1972, she campaigned around the country in opposition to the Vietnam War. But frequently the press ignored the issues and instead repeatedly insisted that she explain how her children could survive with two working parents. Eventually, the exasperated Schroeder told one reporter: "Jim and I get up very early—about 6 A.M. We bathe and dress the children and give them a wonderful breakfast. Then we put them in the freezer, leave for work and when we come home we defrost them. And we all have a wonderful dinner together."[42]

The increasing presence of women in Congress is building pressure for change in the informal legislative processes which have traditionally been structured around the personal and social convenience of men. None is more in need of change than the legislative schedule itself, which includes unpredictable late-night sessions, after-hour receptions, and long recess junkets, all of which presume that every member has a wife at home to care for the children.

Consider the fact that only twice in history has a woman given birth to a child while serving in Congress. California Democrat Rep. Yvonne Brathwaite Burke, who served from 1972 to 1978, bore a daughter during her first term. Yet hundreds of male members have become fathers while holding congressional office. In March 1995, freshman representative Enid Greene Waldholtz (R-Utah) announced her pregnancy, and later that summer became the second woman in history to have a child while serving in Congress.

Waldholtz says that when she first told House Speaker Newt Gingrich that she was pregnant, he gave a typical male response. "He asked if I was okay," she said. "With men it's always, 'Are you okay?' and with women it's always 'Congratulations!' "

The Republican leadership promised to accommodate Waldholtz as much as possible during her pregnancy, including providing a small room near the House floor where she could care for her baby without having to run for votes from her office in a building across the street. Waldholtz also arranged to have two doctors—one in Georgetown and one in Salt Lake City. "[My husband] Joe and I feel very strongly we will do what it takes to make this work," she said shortly after announcing her pregnancy.[43] In the fall of 1995, Rep. Susan Molinari (R-N.Y.) and her husband Rep. Bill Paxon (R-N.Y.) announced that they, too, were expecting their first child.

The chaotic congressional schedule is particularly hard on women, and calls for a more "family-friendly" schedule have been heard. Rep. Lynn Schenk (D-Calif.) says, "[Y]ou see the younger men who are used to working with women, who have been raised by feminist mothers or married to women who have careers—they want some of the same things."[44]

The difficult circumstances faced by female members of Congress have prompted them to form close friendships and support groups with each other. Rep. Tillie Fowler (R-Fla.) says many of the women in Congress get together for monthly dinners to talk not only of political or legislative issues, but of family issues, such as marital strains or children with drug problems.

"We try to keep relationships going, and we feel we're working on that as women as a whole, because it's so true that we are the only people with this experience," Fowler said. "The only other person who can understand what you're going through is another woman, as far as the stresses and the range of things we deal with. And so we need to get to know each other better. We might have philosophical differences on certain things, but as women members we can be a support system here. And I think that is very true. We need to build that networking among ourselves. Some of the older women were saying that when there were fewer of them here it was easier to do. Now there are more of us, so we better work at it."[45]

Women are often forced to make an agonizing choice between having a family or a career in politics. "I think one of the reasons I've never married and had children is because of the guilt I would feel taking time from them," says Rep. Marcy Kaptur (D-Ohio). "To me, one of the great achievements of my life has been not wounding a child. To raise children in this job? You can count on one hand the number of women in this job who have." Kaptur explains, "I'm not a widow, and I don't have children, and I don't have a husband, and that tells me I have better odds of being able to stay."

Louise Slaughter says her family understands that her constituents have a strong claim on her time, but they resent it nonetheless. Her husband says, "It's been hard for our family to accept it, in many ways. I don't wish that Louise wasn't doing what she's doing. The problem is it's just such a totally consuming thing. But you'd never want it not to happen."[16]

Slaughter believes that a woman can hold office while raising a family, but she advises, "I think the important thing for a woman in this position is that she has to have an enormous amount of energy. But none of us should ever come to decide that the things our family needs come second or last."[47]

When recently defeated Marjorie Margolies-Mezvinsky (D-Pa.) was in Congress she discovered that being a mom is a particularly tough challenge for women in Congress. Because she came to Congress with a husband and 11 children in their combined family, she looked to her female colleagues, often senior representatives who have raised kids, for guidance. But like the other mothers in Congress, she felt guilt. "It's an inner demon," she says. "Ultimately, you have to tell yourself that guilt is a wasted emotion, that you're doing the best you can, and that it's important that you are both a mom and a congresswoman."[48]

Margolies-Mezvinsky says that when she was deciding whether or not to run for Congress she almost convinced herself that it would be too rough, but it came down to a decision that the entire family made. Rep. Tillie Fowler (R-Fla.) did the same thing. Before she decided to run, she had a long family discussion. Fowler said her children have always been a major issue in her political career. When she first entered politics by serving on her local city council, her children were ten and 12 years old. "I was so concerned about the whole thing. I went to a pediatrician to talk about what it would do to my children. I talked to friends who had teenagers. It's part of being a mother. I don't think men worry about that. My friends who have teenagers said, 'Do it now, there will be more problems when they are teenagers. Get on into it. It'll be better.' And they were right."

Running for national office in the U.S. Congress, however, was a more difficult situation for Fowler, and she waited until her children were 18 and 20 before she ran for the House in 1992. "I think it would have been very difficult if they were too young, and I'm not sure I would have made the choice. . . . There are different types of support systems that different families have. I think every woman has to look at her situation and determine how that would work for her family."[49]

Rep. Sue Myrick (R-N.C.), one of the seven Republican women elected in 1994, also suggested that women should run for local or state office while their children are young and move into the national arena once their sons and daughters are grown. "Run for city council when your children are small," said the mother of two who served as a Charlotte city council-woman and later mayor before coming to Congress. "It would be very difficult to be a woman in Congress with small children. You can't be a superwoman."[50]

Rep. Lucille Roybal-Allard (D-Calif.) agreed that she would not have run for Congress if she had small children. Allard, who succeeded her father in Congress, did not run for the House until her children were grown.

"I know I wouldn't have run if I had small children," Roybal-Allard said. "It's a tremendous sacrifice to the family. There are a lot of decisions as to relocating your children, the kinds of schools in the area, if there are safe communities. It makes a big difference as to whether a woman will run."

Roybal-Allard said the women in Congress have formed a "support group" to help each other out with some of the problems that are unique to women. "It goes beyond legislation. There is a friendship that's developing among the women. If someone's in trouble or needs advice, you feel comfortable going to them. Say you've had a day where you've lost everything, it's important to have someone to go to and talk to. We do have unique problems, particularly women who have small children. They may say my son or daughter called the office with a problem. I think that happens more with women then men."[51]

Though Fowler, Roybal-Allard, and Myrick, like most of the women who preceded them, chose to wait until their children were grown before running for Congress, many of their female colleagues in the class of 1992 are bucking the trend. The crop of women elected in 1992 included Rep.

Cynthia McKinney (D-Ga.), the single mother of a seven-year-old son, and Rep. Carolyn Maloney (D-N.Y.), mother of 12- and 6-year-old daughters.

"For me the most difficult part about being in public life is being away from my children," Maloney said during a 1994 forum sponsored by the women of the class of 1992. "I remember earlier this year Vice President Gore was going to my district and it just happened to be my daughter's birthday. So I told him I'd love to go [with him], and we flew home on Air Force Two and had four or five meetings. But in between, I rushed home to be with my daughter on her birthday, to blow out the candles on her cake. I find that, for me, that has been one of the most difficult parts of being in Congress. The strain of juggling not only your work here, but your private life with your husband and children."[52]

Cynthia McKinney (D-Ga.) faced similar difficulties when she won election to the House in 1992, and she chose not to move her son, Coy, to Washington. Instead, she continues to rely on her parents to take care of him during the week until she comes home on the weekends. McKinney said Coy experienced some anxiety when she first decided to run for office.

"He was saying at one point what he thought people wanted to hear, that he was happy and proud," McKinney said. "But there was one interview where he didn't do so well, and later he said, 'I really don't want you to go.' He said, 'Mommy, I wish you could stay here and play football with me.' I think he was afraid at first."[53]

Former representative Karan English (D-Ariz.), whose four children range in age from 12 to 20, admits: "My kids often say they miss me, and I miss them too. But that gets back to my goals in coming here in the first place. I'm driven by maternal instinct. I'm trying to do what's best for my children, my community, and the whole country."[54]

Deborah Pryce (R-Ohio) says soberly, "I think that moms have it worse and they always will, and maybe it will change, but I don't know." Pryce, one of only three Republican House women in the 1992 class, also noted the broader problem of alienation faced by Capitol Hill women. "I could use some good girlfriends here in Washington," she said. "It's a lonely feeling for a woman who doesn't have her family here. . . . I feel isolated for the very first time ever. Ever."[55]

While men in Congress have their wives perform a variety of supporting duties, women in Congress do double duty. When former representative Blanche Lambert (D-Ark.) used to complain to the men in Congress that she didn't have time to pick up her dry cleaning, they would laugh. "You're laughing," she would respond, "but I bet your wife picks up yours. Women don't have that." Sen. Dianne Feinstein (D-Calif.) explains, "Women always keep house. It comes with the gender. Every career woman with a family does the laundry, scrubs floor, cleans the bathrooms, changes the beds. The man generally does not."[56]

Even the congressional women without young children find things stacked against them. Rep. Patsy Mink (D-Hawaii) feels that many of the problems faced by women in Congress have deep roots in the American culture that will be difficult to overcome. "It's tough," she says. "Men, by their custom and upbringing never felt they had to be at home, and therefore the voters have the same feeling." On the other hand, complains Mink, women are expected to stay at home and raise the kids. "A lot depends on a supportive husband. Many women in politics have trouble with their husbands. Men coming to Congress often don't have wives in entrenched careers. When they do, it's tough on them too."[57]

Indeed, with the increasing number of women in Congress, the problems of male spouses have become more visible. Because of the historically small numbers of women in Congress, the treatment of male spouses has been an awkward, if not ignored, issue. But the huge number of women elected to the 103rd Congress sparked a change in the long-standing tradition of orientation programs for new congressional spouses. In 1993, for the first time ever, the programs held for spouses of the newly elected members were restructured to accommodate husbands. Special receptions and meetings were held specifically for the 16 new congressional husbands.

Because of the considerably smaller number of women elected to Congress in 1994, there were many fewer male spouses at the orientation for the 104th Congress than for the 103rd. Five husbands of new congresswomen attended the reception organized by Tony Morella, the lawyer-husband of Rep. Connie Morella (R-Md.). Morella gave his group mates some tips like, "It's cheaper to buy evening clothes than to rent," but he emphasized the cardinal rule for dealing with constituent questions: "Tell them, 'Don't ask me, ask my wife.' "[58]

Some of the male spouses also attended the orientation meetings geared toward wives. Rep. Enid Greene Waldholtz (R-Utah) called these meetings the "last gender bastion around here."

"My husband has gone to these luncheons where he was given bags of make-up," she said. She added that the media has had as difficult time getting used to the larger numbers of women on the Hill as have the long-time male members. "There is still, among the media, a fascination of male congressional spouses. I remember during one gathering, the cameras kept focusing on my husband's name tag. He said, 'Look, I was born a man and that's not going to change.' Congress, I think, has adapted better than some other areas."[59]

WOMEN'S LEGISLATION

The legislative agenda of today's congressional women bears a striking resemblance to that of Rep. Jeannette Rankin (R-Mont.), the first woman in Congress. Rankin's priorities were peace, family, and women's rights. She cosponsored the resolution for a constitutional amendment granting women the right to vote in national elections, and when the measure was stalled in committee, she introduced legislation creating a Woman Suffrage Committee, on which she became the ranking minority member.

Rankin, who came to office four years before women were allowed to vote and was the lone woman in either chamber during congressional consideration of suffrage, was given the honor of opening House debate on the legislation in 1918.

"We are facing today a question of political evolution," Rankin told her male colleagues. "Our country is in a state of war. . . . But something is still lacking in the completeness of our national effort. With all our abundance of coal, with our great stretches of idle, fertile land, babies are dying from cold and hunger; soldiers have died for lack of a woolen shirt. Might it not be that the men who have spent their lives thinking in terms of commercial profit find it hard to adjust themselves to thinking in terms of human needs? Might it not be that a great force that has always been thinking in terms of human needs, and that always will think in terms of human needs has not been mobilized? Is it not possible that the women of the country have something of value to give the nation at this time?

"It would be strange indeed if the women of this country through all these years had not developed an intelligence, a feeling, a spiritual force peculiar to themselves, which they hold in readiness to give to the world," Rankin continued. "It would be strange if the influence of women through direct participation in the political struggles, through which all social and industrial development proceeds, would not lend a certain virility, a certain influx of new strength and understanding and sympathy and ability to the exhausting effort we are now making to meet the problem before us."

Rankin concluded her speech by emphasizing the need to make clear to *all* Americans the nation's fundamental commitment to freedom. "Can we afford to allow these men and women to doubt for a single instant the sincerity of our protestations of democracy? How shall we answer their challenge, gentlemen; how shall we explain to them the meaning of democracy if the same Congress that voted for war to make the world safe for democracy refuses to give this small measure of democracy to the women of our country?"

According to the congressional record, Rankin's address was met with "prolonged applause" from her male counterparts. Obviously, passage of suffrage hinged upon the male members of the House and Senate. During the debate, Rep. John Raker (D-Calif.) pointed out that many of the men serving in the House were in fact there by virtue of the women's vote. While in 1918 there was no national mandate allowing women to cast their ballots, several states, including California, did permit women to go to the polls. In speaking of the 20 million Amerian women who were of voting age at that time, Raker argued that the entire Democratic leadership of the House owed their position to women.

"To my Democratic friends I want to say this: The Speaker of this House, the chairmen of the committees of this House, and the officers who constitute the organization of this House hold their positions today as the result of the votes of women. Without the votes of the Democratic Members from California, the Speaker would not be in the chair. These Democratic Members from California would not have been elected without the votes of the women of California. Every man who holds a chairmanship of a committee owes it to the woman vote of the West."

Despite these arguments, many members of the House spoke against the suffrage amendment, citing reasons that were, even for that time, astounding. Rep. Frank Clark (D-Fla.) contended that female voting would, at best, be irrelevant and, at worst, lead to the eventual destruction of the American family and the country as a whole.

"If this resolution should pass," declared Clark, "and the proposed amendment should be ratified by three-fourths of the states of the Union, then we would find a condition where the wife would either follow the husband in the casting of her vote or she would disagree with his views and have her vote counted in opposition to his. If the former is to be the case, then it occurs to me that all will agree that this would be an entirely superfluous and useless piece of legislation, as the only result would be to practically double the number of votes cast without changing in the slightest the political complexion of the state or the nation, but adding largely to the expense of holding our elections. If the latter should be the case, then we would find the husband and wife constantly engaged in political disputation, which would grow warmer, more heated, and more acrimonious as the campaign advanced, until finally a veritable conflagration of domestic infelicity would be kindled, consuming the marital tie, destroying the home, and sending the children, to all intents and purposes, orphans out on the cold charity of the world to become charges on the state."

And what about unmarried women and their right to vote? Clark had an answer to that as well.

"The unmarried woman who has passed marriageable age is the exception to her class, and no general law should ever be passed to fit the exceptions to the class upon which it is intended to operate," he said.

Clark also argued that by granting a woman the right to vote, Congress would be taking away many of the legal protections granted to her at that time.

"No more when charged with crime can she be heard to plead coercion on the part of the husband; no more when marital troubles come can she go into the courts of the country and so easily secure the payment of her counsel's fees in divorce proceedings, alimony for herself pending the litigation, and permanent alimony in the final decree for the support of herself and children. In other words, she cannot exercise the rights of a man and at the same time claim the privileges of a woman. The two are entirely incompatible, and she must relinquish the one or the others. If she relinquishes the privileges of a woman and secures the rights of a man, then, in my judgment, we shall soon see woman becoming more manly and man becoming more womanly. God forbid. It is said that 'nature abhors a vacuum,' and I want to say that about the nearest approach to a vacuum that I know anything about is a manly woman or a womanly man."[60]

Several hours after Rankin's opening statement, the Suffrage Constitutional Amendment was passed by the House on January 10, 1918, by a vote of 274 to 136, barely the two-thirds vote required for passage of a Constitutional amendment. Ten months later, on October 1, the Senate failed to garner the two-thirds vote needed for passage and the amendment was defeated 53 to 31. Fortunately for American women and the nation as a whole, the opposition to woman suffrage was eventually overcome by reason. The House once more passed the resolution in 1919, by a vote of 304 to 90, and a month later the Senate passed it, 56 to 25.

Because Rankin was defeated in her 1918 bid for a Senate seat, she was forced to view the eventual enactment of the Suffrage Amendment from the sidelines as a private citizen. The amendment was ratified by the states in 1920, but Rankin spent 20 years outside of Congress lobbying for a child-labor amendment and for the Maternity and Infancy Bill she had introduced under her own name in the 65th Congress.

Like today's female legislators, the congressional women of the past did not limit themselves to "feminist" issues, but drafted and sponsored bills with broad national implications. In 1932, Rep. Mary Teresa Norton (D-N.J.) introduced the first constitutional amendment to repeal the Volstead Act (Prohibition) and helped pass the Fair Labor Standards Act. Rep. Ruth Bryan Owen (D-Fla.) proposed a Federal Department of Home and Child. She was also an early environmentalist, whose bill eventually created the Everglades National Park.

World War II saw a succession of women on Capitol Hill casting votes for military preparedness. In 1940, Sen. Margaret Chase Smith (R-Maine) broke ranks with most Republicans in the House by voting for the Selective Service Act, the arming of American merchant ships, and lend-lease. After Pearl Harbor she introduced legislation creating the women's naval service called the WAVES. Rep. Clare Booth Luce's (R-Conn.) record in the 78th Congress included proposals for a European alliance (later achieved through the creation of NATO) and racial equality in the armed services. Her postwar legislative initiatives included bills to support jobs for veterans, to eliminate job discrimination against minorities, and to establish civilian control over atomic energy.

After the war, Rep. Emily Taft Douglas (D-Ill.) introduced legislation empowering the United Nations to control weapons and outlaw the atomic bomb. She proposed a program to regenerate European youth reared under Fascism, and also drafted a bill to fund bookmobiles in impoverished areas of the United States. The latter provision was eventually signed into law as the Library Services Act of 1956.

Rep. Helen Gahagan Douglas (D-Calif.), who served from 1945 to 1951, fought successfully for the creation of the United Nations and the Marshall Plan and against a bill that would have given control of atomic energy to the military. She coauthored the McMahon-Douglas Bill, placing atomic patents under civilian control, a bill that the Federation of Atomic Scientists called the most important piece of legislation ever passed by Congress. She also wrote and introduced the first legislation to protect the rights of citizens appearing before congressional committees, such as the House Un-American Activities Committee (HUAC).

In the late 1940s, Rep. Edith Nourse Rogers (R-Mass.), serving as chair of the Veterans Affairs Committee, successfully stewarded bills creating a nationwide network of veterans' hospitals, the GI Bill of Rights, the Women's Auxiliary Corps, and similar women's military services within the navy, coast guard, and marine corps.

In 1943, Rep. Winifred Stanley (R-N.Y.) introduced an amendment to the National Labor Relations Act that made it unlawful "to discriminate against any employee, in the rate of compensation paid, on account of sex." The provision died for lack of support, and it was almost two decades after her departure from Capitol Hill before Congress approved such a provision.

Rep. Leonor K. Sullivan (D-Mo.) served 12 terms, beginning in 1952, during which she became known as the nation's consumer advocate. As chairman of the Banking and Currency Subcommittee on Consumer Affairs, she crusaded against harmful food additives, deceptive advertising, contaminated meat, and hidden consumer-finance charges. In 1961 she introduced a 41-page omnibus bill covering all food, drugs, and cosmetics. Her comprhensive bill was never passed, though she reintroduced it in every Congress. Nonetheless, a series of consumer-protection laws were eventually passed, accomplishing in piecemeal fashion much of her legislative agenda. The legacy of her legislative initiatives includes the banning of carcinogens in food; compulsory federal inspection of poultry; pretesting of all chemical additives used in food; stricter control over the manufacture and sale of pep pills and barbiturates; and the Fair Credit Reporting Act, protecting consumers against false or malicious information from credit bureaus. Sullivan was also responsible for the passage of food-stamp legislation.

Rep. Edith Green (D-Ore.), who served from 1958 to 1975, had a legislative focus on the nation's education. As the second-ranking member of the Education and Labor Committee and the chairman of its Special Subcommittee on Education, she strongly influenced the National Defense Education Act of 1958 and authored the Higher Education Facilities Act of

1963. Her "Green Amendments" to the 1965 Vocational Rehabilitation Act extended job-training opportunities to urban youth, and her work on the Higher Education Act of 1965 broadened student-financial assistance. Among her legislative efforts to end discrimination against women were the Equal Pay Act of 1963 and a provision in the 1972 Omnibus Higher Education Act, which prohibited institutions receiving federal aid from discriminating on the basis of sex.

Rep. Martha Griffiths (D-Mich.) played a major role in extending the provisions of the Civil Rights Act of 1964 to cover sexual discrimination, but the tortuous process by which this was accomplished is replete with irony. The introduction of the provision to prevent discrimination on the basis of sex was actually aimed at killing the Civil Rights Act rather than enhancing it. Griffiths is usually considered the author of the sex provision, but Rep. Howard Smith (D-Va.) actually introduced the amendment in an attempt to *diminish* support for the total bill. Griffiths had intended to introduce the amendment herself, but she recalls, "Judge Smith was Chairman of the Rules Committee and leader of the conservative bloc, who would, if they could, have killed the bill. I realized that Mr. Smith would get more than a hundred votes just because he offered the amendment. . . . Without saying anything to anyone, I decided to let him offer it, and use my powers of persuasion to get the rest of the votes." Griffiths admitted, "I used Smith."[61]

On February 8, 1964, as the House continued its consideration of the Civil Rights Act, staunch segregationist Smith stunned the chamber by offering an amendment that extended the protections of the Civil Rights Act to women. Smith's disingenuous motives quickly became apparent as he began to discuss his amendment.

"[T]o show you how some of the ladies feel about discrimination, I want to read you an extract from a letter that I received the other day," the 80-year-old Smith said on the floor. "This lady has a real grievance on behalf of the minority sex. . . . [S]he says, 'I suggest that you might also favor an amendment . . . to correct the present imbalance which exists between males and females.' Then she goes on to say—and she has her statistics, which is the reason I am reading it to you, because this is serious—'The census of 1960 shows that we had 88,331,000 males living in this country and 90,992,000 females. . . . Just why the Creator would set up such an imbalance of spinsters, shutting off the right of every female to have a husband of her own, is, of course, known only to nature. But I am sure you will agree that this is a grave injustice to womankind and something the Congress and President Johnson should take immediate steps to correct."[62]

Smith's sarcastic amendment, which was met with laughter on the floor, was more than a crude attempt to interject humor into the debate. Smith, who chaired the Rules Committee, felt confident that House conservatives, already reluctant to protect blacks from discrimination, would never vote for a bill that would also protect women. By attaching his amendment to the Civil Rights Act, Smith felt he could defeat the entire package.

Debate on the amendment created some odd alliances. Nearly all opponents of the legislation were prominent liberal men, while those speaking in favor of it were southern segregationists or progressive women. Griffiths had planned to introduce her own sexual-equality amendment but, unlike Smith, hoped for actual enactment of the language.

After Smith brought his language to the floor, Griffiths rose to speak in favor of it.

In her speech she reminded the mostly white male members, "Your great-grandfathers were willing to be prisoners of their own prejudice to permit ex-slaves to vote, but not their own white wives. A vote against this amendment today by a white man is a vote against his wife, or his widow, or his daughter, or his sister."[63]

"I can remember that just before I went up there, once the amendment had been offered, there was uproarious laughter," Griffiths recalled. "Now we had been debating this bill since Tuesday, and this was now Thursday and [Rep.] Lee Sullivan looked back at me—there had never been any laughter on the rest of the bill, but when the amendment was offered, there was tremendous laughter, uproarious laughter—and Lee looked back and she said, 'Martha, if you can't stop that laughter, you're lost.' She and [Rep.] Edna Kelly knew that originally I had intended to offer the amendment, but that I was going to support it for Smith, and they understood why. . . . There was not laughter after I stood up."

In the end, the odd coalition of segregationists and women prevailed, and the amendment passed 168 to 133. When the entire Civil Rights Bill came to a vote, Smith and every one of the southerners who had voted for the sexual-discrimination language opposed the broader package. The act, however, was passed 290 to 130. Later that year it was approved by the Senate and signed into law by President Lyndon Johnson.

Recalled Griffiths: "I always thanked [Smith] afterwards for 'our' amendment. . . . And he said to me, 'Well, of course, you know, I offered it as a joke.' . . . I am sure that the rest of that committee never thought of women, and I am sure that the Congress of the United States had never before considered the effect of a bill upon women, ever, not ever."[64]

Six years later, in 1970, Griffiths again proved pivitol in the passage of legislation containing antidiscrimination language for women. It was in that year that Griffiths successfully pushed through the House a discharge petition to pry the Equal Rights Amendment out of the Judiciary Committee where it had languished without a single hearing since it was first introduced in 1923.

With the possible exception of the Woman Suffrage Amendment, no legislative initiative has resonated more clearly with American women than the ERA. Indeed, the debate on the ERA proved to be the only serious discussion on women's rights since the Suffrage Amendment passed Congress in 1919. Debate over the ERA produced bizarre arguments in opposition, many of them reminiscent of the rhetoric heard 50 years earlier from opponents of the Suffrage Amendment.

"Feminists clamor for equal rights," argued Rep. Emanuel Celler (D-N.Y.). "Nobody can deny that women should have equality under the law. But ever since Adam gave up his rib to make a woman, throughout the ages we have learned that physical, emotional, psychological, and social differences exist and dare not be disregarded. Neither the National Women's Party, nor the delightful, delectable, and dedicated gentlelady from Michigan [Griffiths] can change nature. They cannot do it. Beyond that let me say that there is as much difference between a male and a female as between a horse chestnut and a chestnut horse, and as the French say, *Vive le difference*. Any attempt to pass an amendment that promises to wipe out the effects of these differences is about as abortive as trying to fish in a desert, and you cannot do that. There is no really genuine equality and I defy anyone to tell me what 'equality' in this amendment means. Even your five fingers, one is not equal to the other, they are different."[65]

Despite such arguments, Griffiths's resolution to discharge the ERA from judiciary passed 333 to 22. An hour's debate was then granted for the consideration of the actual language of the amendment. The language, which has yet to be ratified by three-fifths of the states, simply reads: "Equality of rights under the law shall not be denied or abridged by the United States or by any state on account of sex." Griffiths explained that she originally felt an hour's debate was too short for discussion of such an important piece of legislation, but later realized the brief time limit was about all the House could handle.

"Now I personally feel that the Parliamentarian had never explained it to me correctly," recalled Griffiths, "because we had only an hour's debate, but in the long run, no matter what he intended, it worked out to the very best, because all who wanted to speak wanted to laugh at it, and you couldn't have stood two hours of laughter, so we had only one hour."[66]

The House eventually passed the ERA 352 to 15. Griffiths's victory, however, was short lived. Two months later, when the Senate began consideration of the language of the bill, that chamber muddied the water by inserting an amendment exempting women from the draft. With only a few weeks left in the session, there was no time for the two chambers to resolve the difference in language and the ERA was effectively dead for the year.

But Griffiths did not give up the fight. The ERA was again introduced the following year, and this time the Judiciary Committee held hearings on the legislation, led by Rep. Don Edwards (D-Calif.). Edwards reported the bill out of his subcommittee without amendment, but full committee chairman Rep. Emanuel Celler (D-N.Y.) included two amendments that would exempt women from the draft and allow Congress or the states to enact protective labor standards for women.

"Women represent motherhood and creation," Celler said on the floor in defense of his amendment. "Wars are for destruction. Women, integrated with men in the carnage and slaughter of battle, on land, at sea, or in the air, is unthinkable. Can you imagine women trained by a drill sergeant to charge the enemy with fixed bayonets and bombs?"

Another supporter of the Celler amendment, Rep. Thomas Abernethy (D-Miss.), argued: "With all deference to the courage, the beauty, the charm, and the sacrifices that have been made by American women, how many of you believe that this country can be made safe with women standing in times of war at the triggers of cannons?"[67]

Once the ERA hit the House floor in October 1971, however, both Celler amendments were defeated. The amendment exempting women from the draft, which would have effectively killed the ERA had it been enacted, was defeated 265 to 87. The final unamended language of the ERA then passed the House 354 to 24.

Hopes for enactment of the ERA were high as the bill moved on to the Senate for the second time in 1972. That chamber's Judiciary Committee reported the language without amendment on a 15-to-1 vote. Despite obstructionist arguments and amendments similar to those heard in the House, the "pure" language favored by sponsors was never in jeopardy. Final passage came by a vote of 84 to 8 on March 22, 1972. Before announcing the result, the presiding officer warned observers in the galleries that no demonstrations were permitted, but according to the *Congressional Record*, demonstrations did erupt.

Griffiths recalled, "Now, one of the things that really helped in the Senate the second time around was that we did try to organize the wives and daughters of the Senators and the daughters were particularly effective. Various Senators came to me and said, 'Well, you know my daughter is really for this,' and of course it was effective."[68]

The ERA language passed by both houses contained a seven-year ratification deadline, a deadline that Griffiths regarded as unimportant at the time. "I am well aware of the fact that there is a group of women who are so nervous about this amendment that they feel there should be an unlimted time during which it could be ratified," Griffiths said on the floor moments before the House voted in favor of the ERA. "Personally, I have no fears but that this amendment will be ratified in my judgment as quickly as was the 18-year-old vote. . . . I think it will be ratified almost immediately."[69]

Eleven years later, in 1982, after the Congress added an additional three years to the deadline, the ERA expired without having attained the required ratification of 38 states. Attempts to resuscitate the ERA continue to this day. SJRes 25 (ERA) was reintroduced in the Senate in January 1995 by chief sponsor Sen. Ted Kennedy (D-Mass.) and garnered 39 cosponsors. In the House, Rep. Rob Andrews (D-N.J.) introduced HRes.39 in January 1995. The measure calls for an end to the ratification deadline and for Congress to take the necessary action to enact the ERA once it is ratified by the states. It has drawn no cosponsors.

THE MODERN LEGISLATIVE AGENDA

In recent years, as more and more women have joined the House and Senate, the national attention given to women's issues has jumped significantly. In 1969, when there were just ten women in the House and one in the Senate, the *Congressional Record Index* listed 43 House bills introduced on women's issues, 39 of them referring to the Equal Rights Amendment. In the Senate that same year, *no* bills on women's issues were introduced. The *Congressional Record Index* also shows that in 1969, only ten "remarks" on women were made on the House floor, and there was just one speech on women in the Senate. In 1993, on the other hand, 357 bills were introduced on women's and family issues in the House and Senate.

Broadly speaking, the modern women's legislative agenda addresses education, health care, jobs, the environment, government waste, defense priorities, public safety, gun control, reproductive rights (including the Freedom of Choice Act and the Freedom of Access to Clinics Bill), the Supplemental Food Program for Women, Infants, and Children (WIC), antistalking legislation, teenage pregnancy prevention, prenatal care, child care, full funding of Head Start, mentoring programs, and national service.

In 1993, the first year of the 103rd Congress, members not only introduced and debated legislation on women's issues in record numbers, but they also followed through on their words in historic fashion. "Electorally, 1992 was the year of the woman. But legislatively, 1993 has equal claim to that title," said Rep. Pat Schroeder (D-Colo.), former chair of the Women's Caucus. "Issues of concern to women and families truly came of age during the first session of the 103rd Congress, and largely, it was the Congresswomen who set the agenda. We have never come so far so quickly."[70]

During the first year of the five preceeding Congresses—1983, 1985, 1987, 1989, and 1991—an average of just four bills were enacted that dealt with women's issues. In 1993, Congress passed 30 pieces of legislation dealing with women's issues and set a historic precedent for women at the end of its 103rd session by enacting 66 bills that helped women and families. Among those laws were the Family and Medical Leave Act, the removal of restrictions on abortion services to women in prison, the authorization of $225 million for basic research and $100 million for clinical research on breast cancer, language ensuring the inclusion of women and minorities in clinical research studies sponsored by the National Institutes of Health, and the removal of remaining statutory limitations on women serving in the military, including the ban on women serving on combat ships. Members of the Women's Caucus alone introduced 70 bills in 1993 to improve the economic, health, and educational status of women.

Rep. Carolyn Maloney (D-N.Y.), a member of the record-breaking class of 1992, says, "We came to bring real change, and we passed the Family and Medical Leave Bill after seven years of gridlock. We passed the Brady Bill after seven years of gridlock. We passed the Assault Gun Ban and the Crime Bill, NAFTA and the Domestic Violence Bill. For the first time we achieved serious funding for women's health, for research on breast cancer, cervical cancer and ovarian cancer. There is no substitute for a place at the table, and with 48 women at the table, women's health needs will never again be swept under the rug and forgotten."[71]

One of the earliest tangible legislative victories for the newly reinforced women of the 103rd Congress was the Family and Medical Leave Act. When originally introduced in 1985, sponsor Pat Schroeder (D-Colo.) couldn't get a single member of Congress to cosponsor the act. Though eventually passed by Congress in 1990 and 1992, President Bush vetoed the bill both times, and Congress failed to override the vetoes. But in 1993, the recently elected working mothers in Congress, with a total of 67 children, gave a new weight to the floor debate.

Rep. Carolyn Maloney (D-N.Y.) had been motivated to run for Congress in 1992 by her commitment to just such legislative initiatives. In support of the Family and Medical Leave Act, she addressed the House on February 3, 1993. "Mr. Speaker, as a working mother with two children and as the Representative in Congress of tens of thousands of other working parents in New York City, I rise to voice my strong support for the Family and Medical Leave Act. As my twelve-year-old daughter might tell you, this bill is a no-brainer. Every industrialized nation in the world has adopted a policy allowing workers time off to care for a new baby or an ill family member. It is ridiculous, and profoundly embarrassing, that we still do not have such a policy."

Many other women rose to speak in favor of the bill. Rep. Marjorie Margolies-Mezvinsky (D-Pa.): "As a working mother, I know the importance of a strong family leave policy. When I adopted my first child, Lee Heh, in 1970, I was a single parent struggling to balance my obligations to my job and to my child."

Rep. Lynn Woolsey (D-Calif.): "I know from firsthand experience the true value of family leave policies. . . . Mr. Speaker, no American worker should have to choose between caring for a family member and the job that provides for that family."

Rep. Lynn Schenk (D-Calif.): "Mr. Speaker, I stand before this body as a new Member. But before coming to this House, I had and continue to have many other life roles. I am a wife, a stepmother—and a daughter. It is because of this life experience—shared by millions of American women—that I support the Family and Medical Leave Act."

Rep. Marge Roukema (R-N.J.): "In these harsh economic times and with health costs soaring, are you going to tell a pregnant woman or the mother of a child dying of leukemia to, 'Go find another job, if you can?' Are these family values? . . . Families are thrown into crisis when serious illness strikes. I know. I have been there. When my son, Todd, was striken with leukemia and needed home care, I was free to remain at home and give him the loving care he needed. But what of the millions of mothers who work for the thousands of companies that do not have family leave policies?"[72]

In the Senate, Patty Murray (D-Wash.) testified: "When I was 26 years old and worked as an executive secretary in Seattle, I became pregnant with my first child. At that time, even though I was working out of economic necessity, there were no options for working mothers. A family leave policy would have enabled me to devote my attention to the changes in my family. . . . I am of the infamous sandwich generation, charged with caring for my own children and my parents at the same time. I personally understand the emotional consequences."

Sen. Dianne Feinstein (D-Calif.): "Thirty-five years ago, when I gave birth to my daughter, Katherine, there was no maternity or family leave. I left my job to have my child. . . . Today, we have an opportunity to take a stand for our workers. We have an opportunity to support the working parents of this nation, and we have an opportunity, finally, to allow a mother to keep her job to give birth to a child or to care for a sick child or an elderly parent."[73]

Through the personal testimony of such female voices, most of them new to Congress, the act was passed, providing three months of unpaid leave for employees. Forty-two of the 48 congresswomen and six of the seven women senators voted in favor of the bill. But on February 5, 1993, when President Clinton signed the Family and Medical Leave Act, an act that women had fought for a decade to get through the Congress, no female lawmakers were on stage with the president. The only members of Congress asked to speak at the elaborate White House signing ceremony were senators Ted Kennedy (D-Mass.) and Chris Dodd (D-Conn.) and Rep. Bill Clay (D-Mo.). Rep. Pat Schroeder, seated in the second row of the audience, explained, " I had worked on it for nine years, but when it finally passes, it's the guys who take the credit."[74]

The large 1992 class of freshmen women played a major role in some early legislative victories, but before these new women could implement their legislative agenda, they would have to learn some painful lessons about rules and tactics. The real eye-opener occurred in June 1993 when the issue of Medicaid funding for abortions came before the House. The women's caucus task force on abortion rights knew it didn't have the votes to reverse the so-called Hyde Amendment, which prohibited government-funded abortions, but Nita Lowey (D-N.Y.), who chaired the caucus's pro-choice task force, thought it had a strategy to remove the Hyde Amendment without a vote. In preparation for the maneuver, Lowey's task force met with House parliamentarians to be certain of the rules. The Hyde Amendment had come before the House as part of an appropriations bill, and because House rules prohibit legislating on such bills, the women were assured that they could strike the prohibition on procedural grounds.

Unknown to the women, 83-year-old William Natcher (D-Ky.), chairman of the powerful House Appropriations Committee, had worked out a deal with the House leadership to allow Rep. Henry Hyde (R-Ill.) to present his amendment for a vote. The women were astounded that Democrat Natcher, one of their own, would help Republicans defeat their procedural strategy.

An acrimonious debate ensued. Rep. Marjorie Margolies-Mezvinsky (D-Pa.) recalls, "And so here we were, the pro-choice women and the pro-life men, duking it out, and it wasn't pretty. In fact, it was downright ridiculous. The scene resembled a bad high school dance, with the girls huddled in one corner and all the boys in another, each camp eyeing the other warily."[75]

During the floor debate, a number of black women spoke against the Hyde Amendment. Rep. Carrie Meek (D-Fla.) said, "Vote for fairness and vote for the right of poor women to have access to the full range of health care services." Rep. Cynthia McKinney (D-Ga.) pointed out that the Hyde Amendment had created devastating consequences in the lives of low-income women. "The Hyde Amendment is nothing but a discriminatory policy against poor women who happen to be disproportionately black," she said. "[T]his is about equity and fairness for all women, and quite frankly, I have just about had it with my colleagues who vote against people of color, vote against the poor and vote against women."

Henry Hyde responded in his typical acerbic style. "About those people that say the poor are discriminated against, you know what we do? We tell poor people, . . . 'We will give you a free abortion *because there are too many of you people, and we want to kind of refine the breed.*' "

Some of the women began to hiss. Cardiss Collins, a black Democratic congresswoman from Hyde's state of Illinois, asked if Hyde would yield the floor to permit a response. Hyde refused. Collins rose to her feet and shouted, "I am offended by that kind of debate."[76]

Hyde responded patronizingly that he was going to direct Collins to *"some black clergymen in her district"* who could tell her what goes on in her community.

Collins was infuriated and demanded that Hyde's words be striken from the record. She was ruled out of order.* A group of black congresswomen joined Collins at the microphone, and chaos briefly reigned. Rep. Carrie Meek (D-Fla.) turned to one of her female colleagues and said, "Just let me at him. I'll get him by the you-know-whats."[77]

Rep. Pat Schroeder asked to be recognized in order "to try to bring some dignity back to this." She declared, "I say to the gentleman from Illinois [Rep. Hyde], women are not beasts, and that is what we are really hearing here. We are being asked to develop and debate an amendment we did not see, we did not know about, on an appropriation bill where the rules of this House say it does not belong. . . . Mr. Chairman, it seems to me that when the 19th amendment passed, we should have been equal beings. But we are hearing that we have got to go through these incredible procedural back-flips to put all these restrictions on because women of America cannot be trusted."[78]

When all the clamor ended, the vote was taken and the Hyde Amendment remained intact. The women were humiliated. One commented, "I feel like we were raped on the House floor today." Some of them blamed the House leadership for inadequate support, others blamed the parliamentarian for his misleading advice, and many blamed themselves for not being better schooled in parliamentary procedure. Outside the Capitol building the press asked the women how they felt after their humiliating legislative defeat. Rep. Pat Schroeder (D-Colo.) looked into the TV camera and said, "The Year of the Woman just went down the chute."[79]

Not only were the women disturbed by their procedural defeat, but the vote itself produced 11 defections in their own ranks, almost one-quarter of the women in the House. Former representative Maria Cantwell (D-Wash.) said, "I remember lobbying [members] and being shocked. I thought I knew their political positions and all of a sudden they are saying, 'No, I'm not with you on this one.' "

Rep. Deborah Pryce (R-Ohio), one of the defectors on the Hyde Amendment, was torn between party politics and friendship with the other women. "I had mixed feelings about it," she said. "It was a blow to the women in Congress because they were caught off guard and I hated to see that happen."[80]

---

* Rep. Collins's request to delete or "take down" Rep. Hyde's offensive comments was ruled out of order, and Collins was told she would have to bring the matter before the House at a later time. She subsequently did so, stating: "I am sorry that I was not able to have the gentleman's words stricken because I think that it does not serve this body and the history of this body to have people read years from now in the *Congressional Record* words which were indeed inflammatory and, I think, insulting to any number of people who happen to be poor, who may or may not be African-American, all of whom are women, in this country." (*Congressional Record* 139:H4335.) Collins asked Rep. Hyde to have portions of his remarks "stricken down," and he agreed. The quotes shown above in italics were expunged and do not appear in the *Congressional Record*.

Perhaps because they had counted on their procedural tactics, the women had not bothered to take an informal-vote count, even among themselves. They were stunned, but not yet vanquished. They still had a chance in the Senate, where they believed they had the votes to overturn the prohibition on Medicaid funding of abortions. Indeed, the Senate Appropriations Committee approved a bill that would strike the House ban on abortion funding, and Sen. Barbara Mikulski (D-Md.), who led the floor fight, was confident of victory. But once again, the women had miscalculated, and abortion funding was denied.

Rep. Marjorie Margolies-Mezvinsky said that if the Year of the Woman showed how far women had come, the day of the Hyde Amendment vote showed how much further women had to go. She fears that those members who are uncomfortable with the influx of female legislators will use battles such as the Hyde Amendment to intimidate women in Congress.

On July 1, the day after the Hyde Amendment vote, Pat Schroeder organized a meeting with congresswomen, staffers, and the press to try to sort things out. The women were candid in describing how they had been outmaneuvered, and the press followed with stories that characterized the women as vulnerable, emotional, political neophytes. Rep. Nita Lowey (D-N.Y.) said, "It was a terrible debate, and that won't heal for a while. There was a real feeling of pain on the part of these women. So whether the words were truly sexist, there was a perception of that. If we were men, I believe they wouldn't have talked to us that way."[81]

The women were particularly disappointed in the Democratic leadership. "We just didn't have the help," said Rep. Leslie Byrne (D-Va.). "If any other group had an initiative of that type, the Democratic Caucus would have rallied around. That help wasn't forthcoming."[82] The congresswomen arranged a meeting with Tom Foley (D-Wash.), the Speaker of the House, to express their dissatisfaction. Some of the women were reluctant to put Foley on the spot. Others were outspoken.

Rep. Margolies-Mezvinsky recalls that the meeting with the leadership was candid but very rough, producing perhaps irreparable damage. She says there were promises to try to work and communicate better with the Women's Caucus in the future, but the ugliness of the Hyde Amendment debate could not be contained. "[I]n fact, it seemed to have metastasized throughout the body of Congress," said Margolies-Mezvinsky. "It was a horrible, embarrassing moment in the history of this body, and I hope one that will never be repeated again."[83]

Three weeks later, Pat Schroeder put an optimistic spin on the episode. She acknowledged that it was a serious setback, but said it was important that the freshmen women were able to reconfirm how sexist Congress was.

The women had been taught a bitter legislative lesson, but they may have been strengthened in defeat. Rep. Cynthia McKinney (D-Ga.) said, "The women have a real sisterhood now. We may not have realized it going into the debate or even during it. But afterward it was clear we have only each other to look to."[84]

With the Republican takeover, however, the 104th Congress quickly rolled back many of the legislative accomplishments made two years earlier. In August of 1995, the Democratic women of the House released a report detailing what they called "The GOP Legislative War on Women." The report cited 12 measures passed in House committees and on the floor during the first six months of the session that would restrict abortion rights. Among them were a ban on abortions for women inmates in federal prisons, a ban on abortions for women in the military overseas, a prohibition on federal employee health insurance covering abortion, and a measure prohibiting the Legal Services Corporation from taking up any abortion issue.

The 1994 elections—which brought a huge number of both male and female Republicans to office—greatly hurt the pro-choice movement in Congress. In the Senate, there was a net gain of five antichoice seats and a gain of more than 30 antichoice seats in the House. All four leading Senate committees dealing with reproductive issues were handed over to chairs with a 35 percent or less rating from the National Abortion and Reproductive Rights Action League (NARRAL). In the House, all five committees with jurisdiction over reproductive health were handed over to chairs with a zero rating from NARRAL.

The Republican leadership gave anti-abortionists a free hand in 1995, allowing amendments limiting abortion rights to be offered on nearly every appropriations bill, but not all Republican women felt comfortable with such a heavy-handed emphasis.

"It's an image problem for our party when we are trying to stay in [the majority]," said pro-choice representative Deborah Pryce (R-Ohio). "Every time we have to make an issue of it, the party loses. The less time we have to argue about it, the less time Democrats have to attack us on it and the stronger a party we can be."

Pryce concluded: "If Republicans are going to attract women voters, this is not the way to do it."

Even some anti-abortion Republican women expressed discomfort with the numerous votes on the issue.

"I am very pro-life," said representative Barbara Cubin (R-Wyo.). "And I think debate is good, but I don't know how many times you have to debate abortion, or any issue, in one week."[85]

One of the first debates over abortion in the 104th Congress emerged during the confirmation hearings of Dr. Henry Foster, the Clinton nominee for surgeon general. Conservative Republicans opposed the nomination because of Foster's support for abortion rights. At a February 1995 press conference organized by Democrats who supported Foster, Rep. Louise

Slaughter (D-N.Y.) blasted Congress in general for its inability to understand the issue of reproductive rights. "This is not an issue for any kind of legislative body where you have Members saying women can only get pregnant one day a month or there's never been a pregnancy as a result of rape," Slaughter said. "You know this is beyond their scope of their ability to understand."

Slaughter was referring to comments made days earlier by one of the newly elected Republican freshmen, Rep. Dave Weldon of Florida. Weldon was speaking on the floor against the Foster nomination.

But women have not been alone in their push for abortion rights. Following the fight over the Hyde Amendment, a number of congresswomen were disturbed by the popular perception that only women had fought the battle and that only women had lost. They noted that people like representatives Vic Fazio (D-Calif.) and Steny Hoyer (D-Md.) had worked with them and shared their disappointment. Indeed, throughout history, female members have not been alone in their attempts to further their interests. The first member of Congress to ever introduce the Equal Rights Amendment, in fact, was a male—Rep. Charles Curtis (R-Kans.) in 1923. In 1993, of the 357 bills introduced on women's issues, 230 were introduced by men.

Just as men have crossed the lines to influence feminist legislation, women have made a major impact on legislation whose focus cannot generally be described as "women's issues." Women played a major role in the success of the two most difficult and controversial pieces of legislation passed in the 103rd Congress: the Clinton budget proposal and the Omnibus Crime Bill. The freshman women were under pressure from conservatives on Capitol Hill and in their home districts to vote against both proposals, and some of those women were made to pay dearly for their vote in favor of the bills.

During the controversial 1994 debate on the crime bill, women helped ensure that a ban on assault weapons was included in the legislation. In May of 1994, early in the discussion of the crime bill, a bi-partisan group of 20 women from both the House and Senate held a press conference supporting the weapons ban and labeling it a "women's issue."

"We are here today as women Members of Congress and more importantly as mothers, daughters, sisters, and wives to declare that assault weapons are a menace to public safety and must be banned," Rep. Nita Lowey (D-N.Y.) said during the conference. "We are here because crime and violence are women's issues."

The weapons ban, restricting 19 types of semiautomatic assault weapons, was included as part of the larger crime bill, which passed the House on August 21, 1994, by a vote of 235 to 195. The votes of the House's 48 women were nearly unanimous with all but eight women voting for the bill. The Senate enacted the bill four days later by a vote of 61 to 38. Again, women of the upper chamber were united in their support for the crime package, with six of the seven women voting for passage.

Rep. Lynn Woolsey (D-Calif.) recalls, "Even though we were only eleven percent of Congress in 1993, we were fifty percent of the Democratic whip organization that got the assault weapons ban passed. We helped get it passed by two votes, and when it was over, the chairman Charlie Schumer [D-N.Y.] turned around and looked at the back of the House floor and said, 'You women did this for us.' We knew we had, but it was what we came here to do."[86]

Women legislators say while they are most unified on issues relating to women and families, they often share the same perspectives on broader legislation as well.

"There's no question women have a different perspective," said Rep. Sue Myrick (R-N.C.), one of the Republican women elected in 1994. "Women tend to always try to find a solution. We aren't as confrontational as men. We team build. It gives us a definite advantage. We come into situations with a more relaxed, open attitude."[87]

Myrick's Democratic colleague, freshman representative Karen McCarthy (Mo.), echoed the same analysis. "We're more inclusive. We tend to bring people into the scheme in the effort to create unity," McCarthy says. "We always look for bi-partisan support. Our egos are less domineering then men's."[88]

Veteran representative Louise Slaughter (D-N.Y.) agreed: "I think women do have a common perspective on broader issues, and I think that defense has been one of them, though in most people's minds that would not be categorized as a woman's issue. Now this may sound simplistic, but I've often had the idea that if you give boys, little boys, uniforms, guns, and wonderful toys that move and do incredibly grand things, they're going to want to play with them. I think women have a better perspective on the use of force, like, can we talk about this before we all have bloody noses. I think women do bring a different perspective. Pat Schroeder would say it's a matter of testosterone levels. To me, it's just practicality, and I don't want that to be confused with weakness."[89]

One of the most recent examples of congresswomen unifying around an ostensibly "nonfeminist" issue came during the 1994 Senate debate on the retirement of four star navy admiral Frank Kelso. Kelso had served as head of naval operations during the time of the 1991 Tailhook convention, the annual gathering of naval pilots that had degenerated into a drunken sexual assault against about 80 female officers. Although the women's testimony failed to influence the outcome, the debate produced a furor similar to that which erupted during the Anita Hill hearings three years earlier. As with the Hill controversy, the Kelso debate had the appearance of a male-dominated Senate brushing aside charges of sexual harassment and rewarding the man whom female lawmakers held responsible for those actions.

Traditionally, both naval rank and pension automatically fall upon retirement *unless* the Senate votes otherwise, but rarely has the Senate denied retirement at full rank to a chief of a military service. The Senate Armed Services Committee voted 20 to 2 in favor of awarding Kelso the higher rank and increased benefits, despite the dissent of the sole woman on the panel, Sen. Kay Bailey Hutchison (R-Tex.). "The issue," she said, "is his captaincy of the ship—what happened on his watch—and the signal his performance sends to the Navy and the world."

The full Senate was now forced to determine whether the admiral should retire at the rank of two stars, with a pension of $67,467, or whether to allow Kelso to step down with his four-star rank intact and an $84,340 pension. The Tailhook scandal had mobilized women from both chambers of the Capitol and both sides of the aisle to oppose the higher rank and pension. On April 19, 1994, the day of the Senate vote on Kelso's retirement status, nine female House members marched to the upper chamber to stand in silent protest. One day earlier, Rep. Pat Schroeder (D-Colo.) had explained on the House floor the long-range implications of the Senate vote.

"This really is not about sexual harassment; this is about sexual assault," said Schroeder. "I certainly hope that some of my sisters who moved to the other body will take this up, and I hope there is a raging fight on the Senate floor so we can see how many people really feel that there should be a promotion for an admiral who had all this happen under his command and never seemed to be able to get it under control."[90]

When the Senate took up the matter, floor debate quickly turned emotional and sexually divisive.

"The Tailhook matter is a sordid, sleazy stain on the U.S. Navy," said Barbara Mikulski (D-Md.). "[T]here was a series of actions that no one disputes in which several women were sexually harassed, sexually battered, and sexually assaulted. It was a scene of drunkenness, debauchery, vulgarity, and violence."

Mikulski explained, "That is what happened on Kelso's watch and, therefore, he must take the responsibility, pay the price, and send a message that there is no reward either in a pension, a retirement, or a promotion." Mikulski said it was hard to debate this issue because "it is so vulgar I cannot bring myself to even read from the report on the Senate floor. . . . In fact, it is so bad that we, the women of the Senate, do not wish to use the type of language that is described."

Sen. Barbara Boxer (D-Calif.) rose to speak. "Let us talk about Lieutenant Paula Coughlin. She told her immediate supervisor, a vice-admiral, of her experience in the gauntlet. Do you know what he said? 'That's what you get when you go to a hotel party with a bunch of drunken aviators.' Blame the victim. It should not surprise anyone that just two months ago Lieutenant Coughlin resigned her commission citing continuing harassment as the reason for cutting short her promising career. . . . This is what she wrote when she submitted her letter of resignation. 'The physical attack on me by the naval aviators at the Tailhook Convention and the covert attacks on me that followed have stripped me of my ability to serve.' "

Boxer gave personal, emotional testimony on the Tailhook events. "Only the women, the women who were assaulted, are the victims. . . . Any of us who have had any experience with sexual assault, . . . with sexual harassment, will tell you straight from the heart, you do not forget it. I myself had an experience when I was very young, a senior in college, and I can tell you every single detail of what happened to me. . . . You know, Admiral Kelso gets a chance to retire on a pretty good pension, whether it is two stars or four. Lieutenant Paula Coughlin quit the military in the middle of a promising career."

After a number of male senators suggested that the women didn't understand such military matters, that they just didn't "get it," Sen. Carol Moseley-Braun (D-Ill.) responded: "Madam President, the women elected to serve in this body and in the House get it. . . . We believe that sexual misconduct, harassment, abuse, and assault in the military must stop, and that refusal to promote Admiral Kelso for purposes of retirement is the way to stop it. . . . Admiral Kelso's watch will be as much remembered for this disgraceful disregard for women as for any of his purely military achievements. The question today is whether that disregard will be rewarded. The women of the Senate say no."

Sen. Kay Bailey Hutchison, a conservative Republican and the only woman on the Armed Services Committee, explained why she had dissented from the committee's recommendation. "When I voted in committee last week," she said, "I did not know if I would be the lone vote. I did not know if I would be the lone vote in the U.S. Senate. But I did what I thought was right."

Sen. Patty Murray (D-Wash.) said, "The Senate cannot say with one voice 'we do not condone sexual harassment,' and then, look the other way and reward those who are in charge when harassment and abuse occur."

When Sen. Sam Nunn (D-Ga.), a strong supporter of Kelso, questioned whether the Senate would have made a fuss over this issue if Kelso had chosen to retire in 1992, Boxer responded: "It is important to recall that in 1992, Senator Carol Moseley-Braun was not in the Senate. She came here in 1993 with me, Senator Murray, and Senator Feinstein, and we joined Senator Mikulski. Senator Hutchison was not here, either. So I do not know what would have happened in 1992. . . . [B]ut I will tell you one thing. It is 1994, and here we are, and we are making this an issue for good reason."

Barbara Mikulski made a similar point. "In September 1991 there was Tailhook. In October 1991 there were the hearings of Clarence Thomas for the Supreme Court, in which we saw Anita Hill undergo one of the most grueling, humiliating experiences that anyone has ever endured before the U.S. Senate. . . . I had hoped, as the only Democratic woman in the Senate at that time, that America had learned a lesson on sexual harassment. . . . It is no longer business as it was in 1991, or in 1891. It is over."

Sen. Carol Moseley-Braun rose once more: "In conclusion, again, I say to my colleagues that it is no accident that all of the women of this Chamber are of one mind about this issue. That is no accident. We have found in the last year and a half that I have been here, women in this chamber have not really voted as a block on many issues. . . . I say to you that it is no accident that on this issue there is unanimity of opinion among those who are on the receiving end of this scandalous activity. . . . Tailhook represented, at best, a situation of gender insensitivity and gender inequality. At worst, it was a matter of absolute assault. That is why the feelings are so strong on this issue, and that is why the women of this body are of one mind: That there must be some responsibility and accountability of Admiral Kelso with regard to this matter."

At this point, Sen. Ted Stevens (R-Alaska) interrupted once more to challenge Moseley-Braun's personal ability to understand the issue. Moseley-Braun, who later charged Stevens with "chauvinism," was moved to tears. Barbara Mikulski (D-Md.) rose to defend her. "Mr. President, during this entire debate, the women of the Senate and the men who support us in this cause have attempted to conduct this debate with civility and courtesy. . . . The fact is . . . we the women of the Senate are not stupid. . . . This is about the honor code and the code of conduct, and this is not about whether Senator Moseley-Braun gets it. . . . It is whether the rest of the Senate gets it. . . . We hope we win this. But whether we win the vote or not, we feel that we have won a victory here today because we have raised the issue."[91]

The final vote was 54 to 43 in favor of the elevated retirement, but there was bi-partisan unanimity shown in the dissenting votes of the seven Senate women.

To this day, most men in Congress have trivialized the significance of Tailhook. For example, when a jury found the Las Vegas Hilton, the hotel that hosted Tailhook, liable for permitting sexual assault against Navy Lieutenant Paula Coughlin, Rep. Bill Baker (R-Calif.) said flippantly, "Someone throws a party called Tailhook, and some lady decides a month later she's a victim, and we all pay for it in higher hotel costs."[92]

During the extended and heated debate on health care reform, female lawmakers voiced their concerns about the tendency of a male-dominated Congress to overlook women's health. Louise Slaughter (D-N.Y.) recalls, "We weren't trying to do anything except make clear that all the years of neglect meant that diseases that affect women had received no research, no money, no attention. In the case of breast cancer, women were dying at such a clip, and increasingly so, that it was just a disgrace. We pointed out that the large majority of women were paying taxes to help fund medical research, so the underfunding on women's health was not only inhumane, it was unfair."[93]

In February 1994, when Rep. Jim Cooper (D-Tenn.) crafted a reform health package that was considered one of the more likely plans to pass Congress that year, a bi-partisan group of 27 congresswomen wrote to Cooper expressing concern for his inadequate consideration of women's health issues. The women pledged to oppose any plan that failed to offer explicit coverage of women's health care.

"Health care reform presents us with an uprecedented opportunity to correct long-standing incquities in women's health care," the letter to Cooper read. "In order to meet this challenge, Congress must pass a reform plan with a specifically defined comprehensive bencfits package that includes coverage of women's health."[94]

The women cited abortion services, prenatal care, family-planning services, mammograms, pelvic exams, and pap smears as requisite services and benefits in any health care reform plan. Though Congress failed to enact any comprehensive health care reform in 1994, women in Congress have continued their fight into the new legislative session, demanding increased women's services in a revamped health care system.

Despite their ability to coalesce on particular issues, most congressional women admit they will never be able to form a solid voting block based on their gender alone. The 31 Democratic and 17 Republican women in the House cover a broad political spectrum, from conservative to liberal. Steny Hoyer (D-Md.), former chairman of the House Democratic Caucus, says, "I can't think of an issue where I would say all the women would be for that issue." Indeed, when the House passed the family leave bill, considered to be "women's legislation," half the Republican women voted against it.

"I don't see that, as a group, women have made any attempt to do anything that would pull them together . . . as a legislative force," said recently defeated Rep. Karen Shepherd (D-Utah). "If you compare it to the black caucus, I wouldn't say we have come anywhere near having the same amount of effectiveness." Rep. Eva Clayton (D-N.C.), president of the 1992 House Democratic freshmen and a member of the black caucus, declared, "Women have to say we want to be more of a force. We've not reached the potential of our strength."[95]

In 1995, the crop of newly elected Republican women showed a closer affinity to their party ideology than to their female colleagues across the aisle. These new Republican women joined the male GOP freshmen in distancing themselves from the "feminist" agenda in a variety of ways, including a unanimous vote to abolish the Women's Caucus. Six of the seven Republican freshmen women went so far as to present the notorious antifeminist radio personality Rush Limbaugh with a "Rush Was Right" plaque during an orientation dinner. Rep. Barbara Cubin (R-Wyo.) proudly assured Limbaugh, "There's not a FemiNazi among us."[96]

NOTES

1. Barbara Boxer, *Strangers in the Senate: Politics and the New Revolution of Women in America*, Bethesda, Md.: National Press Books, 1993, pp. 44–45.

2. Wendy Kaminer, "Crashing the Locker Room," *Atlantic Monthly*, July 1992, p. 60.

3. Boxer, *Strangers in the Senate: Politics and the New Revolution of Women in America*, pp. 39–40.

4. Florence George Graves, "The Other Woman," *Washington Post*, October 9, 1994, pp. F8–9.

5. New York Times Oral History Program, Former Members of Congress Oral History Collection, No. 11, Reva Bosone. Sanford, N.C.: Microfilming Corp. of America, 1981.

6. Ibid, No. 37, Julia Hansen.

7. Shirley Chisholm, *Unbought and Unbossed*, Boston: Houghton Mifflin and Co., 1970, pp. 82, 86.

8. Patricia Schroeder, *Champion of the Great American Family*, New York: Random House, 1989, p. 25.

9. David Finkel, "Women on the Verge of a Power Breakthrough," *Washington Post Magazine*, May 10, 1992, p. 4.

10. Authors' interview with former Speaker of the House Jim Wright, October 26, 1993.

11. Clara Bingham, "The Women on the Hill," *Vogue*, August 1993, p. 266.

12. Authors' interview with Rep. Patsy Mink (D-Hawaii), December 2, 1994.

13. "Stark Gets His Medicine," *Washington Post*, March 18, 1994, p. D3.

14. Fundraising panel featuring Rep. Leslie Byrne (D-Va.) and other Democratic congresswomen, June 21, 1994.

15. Authors' interview with Rep. Louise Slaughter (D-N.Y.), April 12, 1994.

16. Authors' interview with Rep. Jan Meyers (R-Kans.), January 6, 1995.

17. Susan Taylor, "All in the Family," *MS*, November/December 1994, p. 20.

18. Authors' interview with Rep. Louise Slaughter (D-N.Y.), April 12, 1994.

19. Authors' interview with Rep. Barbara Vucanovich (R-Nev.), October 6, 1994.

20. Authors' interview with Rep. Patsy Mink (D-Hawaii), December 2, 1994.

21. Authors' interview with Rep. Louise Slaughter (D-N.Y.), April 12, 1994.

22. Chisholm, *Unbought and Unbossed*, pp. 80, 85.

23. Gloria Steinem, "Life After Backlash: Our Women in Washington," *MS*, January/February 1993, p. 31.

24. Nancy Traver, "Shock," *Redbook*, November 1993, p. 98.

25. Janet Hook, "Women Remain on Periphery Despite Electoral Gains," *Congressional Quarterly*, October 9, 1993, p. 2708.

26. Press release from Rep. Nita Lowey (D-N.Y.), December 6, 1994.

27. Press release from Rep. Patsy Mink (D-Hawaii), December 16, 1994.

28. Authors' interview with representatives Connie Morella (R-Md.) and Pat Schroeder (D-Colo.), February 13, 1995.

29. Schroeder, *Champion of the Great American Family*, pp. 108–9.

30. Karen Foerstel, "Women's Caucus Holds First Contest in Decade," *Roll Call*, July 11, 1994, p. 1.

31. Karen Foerstel, "The Race Is on for Women's Caucus Chair," *Roll Call*, July 11, 1994, p. 26.

32. Cindy Loose, "They Got the Vote, but Not the Rotunda," *Washington Post*, August 19, 1995, p. A1.

33. Boxer, *Strangers in the Senate: Politics and the New Revolution of Women in America*, p. 112.

34. Karen Foerstel, "Woolsey Breaks Gender Ice, Hill's Hoopster's Win," *Roll Call*, March 29, 1993, p. 8.

35. Kaminer, "Crashing the Locker Room," p. 60.

36. Hook, "Women Remain on Periphery Despite Electoral Gains," p. 2713.

37. Fundraising panel featuring Democratic congresswomen, June 21, 1994.

38. "Message from the President, Harriett Woods," *Women's Political Times*, Winter 1993–94, p. 2.

39. Boxer, *Strangers in the Senate: Politics and the New Revolution of Women in America*, p. 115.

40. Mary Jacoby, "House Erupts Friday Over Waters Speech," *Roll Call*, August 1, 1994, p. 1.

41. Authors' interview with Rep. Patsy Mink (D-Hawaii), December 2, 1994.

42. Boxer, *Strangers in the Senate: Politics and the New Revolution of Women in America*, p. 62.

43. Juliet Eilperin, "Second Ever Rep. Mom, Enid Waldholtz Says She'll Juggle Baby, Budget Vote," *Roll Call*, March 16, 1995, p. 1

44. Marjorie Margolies-Mezvinsky, *A Woman's Place: The Freshman Women Who Changed the Face of Congress*. New York: Crown Publishers, 1994, p. 174.

45. Authors' interview with Rep. Tillie Fowler (R-Fla.), May 24, 1994.

46. David Finkel, "Women on the Verge of a Power Breakthrough," *Washington Post Magazine*, May 10, 1992, pp. 11–12.

47. Authors' interview with Rep. Louise Slaughter (D-N.Y.), April 12, 1994.

48. Margolies-Mezvinsky, *A Woman's Place: The Freshman Women Who Changed the Face of Congress*, pp. 151, 155–6.

49. Authors' interview with Rep. Tillie Fowler (R-Fla.), May 24, 1994.

50. Authors' interview with Rep. Sue Myrick (R-N.C.), February 2, 1995.

51. Authors' interview with Rep. Lucille Roybal-Allard (D-Calif.), August 4, 1994.

52. Fundraising panel for Democratic congresswomen, June 21, 1994.

53. Karen Foerstel, "Ten Single Parents Among Frosh; How are they Juggling Lives?" *Roll Call*, January 8, 1993, p. 30.

54. Traver, "Shock," p. 149.

55. Margolies-Mezvinsky, *A Woman's Place: The Freshman Women Who Changed the Face of Congress*, pp. 154–5, 176.

56. Traver, "Shock," p. 138.

57. Authors' interview with Rep. Patsy Mink (D-Hawaii), December 2, 1994.

58. Sarah Conroy, "For Spouses, a Crash Course on the City," *Washington Post*, January 9, 1995, p. B3.

59. Authors' interview with Rep. Enid Greene Waldholtz (R-Utah), January 10, 1995.

60. U.S. Congress, House, 65th Congress, 2nd session, January 10, 1918, *Congressional Record* 56:771–85.

61. Emily George, *Martha Griffiths*, Washinton, D.C.: University Press of America, 1982, pp. 149–50.

62. U.S. Congress, House, 88th Congress, 2nd session, February 8, 1964, *Congressional Record* 110:2577.

63. George, *Martha Griffiths*, p. 151.

64. New York Times Oral History Program, Former Members of Congress Oral History Collection, No. 32, Martha Griffiths, p. 84.

65. U.S. Congress, House, 91st Congress, 2nd session, August 10, 1970, *Congressional Record* 116:28000–01.

66. New York Times Oral History Program, No. 32, Martha Griffiths, p. 81.

67. U.S. Congress, House, 92nd Congress, 1st session, October 12, 1971, *Congressional Record* 117:35785–87.

68. New York Times Oral History Program, No. 32, Martha Griffiths, p. 81.

69. U.S. Congress, House, 92nd Congress, 1st session, October 12, 1971, *Congressional Record* 117:35814.

70. "First Session Includes Historic Gains for Women," News release, Congressional Caucus for Women's Issues, December 2, 1993.

71. Fundraising panel featuring Democratic congresswomen, June 21, 1994.

72. U.S. Congress, House, 103rd Congress, 1st session, February 3, 1993, *Congressional Record* 139:H365–406.

73. U.S. Congress, Senate, 103rd Congress, 1st session, February 2, 1993, *Congressional Record* 139:S993–4.

74. Authors' interview with Rep. Pat Schroeder (D-Colo.), January 23, 1995.

75. Margolies-Mezvinsky, *A Woman's Place: The Freshman Women Who Changed the Face of Congress*, pp. 2–3.

76. U.S. Congress, House, 103rd Congress, 1st session, June 30, 1993, *Congressional Record* 139:H4293–4326.

77. Margolies-Mezvinsky, *A Woman's Place: The Freshman Women Who Changed the Face of Congress*, p. 6.

78. U.S. Congress, House, 103rd Congress, 1st session, June 30, 1993, *Congressional Record* 139:H4326.

79. Margolies-Mezvinsky, *A Woman's Place: The Freshman Women Who Changed the Face of Congress*, pp. 6–8.

80. Elaine Povich, "Frustration for Would-be Reformers," *Chicago Tribune*, November 28, 1993, p. 8.

81. Linda Feldman, "Women Are Finding a Voice on the Hill," *Christian Science Monitor*, July 23, 1993, p. 4.

82. Beth Donovan, "Political, Tactical Errors Curb Success of Women in the Abortion Debate," *Congressional Quarterly*, October 9, 1993, p. 2710.

83. Margolies-Mezvinsky, *A Woman's Place: The Freshman Women Who Changed the Face of Congress*, pp. 117–119.

84. Donovan, "Political, Tactical Errors Curb Success of Women in the Abortion Debate," p. 2711.

85. Marcia Gelbart, "GOP Women Tell Leaders to Soft-Pedal Abortion," *The Hill*, July 26, 1995, p. 1.

86. Fundraising panel featuring Democratic congresswomen, June 21, 1994.

87. Authors' interview with Rep. Sue Myrick (R-N.C.), February 2, 1995.

88. Authors' interview with Rep. Karen McCarthy (D-Mo.), February 15, 1995.

89. Authors' interview with Rep. Louise Slaughter (D-N.Y.), April 12, 1994.

90. U.S. Congress, House, 103rd Congress, 2nd session, April 18–19, 1994, *Congressional Record* 140:H2370, 2454.

91. U.S. Congress, Senate, 103rd Congress, 2nd session, April 19, 1994, *Congressional Record* 140:S4422–4453.

92. Al Kamen, "The Tailhook Calculation," *Washington Post*, November 16, 1994, p. A23.

93. Authors' interview with Rep. Louise Slaughter (D-N.Y.), April 12, 1994.

94. Press release, including open letter to Rep. Jim Cooper (D-Tenn.), signed by 29 congresswomen, February 14, 1994.

95. Hook, "Women Remain on Periphery Despite Electoral Gains," pp. 2707, 2712.

96. Kevin Merida, "Rush Limbaugh Saluted as Majority Maker," *Washington Post*, December 11, 1994, p. A30.

Representative Jeannette Rankin (R-Mont.), the first woman elected to Congress, became the only member of Congress to vote against both World Wars. Photo courtesy of the Library of Congress.

Senator Rebecca Latimer Felton (D-Ga.) was appointed in 1922 as the first woman senator. Photo courtesy of the Senate Historian's office.

Representative Alice Mary Robertson (R-Okla.) became the second woman elected to Congress in 1920. Photo courtesy of the Library of Congress.

Representatives Alice Mary Robertson (R-Okla.), Winnifred Mason Huck (R-Ill.), and Mae Ella Nolan (R-Calif.), the second, third, and fourth women to serve in the U.S. House of Representatives. Photo courtesy of the Library of Congress.

Senator Hattie Wyatt Caraway (D-Ark.) became the first woman to reach the Senate through the ballot box in 1931. Photo courtesy of the Library of Congress.

At the opening of the 71st Congress, Representatives Ruth Bryan Owen (D-Fla.), Mary Norton (D-N.J.), Florence Kahn (R-Calif.), Pearl Oldfield (D-Ark.), Edith Nourse Rogers (R-Mass.), Eliza Pratt (D-N.C.), and Ruth Hanna McCormick (R-Ill.). Photo courtesy of the Library of Congress.

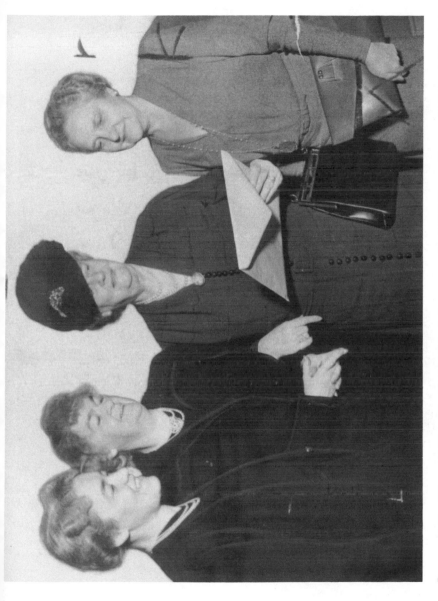

Representative Margaret Chase Smith (R-Maine), Representative Edith Nourse Rogers (R-Mass.), Mrs. Ed Gann, Representative Frances Bolton (R-Ohio). Photo courtesy of the Senate Historian's office.

Representative Clare Boothe Luce (R-Conn.) addresses the 1964 Republican National Convention. Photo courtesy of the Library of Congress.

Senator Margaret Chase Smith (R-Maine), President Lyndon B. Johnson, and Senator Maurine Neuberger (D-Ore.). Photo courtesy of the Senate Historian's office.

Representative Barbara Mikulski (D-Md.) at a 1973 press conference with Robert Strauss, Chairman of the Democratic National Committee. Photo courtesy of the Library of Congress.

Representative Bella Abzug (D-N.Y.) addresses the 1972 Democratic National Convention. Photo courtesy of the Library of Congress.

Representatives Shirley Chisholm (D-N.Y.) and Cardiss Collins (D-Ill.) with Parren Mitchell (D-Md.) and other Black Caucus members after a meeting with President Jimmy Carter. Photo courtesy of the Library of Congress.

In 1994, women members of Congress joined together to urge passage of the Violence Against Women Act. From right to left: Representatives Connie Morella (R-Md.), D.C. Delegate Eleanor Holmes Norton (D), Representative Patricia Schroeder (D-Colo.), Representative Elizabeth Furse (D-Ore.), Representative Carolyn Maloney (D-N.Y.), and NOW President Patricia Ireland. Photo courtesy of the office of Representative Connie Morella.

From left to right: Representatives Patsy Mink (D-Hawaii), Jan Meyers (R-Kans.), Maxine Waters (D-Calif.), two unidentified women, and Representatives Nita Lowey (D-N.Y.) and Patricia Schroeder (D-Colo.). Photo courtesy of the office of Representative Nita Lowey.

In 1994, women members rally together in support for the ban against assault weapons. From left: Senator Carol Moseley-Braun (D-Ill.), Senator Patty Murray (D-Wash.), Representative Maxine Waters (D-Calif.), Representative Nancy Pelosi (D-Calif.), Representative Carolyn Maloney (D-N.Y.), Representative Nita Lowey (D-N.Y.), Senator Dianne Feinstein (D-Calif.), Representative Elizabeth Furse (D-Ore.), Representative Jane Harman (D-Calif.), Representative Connie Morella (R-Md.), Representative Marge Roukema (R-N.J.), Representative Leslie Byrne (D-Va.), and Senator Barbara Mikulski (D-Md.). Photo courtesy of the office of Representative Nita Lowey.

President Bill Clinton signs the Breast Cancer Funding Act in 1994. In attendance, from left to right: HHS Secretary Donna Shalala, Hillary Clinton, Senator Patty Murray (D-Wash.), unidentified woman, Representative Eddie Bernice Johnson (D-Tex.), Representative Jennifer Dunn (R-Wash.), Representative Lynn Schenk (D-Calif.), Representative Connie Morella (R-Md.), Representative Louise Slaughter (D-N.Y.), Representative Marjorie Margolies-Mezvinsky (D-Pa.), Representative Jill Long (D-Ind.), and Representative Anna Eshoo (D-Calif.). Photo courtesy of the office of Representative Connie Morella.

Chapter 4

Congressional Staff

BACKGROUND

Despite the electoral victories that brought historic gains for women in 1992, just 11.7 percent of the House and 7 percent of the Senate was female in the 103rd Congress. The 1994 elections brought no gains for women in the House and an increase of only one in the Senate. Nonetheless, the current influence of women on Capitol Hill can be seen elsewhere. The large and influential Capitol Hill infrastructure represented by the congressional staff, invisible to most of the public, offers women access to power behind the throne. "The reputation of the Senate as a men's club isn't entirely accurate," notes Rick Shapiro, executive director of the Congressional Management Foundation (CMF). "While women are clearly under-represented in the ranks of Senators, an analysis of senior Senate staff reveals a more balanced picture."[1]

Indeed, within the "personal office staff" of the 1993 Senate, 59.7 percent were female. An even higher percentage (67.7 percent) of staff employed in a senator's district office were female. Similar figures are available for House staff, where 60.5 percent of the personal office staff of House members were female and 68.8 percent of the staff in the member's district office were female. Undeniably, congressional staffers wield enormous influence on members and their policy decisions. "If members of Congress were caught without staff, they'd be dead," said Donna Brazile, chief of staff to Del. Eleanor Holmes Norton (D-D.C.). "We're key to running this operation."[2]

Until the 1995 retrenchment under a Republican Congress, the size and cost of the congressional staff had grown steadily throughout this century. In 1933, each House member was allocated only a few thousand dollars for staff, and was allowed to hire only two staff members. By 1957, House members had staff budgets of $20,000 and could hire up to five aides. By 1976, up to 15 aides could be hired on a staff budget of $255,000. In 1992, each House member's allowance for personal staff was $537,480, covering up to 18 full-time and four part-time aides. The growth of Senate staff was just as rapid. Senators' allowances are based on their states' populations, ranging from $814,000 to $1.7 million in 1991. There was no prescribed limit to the number of Senate staff, but the average was about 35 per senator.

The office staff deal with the local political realities, serving as a vital link between members and their constituents—a role that can be the determining factor at the polls. The duties and salaries associated with congressional staff titles vary from office to office, but the most common job categories within the personal office staffs are:

General Counsel/Special Counsel: Attorney responsible for legal research and representation for committee or staff office.

Administrative Assistant (AA): Sometimes referred to as the chief of staff, the AA is the key staff person in a congressional office, overseeing the legislative, political, and administrative side of the member's operation. The AA serves as the primary political advisor to the member and supervises all personnel matters, including the hiring and firing of staff.

Legislative Director (LD): Coordinates the legislative functions of the office. Oversees the work of the other legislative assistants and coordinates legislative policy functions.

Legislative Assistant (LA): Researches legislative issues, writes legislation, and advises member on matters of legislative policy.

Press Assistant: Handles all media contacts. Duties include answering all press inquiries and distributing press releases, bulletins, and special mailings to the press. Serves as spokesperson for the member.

Clerical Assistant: General job classification for those who assist with secretarial duties and mail operations.

Beyond their large numbers within the personal office staffs on Capitol Hill, women are also strongly represented among committee staff and the broader ranks of congressional employees, all of which have been growing steadily through the years. The combined overall staffs of the House and Senate was just 1,430 persons in 1930. That total grew to 3,556 by 1957, 10,739 by 1970, and 20,000 by 1990. This is over four times the size of the legislative staff employed by *any* other major nation in the world.

By 1993, the total legislative-branch payroll was costing $157,762,000 and employing 36,779 people, including 12,954 House staff, 7,723 Senate staff, and the staffs of congressional caucuses and organizations like the General Accounting Office (GAO) and the Government Printing Office (GPO).

Historically, virtually all congressional power has been exercised through the committee structure, and, as a result, committee staff are among the most influential of all congressional aides. Since World War II, committee staffs have grown more than fourfold in the Senate and close to 12 times in the House, though that growth has stabilized over the last 15 years. The elected members of Congress are the chief architects of the coalitions needed to pass legislation, but much of the 'nitty-gritty' of writing the bills, speeches, and reports and organizing support is left to the committee staff.

The chairmen of the congressional committees hire all committee staff who work for the majority party in the House or Senate, and the ranking members of the minority party hire the staffers for their side of the committees. In either case, the committee staff articulate the views of those who hire them. John Jennings, counsel and staff director for a major House committee, says staff must always have the confidence of their employers if they are to be effective. "Everything a committee staffer does must be supportive of the chairman or ranking member. All staff work must be approved by, or channelled through, the member of Congress." Jennings concludes, "The influence they [staff] have is in direct proportion to the perception of whether they are accurately reflecting the views of the chairmen or ranking minority members. Members of Congress, lobbyists, and members of the executive branch all gauge committee staff members' influence by how closely they reflect the views of the chairman or ranking minority member."[3]

SPRINGBOARD TO ELECTION

Staff experience in Congress has not only trained thousands of young women for policy positions off the Hill, but, perhaps most importantly, often serves as a launching board for electoral office. For younger aides, staff positions can provide experience in crafting legislation, teach them political skills, and help them build the networks of supporters in the home state, which develop credentials for a later elective career. Approximately 15 percent of the members who served in the 101st Congress came to their positions through staff experience, and many of them rose to leadership rank. Former House Speaker Tom Foley (D-Wash.), former House Minority Leader Robert Michel (R-Ill.), and former Senate Majority Leader George Mitchell (D-Maine) all worked as staff aides. Of the top four leaders in the 104th Congress, only Senate Majority Leader Bob Dole (R-Kans.) did not follow the staff route to Congress.

A 1994 study showed that candidates who once worked for Congress have a greater probability of winning a primary election than any other type of candidate, including elected officials or incumbents. Between 1978 and 1988, staff candidates made up just over 4 percent of nonincumbents running for Congress, yet they accounted for almost 15 percent of those who won election.[4]

Studies of this phenomenon have focused on the House, because, historically, nearly all freshman senators with staff experience have already served in major statewide office or in the U.S. House of Representatives. Susan Webb Hammond's 1989 study revealed that since the early 1970s, congressional staff jobs have become a more frequent route to House election than previously, and former legislative aides, once in office, achieve leadership positions in the House more quickly than their colleagues. Hammond notes that in recent years, congressional staff positions have become more "professional," serving a brokerage function of gathering, assessing, and distributing information, while also bargaining, negotiating, and compromising as legislation is drafted and coalitions assembled. As a result of these changes, which accelerated in the 1970s, the opportunities for female staff to learn political and policy skills and to build networks useful in electoral campaigns have increased from the times when they served primarily as clerks or secretaries.

The proportion of all House members who have staff experience rose from 5 percent in 1961–1962 to 12 percent in 1983–1984, and has continued to rise since then. Prior to 1972, one to three former staff aides, on the average, were elected with each freshman class. After 1972, the number of former aides elected has never fallen below five, and is usually closer to ten. Occasionally, upon a member's retirement, the incumbent will actually designate an aide as an "heir apparent," stationing the staff member in the district for a strategic period prior to the election. Interestingly, former staff elected to Congress are disproportionately Democratic.

Previous experience as a congressional aide has been shown to lead freshmen in the House to higher positions of power. Among the freshmen elected during the period of 1974–1982, 74.5 percent of those with congressional staff experience obtained positions on major committees, compared to just 56 percent of their colleagues with no staff experience. The figure is even higher for Democratic freshmen with staff experience, 80 percent of whom obtained positions on major committees. About 60 percent of freshmen with previous staff experience acquired committee *leadership* positions, as opposed to just one-third of those without such experience.[5]

Because women have been historically underrepresented in the policy and leadership positions on congressional staffs, they have been, until recently, somewhat less likely to use staff experience as a stepping stone to electoral office. Still, the number of women who have served in Congress after working as congressional staff is not inconsequential, and it is growing.

Rebecca Latimer Felton (D-Ga.), the first woman senator, had earlier spent six years on Capitol Hill, from 1874 to 1880, as secretary and clerk to her husband, Rep. William Felton (D-Ga.). In Georgia's 7th District she came to be known as "Our Second Representative from the Seventh." Florence

Kahn (R-Calif.) served as campaign aide for her husband, Rep. Julius Kahn (R-Calif.), from 1900 until his death in 1924, preparing her for her own congressional career from 1925 to 1937. Prior to her election to the House in 1929, Rep. Ruth McCormick (R-Ill.) worked as secretary to her father, Rep. Marcus Hanna (R-Ohio). Rep. Effiegene Wingo (D-Ark.) worked in her husband's congressional office during his final four years in the House, and succeeded him in office upon his death in 1930. Representatives Vera Buchanan (D-Pa.) and Maude Kee (D-W.Va.) served as secretaries to their husbands, Rep. Frank Buchanan (D-Pa.) and Rep. John Kee (D-W.Va.), until their deaths, at which time they succeeded them in office, both in 1951.

Sen. Margaret Chase Smith (R-Maine) went on the Washington payroll of her husband, Rep. Clyde Harold Smith (R-Maine), when he won election to the House of Representatives in 1936. She handled his correspondence, helped with speech writing, assembled employment data for his work on the Labor Committee, and returned to Maine periodically to update constituents on legislative progress. Just prior to the filing deadline for the 1940 Maine primaries, her husband suffered a severe heart attack, and Margaret filed for the primary, fully intending to withdraw when her husband recovered. The press release from her husband's congressional office indicated that Congressman Smith's wife and "partner in public life" would run in his stead. Within days, Rep. Clyde Smith died, and Rep. Margaret Chase Smith began her own career, first in the House and then Senate, that spanned over three decades.

For more than 20 years before her election to the House in 1946, Eliza Jane Pratt (D-N.C.) had served as an administrative assistant for a succession of congressmen. Beginning in 1924, she worked as AA to Rep. William C. Hammer, Rep. Hinton James, Rep. J. Walter Lambeth, and finally, Rep. William O. Burgin. She became as well known in North Carolina's 8th District as the congressmen she worked for. After Burgin died in April 1946, Pratt won the special election to succeed him. She left after one term, citing financial difficulties and the high cost of campaigning. Nonetheless, she remained on Capitol Hill, serving with three federal agencies and then returning to the congressional staff, serving as AA to Rep. A. Paul Kitchin from 1957 until 1962.

Rep. Leonor Kretzer Sullivan (D-Mo.) served as campaign manager and administrative aide to her husband, Rep. John Sullivan, from 1942 to 1951 when he died. She then worked as secretary to Rep. Theodore Irving until she resigned in 1953 to successfully campaign for her own seat in Congress. She served with distinction from 1953 to 1967.

Rep. Catherine Norrell (D-Ark.) worked as a staff assistant in the congressional office of her husband, Rep. William Norrell (D-Ark.), prior to his death. In the special election held on April 18, 1961, to fill the vacancy left by the death of her husband, Norrell defeated four other candidates.

Sen. Nancy Kassebaum (R-Kans.) worked as an assistant to Sen. James Pearson before her election to the Senate in 1979. Olympia Snowe (R-Maine) served as a district staff assistant for Rep. William Cohen, whom she succeeded in 1979. She then went on to win a Senate seat in 1994. Sen. Barbara Boxer (D-Calif.) worked on the district staff of former Rep. John Burton from 1974 to 1976, before her 1983 election to the House and her election to the Senate in 1992. Rep. Cathy Long (D-La.) was staff assistant to Sen. Wayne Morse and to Rep. James Polk before she won a special election in March 1985 to fill the vacancy left by the death of her husband, Rep. Gillis Long. Rep. Elizabeth Patterson (D-S.C.) worked as a staff assistant to Rep. James Mann (D-S.C.) before her successful 1986 campaign for the House seat in South Carolina's 4th District. Rep. Rosa De Lauro (D-Conn.) served as administrative assistant to Sen. Christopher Dodd in the 1980s, before she herself was elected to Congress in 1990.

Six of the women elected to the House during the landmark elections of 1992 were former staffers. Rep. Nydia Velazquez (D-N.Y.) worked as a special assistant to Rep. Ed Towns (D-N.Y.) in 1983, and now serves as a colleague in the House alongside her former boss. Former representative Blanch Lambert (D-Ark.) worked as an aide to Rep. Bill Alexander (D-Ark.) for four years in the early 1980s, and then actually defeated him in the 1992 primaries, after which she won the general election to the House. Former representative Karen Shepherd (D-Utah) worked in the office of former sen. Tedd Moss (D-Utah) before her election to the House. Rep. Jane Harman (D-Calif.) served as chief counsel to Sen. John Tunney (D-Calif.) and later as chief counsel and staff director on the Senate Judiciary Subcommittee on Constitutional Rights. Rep. Pat Danner (D-Mo.) worked as a district aide to the late representative Jerry Litton (D-Mo.) from 1970 to 1975. Rep. Tillie Fowler (R-Fla.) served as an LA to former representative Robert Stephens, Jr. (D-Ga.) from 1967 to 1970.

Rep. Fowler recently recalled her early work as an LA: "I came up here in the summer of 1965, while I was still in law school, and worked as an intern for [Rep.] Bob Stephens. I became very interested in the process up here. In 1967, near the end of my senior year in law school, I came back to Mr. Stephens to ask his advice on some job offers. He said, since his LA was leaving in June, would I be interested in being his LA? Back then, most offices had only one LA, and very few women. I just about fell off my chair, and I said I would love it. It was a great opportunity."

Fowler said that until Rep. Stephens's unexpected offer, she had not planned to work on Capitol Hill. "There were no openings, and very few women in really professional positions. At that time, Rep. Stephens's office staff was small. We had an AA, an LA, a couple of case workers, and a receptionist. That was it. There was no district office, because in those days, you moved your Washington staff to the district when you closed down for the summer."

Despite the virtual absence of women in "professional" positions, Fowler said she had no difficulty adjusting to staff work on the Hill. After all, she said, there were only five women in her law school. "On the whole, I had a very positive experience on the Hill. Most people were very supportive. There were a couple who were not, but I was fairly comfortable here. I wanted to do a good job, and I received a lot of valuable experience. Rep. Stephens spent two and a half years on what was then the Banking and Currency Committee and the Consumer Subcommittee. That was when we did Truth in Lending. I became very interested in the consumer area through my work on the subcommittee, and I have maintained that interest to this day."

Fowler believes that her staff experience was a good political background that could work for women generally. "It helped me in my election," she said. "My knowledge of congressional committees turned out to be an important issue in my campaign. Comments had been made that a new Republican woman would not have a chance to get on a good committee. So I came up here and met with [minority leader] Bob Michel and explained my background to him. The fact that I had worked on the Hill and knew the Hill helped me with him. I explained to him the importance of getting a seat on the Armed Services Committee, and asked if he would give me a letter supporting such an appointment. He gave me a letter committing to placing me on the Armed Services Committee, and I used that letter in my campaign, and it became a really big issue. So I was able to successfully handle one of the biggest issues in the campaign, because I knew the process from my staff experience."

Even such fundamental matters as finding one's way through the endless maze of Capitol Hill tunnels was eased by Fowler's staff experience. "I never got lost. I still knew my way, perhaps subconsciously. I remember new members running around totally lost, not knowing which way to go. I really sympathized with them. Just knowing how to get through the building from place to place, not to mention knowing the procedures, was a trememdous help to me. I already knew the basic procedures, such as how to handle House bills, how to get legislation to the floor, and so on. My experience also helped me in hiring my own staff, because I sort of knew what I needed, that I needed a balance to make it work."

Today, Fowler can recognize that major changes have occurred. "You've got so many more women in professional positions here. They particularly are getting better jobs as LAs, really top positions. Then you've got women on committee staffs. It's great."[6]

Clearly, female staffers, formerly relegated to dead-end clerical jobs, are seeing unprecedented opportunities available to them. They are gaining confidence in their own abilities as they see other women succeed politically, both in elected office and in top staff positions. Staffer Donna Brazile remembers how she was influenced by several top female staffers early in her career on the Hill: "When I first came here, I knew people like Carlottia Scott [AA for Rep. Ron Dellums (D-Calif.)] and Harriet Pritchett [AA for Rep. William Clay (D-Mo.)]. They were regarded as mother figures. Brenda Pillors, who worked for both Shirley Chisholm and now Ed Towns, and Ranny Cooper, who works for [Sen. Edward] Kennedy, are women whom we looked up to like moms during the old days. There was a special kind of relationship that a young female staffer had with these role models. These people had the qualities of being members without the titles. These were AAs, but they had the stature of a member from a staff person's point of view. You didn't get close enough to the Schroeders and the Chisholms and these other great people to know them personally, but you got close enough to their AAs to know them nonetheless. Most AAs, most chiefs of staff, are the alter egos of the members. This is another kind of powerful female presence on the Hill."

As women increase their numbers in elected office, their success encourages others to run. "When I worked for Geraldine Ferraro in 1984, I decided that I would some day run for office," said Brazile. "I was so impressed with her. I worked on women's issues. We had an opportunity to raise women's issues to a new height. I had just come off of the Jackson campaign, and Jesse gave me guts and energy. But to work for a woman! It energized me. Because of Ferraro, I saw myself, for the first time, as some day running for office."

Some female members believe they get along better with their staff than do their male couterparts. Former representative Marjorie Margolies-Mezvinsky (D-Pa.) says women and others who may have been treated like second-class citizens are often more careful of the way they treat their staff. "Some of us," she says, "treat our staffs as extended family."

Margolies-Mezvinsky believes that women on Capitol Hill are bringing a more down-to-earth quality to their offices, making Capitol Hill a more friendly and cohesive place to work. "Maybe it's just that we're used to pitching in and running a family," she says. "You can see it in the way that we relate to our staffs, encouraging a more colleague-to-colleague atmosphere."[7]

Rep. Elizabeth Furse (D-Ore.) says, "Right from the beginning, we set the standard that people would care about one another in this office. . . . I can't imagine women throwing things at their staff, which I understand some members of Congress do. I think it's just the most horrible behavior that goes on."[8]

On the other hand, some female aides admit that there are other difficulties when working with female members. "I sometimes think I would not want to work for a woman because she would expect more of me," says one top female staffer. "Every kid who's ever worked for me has said that I've expected so much out of them. The women have complained that sometimes I expected more out of them than the men, that I was softer on the men. Maybe I was, but all of them, when they left here, went out and got good jobs."

Donna Brazile, who has worked in a variety of staff positions, says, "I've worked for both male and female members, black and white, north and south, conservative and liberal, but there is a difference in working for a female member. In a white male's office, there's a tendency to be one of the boys, to go along and get along, to get the work done and not to make waves. I've worked with Claudine Schneider, Lindy Boggs, and Eleanor Holmes Norton, and it's different. In the office of a woman or an African American, you're more of a pioneer, a crusader. You're working for someone who is breaking new ground, who may be the first woman or first black elected to that office. There's more of a historical burden for the member and the staff to perform the job exceptionally well, because they are making history. Public policy takes on a new emphasis, because you're not just making policy for the members of your district. You're making policy for the nation."

Rep. Carrie Meek (D-Fla.), elected in 1992, says she gets a thrill whenever young female staff interns come to her office asking to have their pictures taken with a woman in Congress. Meek says that ten or 15 years ago these young women wouldn't have thought they could aspire to Congress. Now they see it can be done.

THE POWER OF STAFF

Some Capitol Hill observers have gone so far as to contend that staffers have as much influence, perhaps more, than the members themselves. When Rep. Norman Dicks (D-Wash.) was elected to Congress after spending eight years as a staff aide to Sen. Warren Magnuson (D-Wash.), he commented: "People asked me how I felt being elected to Congress, and I told them I never thought I'd give up that much power voluntarily."[9]

Congressional staff are well aware of their power. "I think staff have influence over every aspect of a member's life, from their reelection to their public policy position down to their public relations profile," says Brazile. "This is like a small business. A member hires a chief of staff to be the CEO of his or her company. There are staff people who are more powerful than the member in some respects. I know some offices where a staffer is so essential that the member could not function or win without that staff person. . . . I know some chairmen of committees who, without their staff people, would have no clue to the business at hand."

Susan Webb Hammond, a political science professor at American University who has written extensively on congressional staff, says that aides are more professional, better educated, and more likely to regard their work as a career than did the staff of 15 years ago. She agrees that freshmen in Congress today rely more heavily on their staff, and she notes: "I think some of it may relate to the professionalization of Congress. You no longer can really come, bring your campaign manager, and expect to be up and running within two weeks."[10]

One Democratic female staffer who has worked on the Hill for 20 years says the dependence of members on their staff varies considerably from member to member. The staffer, who wished not to be indentified, says, "You have different levels of members. You have members who have to be carried from point A to point B. But there are members who read every newspaper, analyze every piece of paper that comes through the office. There are members who stay in the office until eight, nine, ten at night. You have members like [former representative] Jack Brooks, who after a certain amount of time know the routine so well that they can do it in their sleep. But interestingly, Jack depended on Sharon Mack, his AA. Some of the most successful partnerships I've seen on the Hill are men and women."

Former representative Dennis Eckart (D-Ohio) agrees that the congressional staff has increased its influence over the years, but he notes that "they have that stature and influence because they multiply the talent and reach of the members themselves."[11]

Donna Brazile says, "Politicians can get a sense of how well they are doing their job through opinion polls or, ultimately, at the ballot box. But staff people see their work reflected through their member, when the member introduces a bill, speaks on the House or Senate floor, or goes before his or her constituents at a town meeting. It's difficult to be a staff person in a system designed for members. In this form of democracy, the member has the absolute authority and power. The role of the staff member is to enhance that member's position and effectiveness."

The newly elected women in Congress are making good use of veteran female and male staffers. Freshman senator Patty Murray (D-Wash.) makes no apology for her heavy reliance on her seasoned Legislative Director Carole Grunberg and Administrative Assistant Michael Timmeny. "I know what the issues are; they are in my heart. What I need is someone to make a road map for me. And that's exactly what Carole and Michael do."[12]

The increasing number of women in elected office is probably contributing to greater numbers of female staffers, and thus to an increasing influence of women generally. Rep. Louise Slaughter (D-N.Y.) believes that women members tend to hire more female staff.

"We have from the outset had a larger number of women [in the office]," Slaughter said. "The one thing that I have said from the outset was that women were going to be considered for any job here, that they were not going to be treated any differently. We've had some really amazing women go through here."

As women staffers continue to multiply their numbers on the Hill, their influence on members, and ultimately on national legislation, also multiplies. Slaughter recounts the closed door meeting in 1992 of Democratic members of the Budget Committee along with their staff aides. The members, 22 men and Slaughter, were discussing a funding increase for the National Institutes of Health. After a consensus was reached on an $800 million increase, Slaughter suggested that the entire amount should go toward research for women's health problems such as breast and ovarian cancer.

After being greeted with polite condescension, Slaughter pushed on with even greater conviction, detailing how the number of women who will be struck with breast cancer in one year will roughly equal the number of men who died in the entire Vietnam War. When she stopped talking, the female aides sitting behind the congressmen suddenly stood up and began to applaud.

"There was no question that the women in the room, when they rose to their feet and applauded, I'll tell you, their members paid attention,"[13] Slaughter recalled.

In the end, the 22 men, along with Slaughter, agreed that $500 million of the $800 million NIH increase should be set aside for women's health research.

But many observers on and off the Hill see the growing influence of staff as a negative, if not dangerous, reality. Before his election to Congress, Sen. Trent Lott (R-Miss.) had been a congressional aide to Rep. William Colmer (D-Miss.), whom he succeeded upon Colmer's retirement. Today Lott says, "I think we have too much staff, too many around here. I have always felt that Senators rely too much on staff. In fact, sometimes staff members think they are the Senators. They start speaking for us. . . . I think it is a bad practice."[14]

Some analysts on the political right regard the congressional staff as a powerful empire of unelected junior lawmakers, and they are troubled by the increasing reliance of congressmen, particularly freshmen, on their staff. David M. Mason, director of the Heritage Foundation's Congressional Assessment Project, says: "I think it is a very bad sign if we've gotten to the point when someone with a business background or a nonpolitical background can't manage without professional help when he comes to Congress."[15]

Conservative political analysts, who distrust Congress generally and staffers in particular, claim that many congressmen have become products of their staff. Eric Felten, editorial writer for the *Washington Times* and author of *The Ruling Class: Inside the Imperial Congress*, says: "When legislators ask questions at hearings, more often than not, their every remark has been scripted in advance by staff aides. What about follow-ups? Look for a staffer to lean over and whisper them into the member's ear. Most legislation gets its start at staffers' desks. Even when lawmakers give their aides broad outlines, the staff fills in the text. And when it comes time for that text to be voted on, few lawmakers will have read it, though again their aides will be there to tell them whether they ought to vote yes or no. It is not uncommon to see legislators rushing in for a roll call, looking for a staffer to flash a thumbs-up or -down so they will know how to vote."

Felten concludes: "Unlike senators or representatives, who are accountable at the ballot box, staffers work behind the curtains. They are the new rulers on Capitol Hill, a nameless faceless mandarinate that pulls the strings and feeds off the worst impulses of the institution it claims to serve."[16]

Felten's demonic vision of staffers is widely regarded as partisan propaganda, but his perception of the size of staff power is shared by many. In his recent book, *Arrogant Capital*, Kevin Phillips lists congressional staffers alongside lobbyists and lawyers as part of the "parasitism" on Capitol Hill. Phillips advocates dramatic cuts in the size of the congressional staff, which he says "spends much of its time interfacing with the capital's huge corps of lobbyists and preparing for its own vocational graduation into that corps." Phillips concludes, "Force the staffs of Congress to shrink by 30 to 40 percent over the remainder of the 1990s, and the odds are that the ranks of Washington lobbyists would also shrink by a meaningful percent."[17]

A NEW ERA: LESS GOVERNMENT, LESS STAFF

One of the first changes implemented by the new Republican leadership of the 104th Congress was to slash the number of staffers. Overnight, Republicans gained control of both houses of Congress for the first time in 40 years, putting the jobs of almost 2,000 Democratic staffers, and a number of Republicans, at risk. The employment crunch came on two fronts. As defeated Democratic incumbents and their now unemployed staff departed Capitol Hill, the newly empowered Republicans began implementing promises to cut staff generally, with particular emphasis on committee staff.

As the new majority party, the Republicans had the authority to revise committees in the House rules for the 104th Congress. In the 103rd Congress there had been 2,200 committee staff—about 1,700 Democrats and 440 Republicans—assigned to 22 committees. In the 104th Congress, Republicans abolished or consolidated panels like the Post Office and Civil Service, Merchant Marine and Fisheries, and the District of Columbia. Republicans cut the total committee staff by 30 percent, down to about 1,500, of which they, as the majority party, hired about 1,200, while the Democrats got only about 300 committee staff. In short, about 400 new Republican committee staff were hired, while 1,460 Democratic committee staff were fired. In the Senate, half of the 800 Democratic committee aides lost their jobs, while the number of new Republican aides actually increased.

Personal office staff were also affected by the Republican takeover. Once again, the partisan effect on Democrats was particularly extreme. Democratic congressional candidates suffered a net loss of 61 seats, and the corresponding loss of Democratic office staff was substantial.

Rep. Patsy Mink (D-Hawaii) says, "The worst of all the Republican changes in the House was the purging of the staff. Staff are so vital. They can be of enormous assistance. The staff cuts are the most egregious consequence of the Republican takeover."[18]

A top female staffer who works as a special counsel in the House said the cuts had the most devastating effect on women and minorities. "The staff cuts have hurt women, particularly the younger women. I was training them. There are hundreds of these kids that are gone. Even the Republicans have reduced some of the women who used to be way up there for them. I think it hurts women disproportionately, women, blacks, and minorities. The last hired, the first fired."

As always, women suffered most in the staff cuts, and in late 1994 there were countless tales of woe on Capitol Hill. Until the Democrats lost control of Congress in 1994, Mina Paddock had been a staffer for the Foreign Affairs Committee during the tenure of three chairmen. Now she was out of work. "I'm fifty-seven years old," she said solemnly. "It's not going to be as easy for me to go out and find something."

Veronica Yuvan, a 24-year-old staff assistant in defeated senator Harris Wofford's office, said, "I'm not really worried about myself, quite frankly. For me, it's just the overall picture. I'm more shocked at the overall picture."[19]

Laurie Cody, a 29-year-old staffer on the House Government Operations Committee, considered returning to Florida after she lost her Capitol Hill job. "I'm not ready to go back home yet," she said. "To me, that's admitting defeat in the big city, and I'm not going to do that." Cody had difficulty explaining to her family in Florida why a Democratic staff member could not work for a Republican-dominated Congress. An aunt called her and apologized, "Oh, I'm sorry. I voted Republican this time. I didn't know I eliminated your job."[20]

Sherry Ruffing worked in the office of defeated representative Dan Glickman (D-Kans.). Just before election day she had brought her newborn daughter to the office, where everyone assured her that her job was secure because her boss could not possibly lose the election. After all, she had worked on recently passed legislation that brought more than 2,000 jobs to Glickman's district. Two days later she was job hunting.

On a personal level, the stories of lost jobs on Capitol Hill sounded like those heard anywhere else in American society. An office manager for a congressional committee didn't have the courage to tell her nine-year-old that she could not afford to give him a birthday party. "With children you can't just continue to put them off to the next year," she said. "The next thing you know they're adults and they've missed out on what their childhood should have been."

Audrey Bashkin, an attorney on the House Science and Technology Committee, said, "Wednesday after the election, I was in shock. Thursday

I felt euphoric, thinking it would all work out. Friday I was scared. Saturday I felt good and energetic. Sunday was bad."[21]

Caught in the double web of public hostility toward Congress and the understandable Republican glee at "payback time," the army of unemployed staffers received little sympathy. On panels like the International Relations Committee, GOP and Democrat staffers are barely on speaking terms since the chairman cut *minority* salaries on February 1, 1995. When Democrats went before the House Oversight Committee to complain of such arbitrary treatment of the minority staff, Chairman Bill Thomas (R-Calif.) claimed that the Democrats had taken similar action when they were in power.

Both Republican and Democratic staff felt the strain at the beginning of the 104th Congress, as House Speaker Newt Gingrich put members and staff on a frenetic schedule in order to bring every item in the Contract with America to a floor vote within 100 days. The high cost in sickness, lost sleep, bad food, quick tempers, and late-night schedules made a mockery of the Republicans' promise of a family-friendly Congress. Ways and Means staffers wished each other "good morning" as they left the office after midnight most nights. "If you're Domino's Pizza or Hunan Dynasty you love us," said Republican Ways and Means spokesman Ari Fleischer. "If you're wives, husbands or children, you forget what we look like."

Rep. Scott Klug (R-Wis.) admitted, "If it's like this in May, there will be a riot like in the old Frankenstein movies, with villagers carrying torches and ladders to attack the castle. I'll be happy to lead it."[22]

PROBLEMS IN THE WORKPLACE

Congressional staff positions have provided women an access to significant Capitol Hill influence in numbers well beyond the meager representation they have acquired to date through the ballot box. But the life of a female staffer is not all sweetness and light. Even the physical facilities of the Capitol reflect the male-dominant history of Congress, at the expense of female staff. Congresswoman Lynn Schenk (D-Calif.) notes that despite many recent changes on Capitol Hill, routine inconveniences for female staff remain unaddressed. She complains, "There still isn't a rest room for the female staffers close to the floor of the House." She notes that women in Congress have been able to establish the Lindy Boggs Room, but that is for members only, not their staffs. Schenk says Republican staffers have approached her asking women on both sides of the aisle to work together to get a ladies room for staffers near the floor of the House. Schenk just shakes her head. "We're still fighting the bathroom issue."[23]

Employees of the Senate and House are not civil service employees. There are no job descriptions or salary scales for congressional staff except those established by the individual member of Congress. Hiring and firing is done on whatever basis the member chooses. Staff may be fired without notice, and there is no appeal process. In short, congressional staff serve at the pleasure of their member. The member determines how much to pay each staffer, sets office hours and days off, and decides how much vacation time and sick leave to allow. The recently passed "Compliance Act," which would apply private-sector laws to congressional employees, may help, but few expect significant improvement in working conditions.

Donna Brazile says, "The pay is not exceptionally good, the hours are crazy, the competition is fierce, and the work atmosphere is pressurized. To tell a 21- or 22-year-old staffer that he or she can't make a mistake, that anything in a memo could appear in the *New York Times*, that's a heavy burden to place on a person so young. There is no job security. In some offices, one mistake and that's it. You work under a hell of a lot of stress. It's a grinding type of job. People don't understand the kind of work we do, the hours we put in, the sacrifices we have to make."

Kirsten Fedewa, who served as press secretary for former senator Bob Kasten (R-Wis.), says that "burnout" is a growing problem among Senate aides, who feel burnt out or underappreciated. Some congressional staff have mentioned long hours, limited prospects for promotions, and intense public scrutiny as reasons for increasing turnover.

Perhaps because of these somewhat arbitrary employment practices, there has been a persistent problem of discrimination against women on Capitol Hill. Brazile says, "Because this institution has always been dominated by men and the culture of men, there has been sexual discrimination and sexual harassment. Men dominate this culture, and they know women are at the door, demanding entry and a place at the table."

One female staffer recalled the atmosphere when she arrived on Capitol Hill in the late 1970s. "It was very rigid, very structured. There were things you did, things you didn't do, and things you could or couldn't do. There was always a lot of fear of committees and committee chairmen. It was the fear of their power. Even the reporters would never talk to members the way they do today. The whole aura was different. Everyone assumed that if you were a woman in any position of responsibility, you were sleeping with the boss. It's that simple. As late as 1983, when my boss put me on his committee, six or seven women asked me if I was his girlfriend. People would call me his wife."

The late Dorothye Scott, who served as AA to both the senate Democratic secretary and the secretary of the Senate from 1945 to 1977, recalled the heavy restraints on the behavior and visibility of staff, particularly female staff. One of her early responsibilities was to put the roll-call votes in the files on the Senate floor, but she was careful never to go there when the Senate was in session. She says, "I remember Frances Dustin who worked for Senator [Ralph Owen] Brewster of Maine [1941–52]. . . . She was the first woman staff member to go on the Senate floor when the Senate was in session. And there was a *big* rhubarb about that because no other woman staff member had ever come in when they were in session like that."

Only years later did Dorothye Scott finally get up the nerve to go on the Senate floor while it was in session. Even then, she had to be summoned there by a senator. "At that time," she recalls, "I think it was more appropriate and wasn't condemned so badly."[24]

One female staffer recalls, "At some point early in my days on Capitol Hill, I was going to the House floor concerning a bill on state boundaries, and I was made to feel very uncomfortable. For example, I was going to the floor and they're telling me, 'There's no bathroom for you.' It was a very rare thing to see women doing anything on the floor, except for the reading clerks."

Thirty-year veteran staffer Hannah Margetich says female staff have always been treated differently than men, though she acknowledges that things have improved over the years. "When I was interviewed for my first job on the Hill [in 1963], I was asked questions like, 'Are you happily married, how many children do you have, how often are your children sick?' At that time, women were hired either as receptionists or appointment secretaries. Very few women were LAs when I first came to the Hill. Women with masters degrees thought that if they came to the Hill they'd get somewhere. It didn't happen. Today women have real expectations."[25]

Another female staffer recalls, "If a woman came across as too strong, they would automatically call her gay. That's how they handled you. You had to act like a man, but be careful you weren't called gay or called a bitch. I've been called a bitch more times than you can imagine. You say it doesn't hurt, but it really hurts when you know you're not. You're always walking the line between being a bitch, being gay, or being somebody's girlfriend. You're much better having a reputation of being a bitch and letting the other women know that you're good to them. It's always the sexuality thing that somehow comes up."

Ironically, these hardships have helped women staffers form special bonds. Margetich recalled the networking of women three decades ago. "We'd get together, go to lunch, share things that were happening in our offices. Things like being called over on a weekend to babysit for a member. Or to walk his dog, or take the member's laundry to the cleaners," Margetich said. "The female staffer was always the one asked to do such things. Never the men. It was accepted. But I think things are getting much better. I hear less complaints from women staff about being asked to perform personal services for the member."

Brazile says that same supportive networking occurs today. "I can go into the cafeteria and see some of my fellow AAs and there's an immediate bond there. We talk girl talk, we talk about families, failed relationships. We talk about interesting new legislation. We share office guidelines, office procedures. Remember, AAs have come through the ranks, through a lot of hard knocks. We talk about our lows and our highs. It's more of an informal support group and we take care of each other. It's a club."

Another female staffer recalls the lack of female companionship and role models when she came to the Hill in the late 1970s. "There was no effective support network for staff. There was some kind of wimpy support group, but I can't remember more than twenty women being in it. Nobody ever called me. I couldn't find people like myself to mentor with. I ended up mentoring with my male boss. It was great but that was very confusing for my identity. There were no teachers or role models for professional women. One thing that I notice happening today that I think was missing when I first came here is the mentoring of women by other women. I wanted so badly to look to women members as role models, but I was afraid. There were very few women members in 1979, and we were all in awe of them. I wish someone had said, let's get all the women staff together and all the women members, because it would have been really good for all concerned."

Margetich, who has served in six House offices since 1963, says some members have great difficulty learning how to treat women and men equally. "A woman joining the staff may be quite capable of running the office, but she will not be given the opportunity. Members have traditionally assumed that a man had to perform that function. Yet the female staff may be doing most of the work. One of the members I worked for once said to me, 'Hannah, I really enjoy working with women more than with men. I get more out of them.' "

Capitol Hill, like American society at large, has a long history of discrimination against women on the basis of pay. A 1974 study by the Capitol Hill Women's Political Caucus (CHWPC), titled "Sexists in the Senate," found that the median salary of women staffers in the Senate was $10,260, compared to $17,670 for men. Though females outnumbered males two to one in the CHWPC sample, males consistently outnumbered females at salaries above $18,000. Thirty congressional offices in the 1974 CHWPC sample employed *only* males at salaries above $18,000, while *no* offices hired only females at those levels. None of the CHWPC data differed appreciably as a function of political party.

The 1974 CHWPC study noted that Congress had exempted its employees from the statutory relief (Equal Pay Act of 1963 and Title VII of the Civil Rights Act of 1964) available to female employees elsewhere who may have been subject to employment discrimination. The report stated: "Those of us working on Congressional staffs find ourselves in the anomalous situation of working for the people who have set up these salutory provisions but being excluded ourselves from coverage by these acts."[26] The report concluded by calling for an investigation into Congressional employment practices. A 1977 CHWPC update actually revealed an erosion of female salaries relative to those of male staffers in the Senate.

In 1980, the CHWPC produced a follow-up study of the staffs in *both* the House and Senate. This report was titled, "The Last Plantation? How Women Fare on Capitol Hill." It revealed a $6,000 difference between salaries for men and women staffers in the House, with women earning an average salary of $15,989 compared to $21,745 for men. Women in the House thus earned 73 cents for every dollar men earned. Things were even worse in the Senate, where there was an $8,000 difference between salaries for men and women staffers. Women earned an average of $16,192, while the average for men was $24,160. Women employed by the Senate thus earned only 67 cents for every dollar men earned.

As in the earlier CHWPC studies, salaries for women staffers in 1980 tended to be clustered in the lower ranges. In the House, nearly 80 percent of all women earned salaries below $20,000, while only about half of the men earned such salaries. In both the House and Senate, eight of the nine lowest paying job categories contained more women than men. Even within the same job type, women tended to earn less than men. The percentage of women in job categories decreased as responsibility and pay increased. Only 16 percent of all women on House staffs held policy-making jobs, compared to 46 percent of all men. In the Senate, 14 percent of women were in policy-making positions, compared to 49 percent of all men. On the other hand, 37 percent of women in the House and 41 percent of women in the Senate held clerical jobs, as compared to just 7 percent of men in both the House and Senate.

The 1980 CHWPC report describes a 1974 letter to staffer Shirley Davis from her boss, Rep. Otto Passman (D-La.), in which he stated that Davis was "able, energetic and a very hard worker," but "that it was essential that the understudy to my Administrative Assistant be a man." Passman closed with the statement, "I believe you will agree with this conclusion." Ms. Davis did not agree, and settled out of court after the Supreme Court affirmed her right to sue. The report concluded: "All Congressional staff members, in the final analysis, find that they serve at the pleasure of their employer, without any of the protections afforded other sectors in society—government or private."[27]

More recently, studies by the Congressional Management Foundation (CMF) have revealed little improvement in the pattern of discrimination against female congressional staff. In the 1993 Senate, women represented a larger percentage of the personal office staff than men at all salary levels up to $40,000. From that point on, however, male staff represented the majority, and almost three times more men than women earned above $60,000. The average salary for women in the Senate's personal offices was $33,561, compared to $41,659 for men. Women accounted for just one-third of the "leadership" positions among the Senate's personal staff and only 40.6 percent of the Senate's "policy" positions. Just the reverse proportions were evident among the midlevel and clerical staff positions in the Senate's personal offices. Women held 69.7 percent of the "midlevel" positions and 74.5 percent of the "clerical" positions.[28]

"Women caseworkers abound," says a female House aide, referring to the position that deals with constituent complaints and falls near the bottom of the pay scale. "They figure women are good with crying people."

CMF found the same disturbing pattern of discrimination in House offices, where the 1992 figures showed only 41.7 percent of leadership positions and 43.6 percent of policy positions were held by women. Over three-quarters of the clerical positions were held by women. The salary distribution for personal staff in the House was similarly skewed. During 1992, women predominated in each of the salary ranges up to $35,000, at which point men were increasingly in the majority, with more than three and one half times more men than women earning above $70,000.

Things were even worse in 1994, when only 39.1 percent of leadership positions and 40.5 percent of policy positions were held by women, while 71.6 percent of the midlevel and 70 percent of the clerical positions were held by women. In 1994, $40,000 was the salary ceiling above which women became scarce. Over twice as many men as women earned $60,000, and over three and one half times as many men earned over $80,000. The only consolation for Capitol Hill staff is that things are even worse for women in the broader U.S. economy. Within federal executive agencies, less than 10 percent of all senior executive service positions are filled by women. Within the 500 largest U.S. companies, less than 3 percent of corporate officers were women.[29]

Another recent study of congressional staff pay inequities was conducted by the Gannett News Service (GNS) and published in December 1993 in newspapers around the country. That study began by stating, "Congress has two classes of personal staff employees: highly paid men who hold most of the power, and lower-paid women whose careers can be stunted by an institutional glass ceiling."[30] The GNS study of 11,500 members of the personal staffs in Congress found that in 1993 most women were at back-office desks in clerical positions, answering phones and writing letters to constituents. Only about 30 percent of the people making more than $70,000 a year were women, while 65 percent of those making less than $30,000 were women.

Male staffers in the House were paid, on average, $39,200 per year, while women received $32,000, a 22.5 percent difference. In the Senate, male staff received about $37,800 per year compared to $30,400 for women, a difference of 24 percent. The pay gap between male and female staff existed, to one degree or another, regardless of employer: male or female, Republican or Democrat, African American, white, or Latino, newcomer or veteran. Even within the same position titles, women were paid less.

GNS found that, though 60 percent percent of congressional staffers were women, only about one-third of the administrative assistants, the chiefs of staff, were women. On the other hand, 90 percent of the clerical staff positions were held by women. On average, according to the study, female staffers in the House earned less than 82 cents for every dollar male staffers made; in the Senate, women earned about 80 cents for every dollar men made. Though women in the national work force earned only 71 cents for every dollar men made, an even lower standard than on Capitol Hill, the GNS report suggested that Congress had an obligation to set an example for the broader society by addressing their own inequities.

Pamela Brogan, the GNS reporter who covered the study, interviewed a 64-year-old former staff member, Anne Walker, who was fired from her job in 1982 when her boss, former representative Ed Jones (D-Tenn.), allegedly decided that her $45,000 salary "was ridiculous for a woman." Walker took her case to an outside court, where she was awarded compensation. Today Walker says that no improvement in congressional employment practices will occur until Congress obeys the same rules it requires of the private sector and sets up an independent review process for employee complaints. Indeed, a CMF study indicates that staff think the current review process is biased. Forty-nine percent of female staffers polled in the House said they would be unlikely to file a complaint for fear of retaliation.

Janina Jaruzelski, counsel to the House Energy and Commerce Committee, believes it is inappropriate for these pay gaps to continue. "There should be pay equity," she said. "Congress is supposed to be a model. Is it OK to pay women 20 percent less than men?"

Judith Lichtman, president of the Women's Legal Defense Fund, says, "It's a public shame that the Capitol dome operates as a glass ceiling," preventing qualified women from advancing into jobs and pay brackets traditionally held by men.[31]

Karen Rose, a congressional staffer who formerly chaired the sexual harassment task force of the Capitol Hill Women's Political Caucus, says: "On a personal level, this has to affect the morale of women here. I know, and other women know, that there are members who only hire attractive women for the front desk and that others don't hire women for responsible positions."[32]

The long-overlooked inequities within the congressional staff are finally being scrutinized by some within Congress, but predictably it is the women on Capitol Hill, including Republicans, who are leading the charge. "I think some members might be discriminating against women," said Sen. Olympia Snowe (R-Maine), former cochairwoman of the Congressional Caucus for Women's Issues. "These discrepancies in pay and hiring are serious. Some members have a serious problem in their regard for women. I've seen it."[33]

Lynn Martin, ex-Labor secretary and former Republican representative from Illinois, held a press conference on August 5, 1993, to blast her former congressional colleagues for discrimination against women and minorities on Capitol Hill. Martin pointed out that of the 316 House staffers earning more than $100,000—a very elite and influential club—only 53 were women. "If you're making the money, you're making the decisions," she said. "We're talking about a universal policy here. . . . This has got to stop, the waste of talent and ability."

In a prepared statement, Martin wrote: "In the decade since I was a new member of Congress and stumbled into the minefield of how Congress was obviously discriminating against women and minorities, much has changed. Back then many members of Congress resented a mere woman pointing out that 80% of the people on congressional staffs making over $40,000 were men, and 80% of the people making under $20,000 were women. The fact that talent, experience, and ability were being wasted meant little to many of our elected officials; the fact that this was wasting taxpayers' money meant even less. . . . And how has Congress changed during this decade? How have the people's representatives responded to the demographic diversity that is America, where over 60% of the new entrants to the work force in the past 10 years have been women, minorities, and immigrants? Well, evidently in the same way that helps make the Congress one of the least respected institutions in America."

Martin criticized the hiring practices of both Republicans and Democrats, saying "the whole bunch couldn't pass a federal contract review." She noted, "The Appropriations Committee, one of our most powerful and visible institutions in the House, had 29 men and only 1 woman in its top salary ranks. It's not as if the guys are doing such a great job that no one could envisage doing better. . . . They still believe the divine right of kings refers to them."[34]

SEXUAL HARASSMENT

One female special counsel who came to the Capitol in the 1970s says there were few women in positions of responsibility. "In 1978 or 1979, the female staff was mainly secretarial. I saw a few women lawyers. There was a small group of them and they were very active in trying to get things done. But it was a hard thing, because everybody looked at everybody else like you were somebody's girlfriend. There was a lot of hitting on you. There was the attitude that the members were 'the powerful men.' " Among the burdens for female staff on Capitol Hill is the continuing spectre of sexual harassment. As in society at large, sexual harassment exists on Capitol Hill, but until relatively recently it has seldom been reported.

Donna Brazile says when she first came to the Hill, there was sexual discrimination and harassment, but it wasn't discussed. She says conditions have improved considerably since then. "The offices now have sexual harassment guidelines, and that's an important achievement. There are support groups for younger women. In the past, the young women coming up through the ranks always used to complain about how bad things were. Anita Hill gave voice to all of us. Prior to Anita Hill, no one around here talked about it."

Rep. Elizabeth Furse (D-Ore.) says she has heard stories for years that young female pages are given a list of whom not to get in an elevator with. "If it was a page in my office," says Furse, "I would make sure something happened. We're adults here, except the pages. But everyone else can kick somebody in the ankles, and I would hope they would." Former representative Marjorie Margolies-Mezvinsky (D-Pa.) says sexual harassment of female staffers will be tolerated much less readily now that some of the people wielding power are women.[35]

In response to growing evidence of sexual discrimination and harassment on Capitol Hill, Rep. Pat Schroeder (D-Colo.) introduced House Resolution 445 in July 1988, establishing an internal grievance panel of six private-sector members to hear and adjudicate complaints. In her press release, Schroeder said that, despite years of congressional discussion of fair-employment practices, there had been "a certain silence" with respect to discrimination *within* Congress. "My House Fair Employment Practices Resolution," said Schroeder, "offers Congressional employees a form of redress in the House of Representatives if they feel that they have been discriminated against on the basis of race, sex, religion, national origin, age, or state of physical handicap." The House quickly established an Office of Fair Employment Practices (OFEP) to respond to staff complaints, including allegations of sexual harassment. Before the establishment of that office, complaints of sexual harassment were rarely aired publicly. However, when stories of sexual harassment by then representative Jim Bates (D-Calif.) surfaced in 1988, Capitol Hill began to doubt that the silence meant all was well.

Two members of Bates's staff told the House ethics committee that he had made a variety of untoward advances. They said he requested daily hugs from women staffers and asked one if she would sleep with him if they were stranded on a desert island. He also wrapped his legs around the leg of a female staffer in full view of others in the office. The House ethics committee chose to "reprove" Bates, the most lenient action available to the committee. All of the more serious categories of action, from reprimand to censure to expulsion, would have required a vote by the full House, a vote that few members wanted to cast.

The ethics committee instructed Bates to apologize to two women staffers, take "sensitivity" training, and it warned that "any further action by you in the areas which were the subject of the committee's preliminary inquiry may result in a recommendation that disciplinary action be considered by the House."

Bates accepted the committee's finding. "I think I made a mistake," he said. "I didn't really know what sexual harassment was."[36]

Following the Bates scandal, the Capitol Hill Women's Political Caucus (CHWPC), an affiliate of the National Women's Political Caucus, began collecting signatures from members of Congress whose offices had prepared written sexual harassment policies. In February 1990, CHWPC began a study of the rights of women on the Hill compared with women nationally, and the results were not encouraging. Jean Dugan, then cochair of CHWPC and press secretary for the late senator Quentin Burdick (D-N.D.), said it was "pretty shocking to our members that we were the last plantation in terms of sexual harassment." The caucus then decided to prepare its own policy on sexual harassment, and in the process, according to Dugan, "women came forth with anecdotal evidence of sexual harassment experiences on the Hill."[37]

During 1991, the Senate established an Office of Fair Employment Practices (OFEP) similar to the one in the House, and the CHWPC distributed its new sexual harassment policy to members of Congress, asking them to sign on to the CHWPC policy or verify that their office already had a comparable policy in place. By October 25th of that year, 224 House members and 39 senators had signed on to the policy. Some offices already had policies in place that were at least as strong as the CHWPC policy. Other offices felt the need to tighten up already existing policies. Patty Sheetz, administrative assistant to former representative Don Ritter (R-Pa.), said their office signed on to the CHWPC policy because "we'd always had one, but we thought we'd formalize it. We weren't as formal as we now think we need to be."[38]

By 1992, 260 House members and 58 senators were listed by CHWPC as having acceptable sexual harassment policies, in addition to eight House committees and five Senate committees. Those numbers, however, still left 40 percent of the House's personal offices and 42 percent of Senate offices with no formal policy against sexual harassment.

Simultaneous with the CHWPC's campaign, the Congressional Caucus for Women's Issues experienced a surge of inquiries concerning sexual harassment. Then came two highly publicized sexual harassment scandals that would leave Capitol Hill tainted.

First there were "the Adams chronicles," as they became known in the press. Sen. Brock Adams (D-Wash.) had survived 1987 charges by a 24-year-old House committee staffer, Kari Lynn Tupper, that he had drugged her, forced her into bed, and sexually fondled her against her will. Tupper had filed a complaint of simple assault against Adams with the D.C. police, but the U.S. attorney's office decided not to prosecute, citing lack of evidence. For more than a year, no reporter discovered the unprosecuted complaint, and when the *Washingtonian* magazine published a lengthy version of Tupper's side of the story, only the Seattle papers took note. Even then, many in both Washingtons remained skeptical about the charges—until March 1, 1992, when the *Seattle Times* printed allegations from six other unnamed

women who charged Adams with a long history of bizarre sexual molestation. Two other women with similar stories withheld permission to publish
them, because they feared that the details would make them identifiable.
Among the women described in the *Times* article were a Democratic party
activist, a secretary at the Department of Transportation, a lobbyist, a secretary at Adams's law firm, and two congressional staffers.

An Adams aide from the 1980s described how he had stroked her leg and
forcibly kissed her on at least two occasions. But the most powerful of the
published accounts came from a staff secretary who worked for Adams
from the mid-1970s in the House to his 1986 Senate campaign. She described
Adams's habit of putting his hands on female staffers as being so blatant
and frequent that she would always warn new employees of "Brock's
problem." The secretary gradually became a kind of clearinghouse for
complaints from staffers, such as the receptionist who came to her in tears
after being fondled by Adams. The secretary remained with Adams
throughout his Senate campaign, during which she continued to hear
stories of his inappropriate sexual behavior. Soon thereafter she wrote to
Adams announcing her resignation and identifying his sexual behavior as
the cause.

To the dismay of women on Capitol Hill and around the country, the
Senate's Select Committee on Ethics decided on May 22, 1992, that it would
not investigate the allegations of sexual misconduct against Adams, because many of the incidents were said to have occurred before he had joined
the Senate in January 1987. The committee said it had no jurisdiction over
the conduct of an individual prior to his or her joining the Senate and,
therefore could not investigate complaints relating to such conduct."[39] The
committee acknowledged that the accusations by Kari Tupper did relate to
the period after Adams had joined the Senate, but because those charges
had been investigated and rejected by the U.S. attorney for the District of
Columbia, the committee chose to disregard them.

Barely had the dust settled on the "Adams chronicles" when the Packwood scandal erupted. Rumors had been circulating in Washington and
Oregon for years that Sen. Robert Packwood (R-Ore.) often made sexual
advances toward staff. In the wake of the Clarence Thomas hearings,
freelance journalist Florence Graves contacted the *Washington Post* with
information about Packwood that she had gathered while working on an
article about sexual harassment on Capitol Hill.

In the course of the *Post*'s investigation, former Capitol Hill staffers and
lobbyists revealed that, since Packwood's earliest days in Congress, he had
made uninvited and inappropriate sexual advances to women who worked
for him or with him, including ten women who, independently of each
other, gave specific accounts of such behavior toward them. With a close
race for reelection entering its final days, Packwood denied the allegations
and provided the *Post* with statements intended to cast doubt on the

women's credibility. The *Post* then informed Packwood that its story would not be published before the election. The delay in publication probably assured his reelection to a fifth term in the Senate.

Initially, Packwood's office had described the *Post*'s inquiry as a politically motivated "witch hunt." Yet on November 20, 1992, after the election had been won, Packwood sent a three-page statement to the *Post*, saying he would not make an issue of any specific allegation. His statement also apologized for any of his comments or actions that may have been unwelcome or for conduct that may have caused any individual discomfort or embarassment. "My intentions," said Packwood, "were never to pressure, to offend, nor to make anyone feel uncomfortable, and I truly regret if that has occurred with anyone either on or off my staff."[40]

Jack Faust, a Portland lawyer and close friend of Packwood, said Packwood was admitting to some "human flaws." Faust agreed that "denial is not credible," adding, "There's nothing to be gained in a denial. The best thing to do is to accept it, not make an issue of it, and go back to work."

Indeed, Packwood went back to work, despite growing calls from both sides of the aisle for him to resign. Women on Capitol Hill and around the country were outraged over the published accounts of staff who had endured Packwood's harassment. When first contacted by the *Post*, the ten women had been reluctant to talk about their experiences, but several allowed their names to be mentioned to Sen. Packwood during reporters' interviews with him. Four women consented to be identified in print if others agreed as well. Three former staff members and a lobbyist refused to be identified publicly or to Packwood because of their fear that they would suffer professionally or financially. One of these former aides said she had warned Packwood years ago that his behavior might some day threaten his career. Another former aide remained silent about the sexual harassment until after she left employment on Capitol Hill, at which time she wrote a letter to Anita Hill, who had recently suffered through the ordeal of the Thomas hearings. In her letter, the former aide praised Hill for demonstrating more courage than she herself had been able to summon. "My disillusionment with a man and a position I had previously held in such high regard overwhelmed me," she wrote. "I suppose somehow I felt I did something wrong."

The earliest account of Packwood's sexual advances given in the *Post* article dated back to 1969, when the 36-year-old Packwood was the youngest member of the Senate. Julie Williamson was a 29-year-old legal secretary who worked for Packwood's 1968 campaign and then in the senator's new office in Portland, Oregon. She said that one day in 1969, while she was speaking on the phone, Packwood walked in and kissed her on the back of the neck. She told him never to do that again and walked away, but Packwood followed her into an adjoining room where he grabbed at her clothes. "He couldn't get the girdle off and I kept struggling and he just gave up," Williamson told the *Post*. "I was really frightened."

Williamson quit her job within weeks of the incident.

In the mid-1970s, another young woman, Jean McMahon, applied to work in Packwood's Oregon office in Portland. Packwood arranged for McMahon to meet with him to discuss drafting a speech for him, and several weeks later he asked her to meet him at the Oregon motel where he was staying during an annual state Republican conference. During the first visit, only business was discussed, but, according to McMahon, the second visit "ended up in one of those classic unpleasant situations where it was obvious he had other ideas on his mind and didn't want to talk about the speech. . . . I can remember being chased around the table and being grabbed and kissed once."

In 1976, Paige Wagers, then a 21–year-old mail clerk in Packwood's Washington office, was grabbed and kissed by Packwood. Wagers recalled, "It was very hard to get him to let go of me." She eventually pulled away and left the office. Later, a Packwood aide told her that such advances had occurred before and advised her not to enter his office alone. Within a few months, Wagers left to take another Capitol Hill position, but in 1981, while working for the Department of Labor, Wagers ran into Packwood in one of the Capitol's passageways. Wagers felt confident enough to talk about her new job with her former boss, but Packwood suddenly opened an unmarked corridor door and ushered her into a private office. He shut the door, kissed her, and reached out to clear a place on the sofa. Wagers says she pulled away and made it clear that she wasn't interested. She recalls that she felt foolish for allowing herself to be caught once more in such a situation and frustrated at the way she had been treated.

Wagers confided in several of her friends, who advised her not to complain publicly, warning that she would be the one to suffer. "That's the way Washington is," she told the *Post*. "You have to build, you can't have enemies." She expressed frustration with her situation, saying, "[Y]ou know it happened to you . . . and that it's right to say what happened. But because only the two of you were in the room, there is no way you can prove it. You're vulnerable. You're totally out on a limb."[41]

Another former staffer, who agreed to be identified to Packwood but not to be named in the *Post*'s article, described an incident in early 1982, when she was 21 years old. She had stopped off at Packwood's office one evening to deliver some papers and found him drinking wine. She recalls that he walked over to her, pulled her out of the chair, and tried to kiss her. "He stuck his tongue in my mouth," she added. She squirmed out of Packwood's grasp and fled to her home, leaving her purse and coat in her office, despite the winter cold. "I was embarrassed, insulted and feeling like an idiot . . . for ever thinking he thought I was important." She filed no formal complaint, because she thought, "I wasn't important enough for anybody to believe. . . . I didn't know where to turn. I didn't know who to complain to, and he would probably just deny it, have me fired, and that's all I needed at that time." She told several friends of the incident, and resigned from Packwood's office that spring.

Other less detailed accounts were also provided to the *Post*. One former Packwood aide described a 1990 incident in Packwood's office in which he abruptly kissed her, causing her to run from the building, crying. A 22-year-old college intern in Packwood's office complained of his sexually explicit jokes, which, she said, were "very degrading to women." She recalls, "I didn't know what I should do. I just sat there and took it."[42]

In a December 10, 1992, news conference, Packwood seemed to admit wrongdoing, but suggested that he had seen the light. "My actions were just plain wrong," he said. "I just didn't get it. I do now."[43]

Less than two months later, 13 more women revealed acts of sexual harassment by Packwood that had occurred between the late 1960s and mid-1980s. The women involved included congressional employees, campaign volunteers, and lobbyists. Packwood was also alleged to have made sexual advances to a high school student who worked for him as a summer intern in 1982 and 1983. Six of these 13 women agreed to have their names published, and two others agreed to be identified only to Packwood. Some feared that Packwood would attack them personally, putting their government careers at risk, while others felt that speaking out would be futile.

The earliest of the new set of charges dated back to 1969, when 28-year-old Sharon Grant met with Packwood in his Capitol Hill office to discuss a possible staff job. During their talk, Packwood made it clear that he wanted to spend the night with her, and Grant recalls talking her way out of the office. "He didn't know me at all, yet he felt he could have what he wanted with impunity," she said. "I was young, vulnerable, and he felt he could just do what he wanted."[44]

Gena Hutton served as Packwood's local campaign chairman in Eugene and Lane County Oregon in 1980. Packwood arranged to meet her at a Eugene restaurant during one of his trips home. Hutton said that afterward as Packwood walked her to her car, he suddenly grabbed her and kissed her sensuously. Packwood invited her to his hotel room, but she bluntly turned him down. Hutton says she told Packwood's campaign manager, Craig Smith, about the incident, and Smith told her that "it happens all the time," and that they had "talked to him over and over about it."[45] Hutton said Smith advised her to stay out of Packwood's way.

Among the former Packwood staff members who would not publicly identify themselves, several said they had firsthand experiences with Packwood, and some said they had to fend off his advances more than once. One former staff member said Packwood made three unwelcome advances in 1982, one occurring in his personal office. She soon concluded that she had better find other employment. One evening after hours, as she was typing her resume for another job, Packwood came up behind her and put his hand inside her blouse. She told him to stop and walked away from him. Shortly thereafter she took another job.

A Eugene woman, who agreed only to be identified to Packwood, told the *Post* of two 1985 incidents that occurred while Packwood was considering her to chair his 1986 campaign in Lane County. After a campaign meeting at a local restaurant, Packwood grabbed her, made "suggestive movements," and kissed her on the neck. At the time, the woman blamed the incident on Packwood's drinking, but later that year, after a political event in Eugene, Packwood once more kissed her. She pushed him away and later called one of Packwood's top aides to complain. The result was an angry call back from Packwood, telling her never again to discuss such matters with his staff. Needless to say, the woman turned down the Lane County position.

The response of women on Capitol Hill to the Packwood revelations was swift. Whereas in 1991 CHWPC was energized by the sexual harassment charges that arose during the confirmation hearings on Justice Thomas, in 1993 the caucus leaned heavily on the Packwood scandal. In a February 3, 1993, mailing to members of Congress, CHWPC declared: "For the first time in history, the U.S. Senate is conducting an Ethics Committee review involving allegations of sexual harassment. These are serious charges with serious consequences to all who serve in the institution of Congress. The Capitol Hill Women's Political Caucus (CHWPC) would like to take this opportunity to provide you with our recommended office policy on sexual harassment. . . . CHWPC strongly believes that a written policy distributed to each member of your staff can protect you and your employees from misunderstandings about what sexual harassment is and why it occurs. More importantly, it can create a better working environment where all employees understand that sexual harassment will not be tolerated."[46]

The two-page CHWPC policy defined sexual harassment, gave examples, described the "harassers" and the victims, and stated the implications for the Hill: "Every Congressional office is responsible for ensuring a work environment free from sexual harassment. In addition to harming the individual employee, sexual harassment interferes with morale and productivity by stunting professional development and deflecting employees from their professional purpose. It undermines the credibility, reputation and performance of the United States Congress as an institution. Failure to take affirmative steps to prevent the occurence of sexual harassment may subject the Member of Congress, Staff Director, Administrative Assistant, and other supervisory staff, as well as the perpetrator of harassment to law suits, ethics complaints, and grievances filed with the Office of Fair Employment Practices, any one of which may have legal, financial and political consequences."[47]

At the end of the CHWPC policy document, the member of Congress and his/her chief of staff were asked to sign the following statement: "Based on the guidelines set forth in this document, the office of _____ condemns all acts of sexual harassment, pledges to maintain a work environment free from this form of discrimination, and guarantees swift and serious attention to any complaint of sexual harassment."[48] As of spring 1994, 272 House offices and 72 Senate offices had signed the pledge.

Currently, congressional employees may initiate complaints against discriminatory action, including sexual harassment, by contacting the House or Senate Office of Fair Employment Practices (OFEP) within 180 days of the alleged action. Complainants must meet with an OFEP counselor after which mediation may be requested. House employees must file a *Complaint of Discrimination* form within 15 days of the end of the counseling period. A Senate employee may file a formal complaint not later than 30 days after the end of the mediation period.

In the House, an employee wishing a hearing on an alleged act of discrimination must request it within ten days of filing a formal complaint. In the Senate, the OFEP director assigns a board of hearing officers, none of whom may be senators, officers, or employees of the Senate, to consider each complaint. If a House or Senate employee is not satisfied with the result of the hearing, he/she may request a review of that decision. For House employees, the review is conducted by an eight-person panel consisting of two majority and two minority members of the House Administration Committee, two officers of the House, and two House employees. In the Senate, the Select Committee on Ethics conducts the review, unless the Senate designates another entity. If discrimination is found to have occurred in the House or Senate, remedies may include monetary compensation, injunctive relief, attorney fees, employment, employment reinstatement, or promotion.

Despite these attempts to create a formal structure to protect congressional staff against discrimination, the OFEP never gained the confidence of staff, particularly women. The Congressional Caucus for Women's Issues asked the General Accounting Office, the investigative arm of Congress, to determine whether congressional employees were being adequately protected against discrimination and sexual harassment. The congresswomen asked the GAO to determine how effective the OFEP had been in handling complaints and whether congressional employees were being afforded the same level of protection as private employees. "As one of the people responsible for the establishiment of the OFEP, I believe it is essential that we determine whether this office has been an effective means of dealing with discrimination complaints," said Pat Schroeder, then cochair of the Congressional Caucus for Women's Issues. "This investigation is the best way to get a fair and objective assessment of how Congress can hold itself to the same standards as employers in the private sector." Former cochair

Olympia Snowe (R-Maine) added, "Congressional employees should be covered under all anti-discrimination laws. The GAO investigation will help ensure that Congress has in place a system that will provide the best protection for our employees."

In May 1993 GAO released its report, which found that congressional employees were not using the OFEP. The report showed that, despite substantial anecdotal evidence of discrimination, only four employees had filed discrimination complaints with the OFEP since its creation in 1988, none of them citing sexual harassment. Schroeder compared the office to the "Maytag repairman," saying both were inactive. She also explained the absence of sexual harassment complaints in terms of poor promotion of the office to staff and the fear among staffers of retribution for filing complaints.

In response to the GAO report, Schroeder and Snowe introduced the Congressional Employees Fairness Act, legislation that would make Congress subject to the Civil Rights Act, the Americans with Disabilities Act, and the Age Discrimination in Employment Act. The bill would have established an independent office of congressional compliance to hear charges of discrimination in both the House and the Senate. A board of directors made up of nine congressional outsiders would hear and rule on employment complaints. Under the act, congressional employees would have the right to appeal the board's decision to the U.S. Court of Appeals.

In a caucus press release on August 3, 1993, Snowe stated: "Congress must be held accountable to the same laws as all other employers. The legislation we are introducing today ensures that congressional employees will be fully protected under the law."

"We know that discrimination occurs on Capitol Hill," said Schroeder. "Unfortunately, the OFEP is not a place where employees feel they can take their complaints."

The congresswomen expressed concern that the OFEP was too closely connected to members of Congress, the people against whom complaints may be directed. The OFEP is under the control of a key political appointee and all appeals are heard by members of Congress. "The current system doesn't even have the appearance of impartiality," stated Rep. Snowe. "It's no wonder that congressional employees aren't using the system. Under our legislation, Members of Congress and their staff will be completely removed from the process, and cases will be heard by outside experts in employment discrimination law. Moreover, by granting the right to appeal in federal court, we make sure that employees have full opportunity for a fair hearing."[49]

The Schroeder-Snowe bill was never passed, but it became a focal point for the much-ballyhooed "congressional reform" pursued during the 103rd Congress and initiated during the 104th Congress. In June 1994, the Senate Rules Committee marked up a reform package drafted the previous year by the Joint Committee on the Organization of Congress, which had heard testimony from Schroeder and Snowe. The bill would apply fair-labor and worker-safety laws to the Senate, while the corresponding House bill would apply such laws to both the House and the Senate. Among the improvements proposed were the creation of a single bicameral office of compliance. Amendments were considered that would apply the Freedom of Information Act and the Occupational Safety and Health Act to Congress and extend coverage to all congressional support agencies, such as the Library of Congress and the Government Printing Office.

In August 1994, by a vote of 427 to 4, the House approved the Congressional Accountability Act, which would apply to Congress and its support offices all of the laws regarding civil rights, fair-labor practices, disability, family medical leave, health and safety that Congress has applied since 1936 to the executive branch and to the private sector. When the bill went to the Senate, Joe Lieberman (D-Conn.) and Chuck Grassley (R-Iowa) led the charge to complete congressional approval of the bill. "We have gathered a bipartisan group of 20 co-sponsors to move this bill in the Senate," they declared. "We sincerely hope that the Senate will act now to end a worn-out double standard that offends the public and diminishes our standing as an institution. . . . This should be an easy one. The public wants this reform. And it's the right thing to do."[50]

Despite strong bi-partisan support for the bill, it ran up against preelection Republican stalling tactics, which delayed Senate action until 1995 when the new Republican majorities in the House and Senate allowed the GOP to call the bill its own. The House, which had already approved the bill in the 103rd Congress, passed it once more on the opening day of the 104th Congress, by a vote of 429 to 0. The House had incorporated provisions of the compliance bill in its rules when the bill stalled in 1994, but there remained major gaps, including coverage for Senate workers and the roughly 15,000 employees of congressional support agencies. In addition to extending coverage to all employees, the bill created an independent office of compliance to enforce the new protections and gave congressional employees the right enjoyed by other workers to sue and recover damages in federal court for breach of workplace rules.

Final passage in the Senate occurred on January 11, 1995, by a vote of 98 to 1, and President Clinton signed it into law soon after. Though the early support for the bill had come from Democrats, Republican lawmakers now claimed it as part of their Contract with America. Changes in congressional rules had already brought the 36,000 employees of Congress and its agencies under many of the public workplace laws.

The ten laws that now apply to congressional employees are:

1) The Fair Labor Standards Act of 1938, which sets minimum wages and maximum hours. Congressional offices are now required to pay "time and a half" to staff instead of the traditional "compensatory time."

2) Title VII of the Civil Rights Act of 1964 already applied to federal employees, including congressional staff, but now employees would have legal recourse for complaints.

3) The Occupational Safety and Health Act of 1970 sets health and safety standards, which would require some rewiring of Capitol Hill offices and protection of staff from toxic chemicals.

4) The Americans with Disabilities Act of 1990 already applied to Congress.

5) The Family and Medical Leave Act of 1993 will allow unpaid leave for illness, pregnancy, or care of newborn children.

6) The Civil Service Reform Act of 1978 now allows congressional staff the right to join labor unions, form bargaining units, and negotiate with employers.

7) The Age Discrimination in Employment Act of 1967 prevents age discrimination against persons age 40 and over. The House already has a similar rule, but the act would improve legal recourse.

8) The Employee Polygraph Protection Act of 1988 restricts the use of lie detectors on employees, but Congress does not currently use polygraphs.

9) The Worker Adjustment and Retraining Act of 1988 requires 60-day notice of mass layoffs, and would likely have little effect on Congress.

10) The Rehabilitation Act of 1973 provides anti-discrimination protection for disabled persons, but Congress already conforms to most provisions.

Regardless of which party deserved credit for the Congressional Compliance Bill, it was welcomed by all Capitol Hill staff as a step in the right direction. But few expect a golden age to descend on the workplace. "The compliance act may not have any significant effect," says one senior female staffer. "The discrimination is so subtle. If the women have the guts to complain, it would be one thing. But the employer can always tell you that they just didn't like you politically. Your politics were wrong. But it's not your politics. It's being female."

CONCLUSION

Women within the congressional staff are displaying tepid optimism about an improvement in their working conditions in the 104th Congress. On May 17, 1995, the Senate Ethics Committe gave some indication of a willingness to take action against sexual harassment on Capitol Hill when it reported, after a 30-month investigation, that there was substantial evidence that Sen. Bob Packwood may have abused his office through sexual misconduct and other inappropriate behavior. Among many charges against Packwood, the committee's report documented 15 acts of sexual harassment or abuse against female staff during the period from 1969 through 1990. The report amounted to an indictment of Packwood, though it made no judgment about the allegations. Packwood was offered the opportunity for a public hearing, but he chose initially to meet privately with the Senate Ethics Committee on June 27, 1995, to discuss the allegations against him.

Mary Heffernan, a former Packwood employee and complainant, responded to the Ethics Committee report by saying, "There was a great chance that this thing was going to be swept under the rug, and probably what is most profound for me out of this is how significant the evidence had to be, how egregious his behaviors had to be for the Ethics Committee to come out at this juncture." Heffernan is willing to repeat her allegations in public hearings, but she admits, "[T]hat doesn't mean that I will be treated well, or that it won't be a hurtful process."

Gena Hutton, who had served as a local Packwood campaign chairman, agreed: "It's important to me that I be heard, . . . that I be able to say to my daughters, I did this, I took care of myself here, and I kept my voice out there until somebody listened, right to the end."

During the 104th Congress, some Packwood critics who earlier had called for his resignation said they would settle for Senate action to strip Packwood of his Finance Committee chair, but Portland attorney Carleton Grew says, "[Any] other person in this country who committed this kind of activity in their job, besides a U.S. Senator or a high public official, . . . would be fired."[51]

By the spring of 1995, the *Washington Post* editorialized: "The preponderance of charges concern a pattern of truly revolting sexual marauding that occured over a period of years. . . . Almost all of it was directed against members of his own or other Senate staffs, campaign workers and lobbyists, whose positions made them particularly vulnerable to his demands. . . . In the months ahead, as Senator Packwood is heard, judged and possibly penalized, he will not be the only one tested. If the case is proved, each senator's vote will tell us not only what he or she thinks of the Oregonian's conduct but what each of them considers the standard of acceptable behavior for all those who serve in the Senate."[52]

In July, when the Republican-controlled Senate showed no inclination to hold hearings on the allegations against Packwood, five female senators protested. Democrats Barbara Boxer (Calif.), Diane Feinstein (Calif.), Carol Moseley-Braun (Ill.), and Patty Murray (Wash.) were joined by Republican Olympia Snowe (Maine) in signing a public letter that said, "The Senate is the people's home, not a private club. Serious allegations of misconduct by any member of the Senate should be fully and publicly aired." Sen. Barbara Mikulski (D-Md.), a member of the ethics committee, issued her own statement in support of public hearings. Republicans Nancy Kassebaum (Kans.) and Kay Bailey Hutchison (Tex.) declined to sign the letter or support public hearings.[53]

In response to the women's letter, Senate Ethics Committee vice chairman Richard Bryan (D-Nev.) issued a statement advocating public hearings, and Sen. Boxer said she would seek a vote on a binding resolution if the committee failed to take action. The committee chairman, Republican Mitch McConnell (Ky.), indicated displeasure with both Bryan and Boxer, threatening to hold hearings on prominent Democrats if Boxer forced the issue on Packwood. "I'm not threatening you, I'm promising you," McConnell told Boxer, who responded, "Is this what the ' revolution' is about: close the door on the boys' club?" She said that if the Republicans refused to hold hearings, "it will make the Anita Hill case look like a birthday party."[54]

Republicans like Senate Majority Leader Robert Dole began intensive "Boxer-bashing," and on July 31, a divided ethics committee voted *not* to hold public hearings on the allegations of Packwood's sexual and official misconduct. The committee did agree to make public all "relevant" information gathered during the 31-month inquiry, but Boxer was unmoved. "It's like cancelling a trial, . . . determining guilt or innocence on the basis of a pile of papers."[55] The committee also began consideration of disciplinary action against Packwood.

On August 2, after a highly partisan debate, the Senate narrowly defeated, by a vote of 48 to 52, the Boxer proposal to change Senate rules to require public hearings in all major ethics cases, including the Packwood inquiry. Sen. Mikulski (D-Md.) said the vote once again makes women the victims by denying a public voice and visibility to those alleging Packwood's misconduct. The very next day, the ethics committee revealed two new allegations of misconduct against Packwood, one of them an explosive charge by a young woman that Packwood had made unwanted sexual advances toward her when she was a 17-year-old summer intern on Packwood's staff. The incident, which included grabbing and kissing the girl, had been anonymously reported in the earlier *Washington Post* accounts, but was now a formal allegation.

Sen. Boxer was outraged by the new charges. She told reporters that the involvement of a minor added a new dimension to the scandal and that the earlier Senate vote against holding public hearings would have been different if that had been known. Committee members said the panel's staff had not told them of the new charges until the day after the Senate's vote against hearings. Boxer commented that "the timing was very odd."

Sen. Alan Simpson (R-Wyo.), a chief interrogator of Anita Hill in 1991, attempted to intimidate potential witnesses against Packwood by warning that they would pay a personal price if public hearings were held. "People get destroyed in the process," he warned. Packwood himself then took the offensive against the women who had brought the accusations. "I was trying to keep a lid on my powder, but now it is time to fight fire with fire," he said. "I have avoided public confrontation with the accusers, however, they have not shown me the same measure of respect. I will not deal with the personal attacks as I have in the past."[56]

The ethics committee responded to the new allegations by postponing a decision on the Packwood case until after Labor Day.

By the fall of 1995, Packwood's political fortunes had disintegrated. Incriminating sections of his diary became public, including his claim that he had made love to 22 staffers and had "passionate" relationships with 75 others. On September 6, the Senate Ethics Committee voted unanimously to recommend that Packwood be expelled from the Senate, and on the following day Packwood told a somber Senate that he would resign his seat. He then stepped down as chairman of the Senate Finance Committee and specified October 1, 1995 as his date of departure, making him the first senator since the Civil War to be forced from the chamber.

The process of judging Packwood and confronting sexual harassment on Capitol Hill was a painful and defining period for Congress and its staff during the 104th Congress, but there will also be a host of reforms and rules changes introduced by the Republicans that will significantly affect female staff. A recent CMF survey of 1,400 Senate and House staff revealed long-standing complaints about burnout, long hours and low pay, and consequent support for trimming the number of congressional committees and subcommittees, limiting members' committee assignments, cutting back on late-night and weekend sessions, and complying with the overtime requirements of the Fair Labor Standards Act. All of these provisions were part of Newt Gingrich's House rules changes in 1995.

The CMF survey revealed that 67 percent of staff "never had enough time to get anything done." Significant numbers of Senate and House staff listed "job burnout" and the "unpredicatability" of their schedules as major problems. Richard Shapiro, CMF's executive director, says, "For the past decade or so, Congress has taken the brute force approach—if everybody works longer and harder, we can get the work done. What we're hearing is: It ain't working." Shapiro noted that while staff size has remained relatively stable over the past decade, the demands on that staff have significantly increased. For example, the amount of district casework and constituent correspondence has more than doubled since 1992. The survey concluded that strict application of the Fair Labor Standards Act would "ensure that Congress begins considering the costs—financial and personal—of asking staff to routinely work evenings and weekends." Those costs are particularly high for women.[57]

The ranks of the army of congressional staff have been thinned with a heavy partisan hand. With the GOP takeover of Congress, the staff has become overwhelmingly Republican, but their interests and influence on Capitol Hill have not significantly changed. There is bi-partisan hope that fair-employment practices, reasonable workloads and "family friendly" schedules will improve the work environment for staffers, women in particular. The workplace reforms in the 104th Congress should help to increase the number of female staffers on the Hill, and women's relatively recent ascension to staff leadership positions has all but assured that their growing influence on the legislative process will be irreversible.

The increasing number of female members of Congress remains the best hope for the recruitment of female staffers, particularly in leadership positions. Rep. Patsy Mink says, "I am generally pleased with how many women I see in top staff positions. There were hardly any women in top positions when I first came here. There were no women AAs, no chief counsels. Just secretaries and maybe some LAs. I don't think I had any women on my staff on the Hill during my first term. Right now I have an all-female office in my district, and my two top staffers on the Hill are women."[58]

Hannah Margetich sees no significant difference between working for a Republican or a Democrat. "As a matter of fact," she said, "the Republican I worked for was the first member I worked for who treated women equally. My AA in that office was a woman. That was the first female AA I had ever worked for."

A female committee staffer recalls that the Republicans on her committee "had far more women than the Democrats did. The Republicans were way out there. The Democrats had men, men, men. It was the old boys, and they were boring and they were stupid. I think the Republicans have always realized the value of women."

Staffer Donna Brazile agrees that women's issues are now crossing party lines, and she recalls with pride her work on Republican Claudine Schneider's 1982 reelection campaign. "I worked very closely with Claudine Schneider on Title IX, and she taught me a great deal about reproductive rights and pay equity. This is a Republican! I learned a lot about Republican and Democratic politics in this Congress. Even though there are vast differences between Republicans and Democrats, blacks and whites, males and females, there are issues that can bring all of us together and tie us together."

Brazile believes circumstances have improved dramatically for congressional staff. "There are more minorities now in positions of influence in this Congress, and there are more opportunities. When I first came to Capitol Hill, I never envisioned myself as a chief of staff. First, you had only a dozen African American members and maybe fifteen women members. Everyone was hiring white men because they thought white men had the experience. White men have had the opportunities that we as women and minorities have not had. Now we're trying to take advantage of those opportunities. Today, the speaker wouldn't dare put together a delegation to go to a major international conference without including one female member. There's more sensitivity towards women members and female staff. I only hope that we can keep this going so that we can remove any obstacles or barriers or any harassment of women in this workplace."

Still, Hannah Margetich believes that it will take about 20 more years for sexual bias to disappear from Capitol Hill, as old members leave and are replaced by a more enlightened tradition. "Twenty years ago there were many women among the congressional staff, but all in low positions. There would be three or four secretaries in an office, and they did most of the work. Women prepared the legislation and wrote the letters, but the male staffers discussed the legislation with the members, met with the lobbyists, and played the visible role in the office. That legacy has not completely disappeared."

Despite the many frustrations she has experienced as a Capitol Hill staffer, Brazile is optimistic: "Seeing some of the men employing women as AAs is very refreshing. We don't feel like window dressing any longer. When you're only one of anything, one black, one female, you're a token. When you're two, you might feel like window dressing. But when you start getting three or four and into the teens, you know there's serious movement and serious power. I think it's the power of the female electorate and the power of women's issues that are finally becoming mainstream issues. Women make a difference. We sensitize an office. We make sure that a press release doesn't go out without proper reference to gender, and so on. Men don't want to antagonize half of the population.

"I've always said, I never want to be in 'the room' by myself, meaning I don't want to be the only woman, or the only black. It's not a comfortable position to be in. When I was a 21-year-old kid I was intimidated by this institution that was full of blue suits, red ties, gray hair, and white faces. Now I feel like it's family. When you walk the halls and see so many women, so many dark people, so many minorities, it feels good."

NOTES

1. Karen Foerstel, "One-Third of Senate's AAs, Press Secretaries, and LDs Are Women," *Roll Call*, December 9, 1991, p. 30.

2. Authors' interview with Donna Brazile, chief of staff to Del. Eleanor Holmes Norton (D-D.C.), January 31, 1994. All subsequent quotes attributed to Donna Brazile are from this interview.

3. John F. Jennings, "The Congressional Committee Staff Member: The Hidden Link in the Legislative Process," *NASSP Bulletin*, November 1989, p. 14.

4. Paul S. Herrnson, "Congress's Other Farm Team: Congressional Staff," *Polity*, Fall 1994.

5. Susan Webb Hammond, "Congressional Staff Aides as Candidates and as U.S. Representatives," *The Social Science Journal*, v. 26, no. 3, July 1989, p. 277.

6. Authors' interview with Rep. Tillie Fowler (R-Fla.), May 24, 1994.

7. Marjorie Margolies-Mezvinsky, *A Woman's Place: The Freshmen Women Who Changed the Face of Congress*, New York: Crown Publishers, 1994, p. 50.

8. Ibid., p. 55.

9. Eric Felten, "Little Princes: The Petty Despotism of Congressional Staff," *Policy Review*, Winter 1993, p. 51.

10. Eliza Newlin Carney, "Business as Usual," *National Journal*, May 1, 1993, p. 1038.

11. Ibid.

12. Ibid.

13. Authors' interview with Rep. Louise Slaughter (D-N.Y.), April 12, 1994.

14. Richard E. Cohen, "People of Influence," *National Journal*, June 15, 1991, p. 1390.

15. Carney, "Business as Usual," p. 1038.

16. Felten, "Little Princes: The Petty Despotism of Congressional Staff," pp. 52, 57.

17. Kevin Phillips, *Arrogant Capital: Washington, Wall Street, and the Frustration of American Politics*, Boston: Little, Brown and Co., 1994, p. 197.

18. Authors' interview with Rep. Patsy Mink (D-Hawaii), December 2, 1994.

19. Kim Masters, "For Congressional Staffers, Feelings of Pain and Privilege," *Washington Post*, November 10, 1994, p. D2.

20. Stephen Barr, " 'Outs' on Hill Scramble to Stay 'In,' " *Washington Post*, November 18, 1994, p. A24.

21. Cindy Loose, "Republican Victory Has Some 'Hill Rats' Scurrying for New Jobs," *Washington Post*, November 20, 1994, p. A23.

22. Guy Gugliotta, "Breakneck Pace Frazzles House," *Washington Post*, March 7, 1995, pp. A1, A6.

23. Ibid., p. 45.

24. *Dorothye G. Scott, Administrative Assistant to the Senate Democratic Secretary and the Secretary of the Senate, 1945–1977. Oral History Interviews*, Senate Historial Office, Washington, D.C., 1992, pp. 50–51.

25. Authors' interview with Hannah Margetich, February 14, 1994. All subsequent quotations attributed to Hanna Margetich are from this interview.

26. "Sexists in the Senate? A Study of Differences in Salary by Sex Among Employees of the U.S. Senate," Prepared by the Capitol Hill Women's Political Caucus, May 1975.

27. "The Last Plantation? How Women Fare on Capitol Hill," A Study Prepared by the Capitol Hill Women's Political Caucus, September 1980, pp. 2–3.

28. "1993 U.S. Senate Employment Practices: A Study of Staff Salary, Tenure, Demographics and Benefits," A Congressional Staff Foundation Guidebook, Washington, D.C., 1993.

29. "1994 U.S. House of Representatives Employment Practices: A Study of Staff Salary, Tenure, Demographics and Benefits," A Congressional Management Foundation Guidebook, Washington, D.C., 1994, pp. 9, 11, 28.

30. Pamela Brogan, "Big Gender Gap Found in Congressional Staff Pay," *Sacramento Bee*, December 18, 1993, p. A1.

31. Ibid.

32. Pamela Brogan, "A Congress of Two Classes," *The Cincinnati Enquirer*, December 26, 1993, p. A6.

33. Brogan, "Big Gender Gap Found in Congressional Staff Pay," p. A1.

34. Press release by Lynn Martin, August 5, 1993.

35. Margolies-Mezvinsky, *A Woman's Place: The Freshmen Women Who Changed the Face of Congress*, pp. 50–51.

36. Michael Oreskes, "Ethics Committee Scolds Lawmaker, *New York Times*, October 19, 1989, p. A24.

37. Susan B. Glasser, "Members Hustle to Add Their Names to Anti-Harassment Policy Statement," *Roll Call*, October 14, 1991, p. 7.

38. Ibid.

39. "Senate Committee Won't Pursue an Inquiry on Brock Adams," *New York Times*, May 23, 1992, p. A9.

40. Florence Graves and Charles E. Shepard, "Packwood Accused of Sexual Advances," *Washington Post*, November 22, 1992, pp. A1, A26

41. Ibid.

42. Ibid.

43. Ibid.

44. Florence Graves and Charles E. Shepard, "List of Packwood Accusers Grows," *Washington Post*, February 7, 1993, p. A14.

45. Ibid.

46. February 3, 1993, memo and attached policy statement to members of Congress from the Capitol Hill Women's Political Caucus, signed by Karen Rose, Chair and co-Chairs Menda Fife and Bonnie Piper.

47. Ibid.

48. Ibid.

49. News release, Congressional Caucus for Women's Issues, August 3, 1993.

50. Senators Joe Lieberman and Chuck Grassley, "The House Passed Coverage Bill: Now Senate Must Act," *Roll Call*, September 12, 1994, p. A5.

51. Interviews on the McNeil/Lehrer News Hour, Maryland Public Television, May 18, 1995.

52. "Senator Packwood and His Peers," *Washington Post*, May 19, 1995, p. A24.

53. Helen Dewar, "5 Female Senators Seek Packwood Hearings," *Washington Post*, July 11, 1995, p. A4.

54. Helen Dewar, "Packwood Hearings Issue Unresolved," *Washington Post*, July 13, 1995, p. A8.

55. Helen Dewar, "Ethics Panel Rejects Packwood Hearings," *Washington Post*, August 1, 1995, p. A1.

56. Helen Dewar, "Packwood Launches Media Defense," *Washington Post*, August 17, 1995, p. A7.

57. Guy Gugliotta, "Hill Staff Survey Echoes Calls for Reorganization," *Washington Post*, December 15, 1994, p. A18.

58. Authors' interview with Rep. Patsy Mink (D-Hawaii), December 2, 1994.

Chapter 5

Prognosis

After almost 90 years of political struggle, women have managed to capture less than 11 percent of the U.S. House of Representatives and only 8 percent of the Senate. There are still eight states—Alaska, Delaware, Iowa, Mississippi, New Hampshire, North Dakota, Vermont, and Wisconsin—that have *never* elected a woman to Congress. If women continue to win congressional seats at this pace, it will take centuries to reach parity with men. There are some who are beginning to doubt whether the goal of parity is realistic, or even relevant in an increasingly conservative society. Sen. Nancy Kassebaum may be the most "moderate" of the Republican women, but she calls herself "a U.S. senator, not a woman senator," and sees no particular advantage to increasing the numbers of women in Congress. "Women don't march in lockstep, nor should they," said Kassebaum. "It diminishes women to say that we have one voice and everything in the Senate would change if we were there." She says she does not wish for more women senators so much as she wishes for more moderate Republican senators.

With the Republican takeover in Congress, the independent-minded Kassebaum has become an unexpected political force, the first woman to chair a full committee since Margaret Chase Smith in the 1950s. Yet, like all the Republican women, she avoids criticism of the male-dominant power structure. "I guess I'm not enough of a feminist that I worry too much about those things," she admitted. "I used to say when I came here if I worried about whether I've been slighted, I would not get much else done."[1]

Lynn Martin, former Republican congresswoman and secretary of Labor, takes a similar view. "You belong to your party," she said. "You don't just vote by sex. The ballot says Lynn Martin (Representative), not Lynn Martin (Feminist)."[2]

Democratic women have, in the past, successfully campaigned against the exclusionary, male-dominant culture of Capitol Hill, but Republicans have been reluctant to attribute the paucity of women in Congress to discrimination. Back in the 1970s, conservative activist Phyllis Schlafly claimed, "The fact that there may be only eighteen women out of 535 members of Congress does not prove discrimination at all. The small number of women in Congress proves only that most women do not want to do the things that must be done to win elections."[3]

Just what is it that women must do to win elections? File for candidacy, of course, something women have historically been reluctant to do. And if women show the initiative to run for office, they must then raise money, lots of money, something women have shown an encouraging ability to do. But what kinds of campaigns should they run? In 1925, Rep. Florence Kahn (R-Calif.) advised Republican women planning to run for office "to obliterate sex in politics." This campaign strategy may have seemed quite pragmatic at the time. After all, when Kahn joined Congress, no woman had yet survived more than a single term. Jeannette Rankin, the first woman in Congress, had made gender a major issue, and she lasted only one term. Indeed, Kahn's unisex politics kept her in Congress for six terms and may have set the standard for Republican women since then.

The most prominent Republican woman ever to serve in Congress, Sen. Margaret Chase Smith, spent almost 33 years in the House and Senate, during which she frequently expressed resentment at being singled out as a woman. In a November 1994 interview, the still feisty 96-year-old Smith told us once more, "I was elected as a person. I served as a member. I was never considered a woman in Congress. I was a member."[4]

Today's Republican women, though basking in their party's newly won majority status, remain reluctant to assert themselves as women. In December 1994, when Rep. Barbara Vucanovich was elected secretary of the Republican House Conference, becoming the second woman in the top Republican leadership, her press release simply said, "This shows that Republicans are more concerned about ability than quotas."[5] Rep. Jan Meyers (R-Kans.) is one of three women to assume committee chairmanships in the 104th Congress—an unprecedented accomplishment—yet she claims that no particular significance should be attached to a woman serving as committee chair. By way of explanation, she adds, "I'm not into quotas." Freshman Republican women like Rep. Enid Greene Waldholtz (Utah) and Rep. Sue Myrick (N.C.) take the same line, rejecting gender as a campaign issue and, in fact, denying that there are such things as "women's issues."

The contrasts between the elections of 1992 and 1994 are startling with respect to women. The Democrats not only dominated the 1992 elections at the polls, but they defined the terms of the campaign debate. In particular, gender was a dominant issue, and it brought the largest number of new women into Congress in history. By contrast, the 1994 Republican landslide at the polls was accompanied by gender-blind campaigns and virtually no increase in the total number of women in Congress. The 1994 elections highlighted the changing roles of female politicians. A record 11 general election races pitted women against women. The philosophies of the newly elected women ranged from the Christian right to the liberal left, and the election results ended the stereotype of "Republican women" as a contradiction in terms.

The numbers of Republican women in the House have not equalled Democratic women since the 72nd Congress (1931–33), and even today Democratic women retain a significant majority. But with Republican women outnumbering Democratic women by almost two to one in the 1995 freshman class, there is a wider variety of ideologies and political priorities defining, or obscuring, the "woman's agenda." As the phenomenon of women challenging women in primary and general elections becomes commonplace, women's issues will be increasingly preempted by the ideological debate. The success of conservative women at the polls will vary with the national political winds, but they will probably continue to grow as a political force on Capitol Hill. Nonetheless, there are some signs that the Republican insistence on gender-blind campaigns has undercut the electability of female candidates throughout politics. Perhaps more disturbing than women's static showing in the 1994 congressional races was the actual decline in the number of women elected to *state* legislatures, the starting point for many women in politics.

Several months before the 1994 elections, Rep. Louise Slaughter (D-N.Y.) warned of a pendulum swing against women. "Historically, during wars or whenever men are scarce, women have demonstrated that they could do whatever needed to be done," said Slaughter. "But when the problem was over and the men came back to work, they said, 'I'm sorry, you really shouldn't do that, you're not capable of doing that, so just go back in the kitchen and do what you're supposed to do.' We've got to watch out for the circumstances that cause this reaction. It's cyclical, and back through history you can see where it has happened. We've got to guard against it and make sure that it does not occur again."[6]

That reaction may be recurring now on Capitol Hill, but there is no consensus on how, or even whether, to fight the pressures against women in Congress. With the Republican takeover of Congress in 1994 and the static growth in the number of women members, even some Democratic women seem to have concluded that a feminist campaign will no longer fly.

"I think 1992 may have been the last election where gender was a significant issue, an issue you could rally around," said freshman Democrat Karen McCarthy (Mo.). "I think we're beyond that now. The idea of having more women in Congress has not gone away, because women do bring a unique perspective to Congress that would be left out if we were not present, but I didn't see it in 1994 as the sort of rallying cry that it was in '92. Whether we'll return to the issues of women and minorities, I don't know."[7]

Ironically, even as campaigns become sanitized of sex, gender voting patterns are intensifying. One thing seems certain. The 1996 congressional and presidential races will be conducted in the context of the widest political gender gap ever seen by public opinion analysts. The *Washington Post* anticipates "an unprecedented political war of the sexes." Republican pollster Bill McInturff calls it "the permanent gender gap." He explains, "What was an artifact of the '80s is now being institutionalized and locked into place."

Democratic pollster Celinda Lake says the gender gap in the 1980s was specifically related to President Ronald Reagan, but now the split encompasses virtually all of politics. Even among conservative "born again" Christians, women believe the Republican congressional budget cuts are going "too far," while born-again men support the cuts by 56 percent to 29 percent.

"There is a real chasm between the genders," says Democratic pollster Guy Molyneux. "We are looking at unbelievably high gender gaps.... This is being driven by women turned off and white men turned on by the Republican agenda." GOP pollster Ed Goeas found that Newt Gingrich had a 54 percent positive to 35 percent negative rating among white men, compared to decisively negative ratings from white women, 37–47, and disasterous ratings among black women, 20–51. Still, Goeas saw the "feminization of Bill Clinton" as the sustaining force behind the split, claiming that Clinton "has aggravated the gender gap more than Reagan was able to do from the other direction." The positive-to-negative ratio for President Clinton among white men was 35–56, while among white women it was 51–40, and among black women an astounding 72–21.

In 1994, white men identified with the Republican Party by a decisive 53 percent to 37 percent for the Democrats and 10 percent independent. On the other hand, a plurality of white women and a whopping 88 percent of black women identified with the Democratic Party. Molyneux says "women are strong on the role of family and society, and they tend to be concerned about what can go wrong. Men . . . discount heavily what can go wrong until it is absolutely thrust in their face."

Married women are somewhat critical of GOP policies in Congress, with 41 percent negative and 36 percent positive, while unmarried women— never married, divorced and widowed—are overwhelmingly hostile to the Republican agenda, 48 to 27 percent. Unmarried women in 1994 backed Democrats over Republicans by a 32 percentage-point margin, while married men supported the GOP by a 12-point margin.[8]

Both Republican and Democratic pollsters agree that 1996 will bring an increasingly factionalized electorate, with gender differences crossing traditional partisan lines. If continued, this may bring agonizingly slow but steady growth in the numbers of women in Congress over the next decade, but whether women will assume genuine power within the halls of Congress is less certain. If women maintain their historical pattern of entering Congress later in life and leaving office sooner than their male colleagues, they will never reap the benefits of the seniority system that rules Capitol Hill. Their meager numbers in Congress will, for some time to come, limit their representation on powerful committees and in the leadership posts, which ultimately decide committee membership. It was certainly encouraging to see women assume three committee chairmanships in 1995, one in the Senate and two in the House, but that accomplishment is offset by the reality that there are 34 other full committees, as well as countless other joint and select committees, all of which are chaired by men.

Two Republican initiatives during the 104th Congress may have some positive affect on the ability of women in Congress to acquire committee and leadership power. For one, the Republicans introduced a rule change that would limit all committee chairs to a maximum of six years tenure. This may prevent a small elite from hoarding committee power for decades, making committee chairmanships available on a more regular basis to less senior members, including women. Another Republican initiative, a constitutional amendment imposing term limits on all who are elected to Congress, was defeated. It may be reintroduced, but the difficult and extended process of passage and ratification makes its success problematic.

Many believe that term limits are the only way to destroy the seniority system, which denies power to the relative newcomers, such as women. But women in Congress, including Republicans, have their doubts. Rep. Nancy Johnson (R-Conn.) defied her party's leadership by voting against term limits. "The ultimate solution to term limits is reform in Congress, and what the Republicans have done is to limit the term of any [committee] chairman to six years," she said. "That's as it should be. There are constuctive solutions." In explaining her opposition to terms limits, Johnson also took a swipe at the predominantly female congressional staff, claiming, "If you limit the terms of Members and you don't limit the terms of staff, you're going to transfer a lot of power to staffers who not only live in Washington, but tend to become part of the Washington mindset. . . . I worry about staff power and the bureaucracy driving the legislative process."[9]

Women will likely continue to increase their ranks on the Hill, but the huge gains during 1992, the Year of the Woman, were probably an aberration caused by a confluence of events. The 1992 elections—which followed such high-profile news stories as Anita Hill and Tailhook—clearly showed how gender and women's issues can be used to attract voters. But absent such circumstances in the future, it is unlikely that women will ever repeat the record gains of 1992. Though women still represent only a small minority of Congress, they have increased their ranks to the point where they are no longer automatically perceived as political outsiders and agents of change. In this sense, they are the victims of their success, modest though it may have been.

The reality is that women have gained such a negligible slice of power that any optimism would be inappropriate. Even in the early days of the 103rd Congress, following the spectacular increase in elected women, those in the know were sober and realistic. When Rep. Barbara Kennelly (D-Conn.) was asked to name the most powerful women in Congress, she responded with surprise, "Why, none of us."[10]

NOTES

1. Kevin Merida, "Kassebaum's Evenhandedness Earns Respect in Senate Debate," *Washington Post*, May 14, 1995, p. A4.

2. Wendy Kaminer, "Crashing the Locker Room," *Atlantic Monthly*, July 1992, pp. 67–68.

3. Valentine Moghadam, ed., *Identity Politics and Women: Cultural Reassertions and Feminisms in International Perspective*, Boulder, Colo.: Westview Press, 1994, p. 373.

4. Authors' interview with Margaret Chase Smith, November 14, 1994.

5. Press release from Rep. Barbara Vucanovich (R-Nev.), December 6, 1994.

6. Authors' interview with Rep. Louise Slaughter (D-N.Y.), April 12, 1994.

7. Authors' interview with Rep. Karen McCarthy (D-Mo.), February 15, 1995.

8. Thomas B. Edsall, "Pollsters View Gender Gap as Political Fixture," *Washington Post*, August 15, 1995, pp. A1, A11.

9. Interview on the "McNeil-Lehrer News Hour," Maryland Public Television, March 13, 1995.

10. *Washington Post Magazine*, May 10, 1992, p. 16.

Selected Bibliography

Abzug, Bella and Kelber, Mim. *Gender Gap, Bella Abzug's Guide to Political Power for American Women*. Boston: Houghton Mifflin and Co., 1984.

Boxer, Barbara. *Strangers in the Senate: Politics and the New Revolution of Women in America*. Bethesda, Md.: National Press Books, 1993.

Carroll, Susan J. *Women as Candidates in American Politics*, 2d ed. Bloomington, Ind.: Indiana University Press, 1994.

Chamberlain, Hope. *A Minority of Members: Women in the U.S. Congress*. New York: Praeger, 1973.

Chisholm, Shirley. *Unbought and Unbossed*. Boston: Houghton Mifflin and Co., 1970.

Cook, Elizabeth Adell, ed. *The Year of the Woman*. Boulder, Colo.: Westview Press, 1994.

Ferraro, Geraldine. *Changing History: Women, Power and Politics*. Wakefield, R.I.: Moyer Bell, 1993.

George, Emily. *Martha W. Griffiths*. Washington, D.C.: University Press of America, 1982.

Gertzog, Irwin N. *Congressional Women: Their Recruitment, Treatment, and Behavior*. New York: Praeger, 1984.

Jordan, Barbara and Hearon, Shelby. *Barbara Jordan: A Self-Portrait*. Garden City, N.Y.: Doubleday and Co., 1979.

Josephson, Hannah. *Jeannette Rankin, First Lady in Congress: a Biography*. Indianapolis: Bobbs-Merrill, 1974.

Kinkaid, Diane, ed. *Silent Hattie Speaks: The Personal Journal of Senator Hattie Caraway*. Westport, Conn.: Greenwood Press, 1979.

Margolies-Mezvinsky, Marjorie. *A Woman's Place: The Freshman Women Who Changed the Face of Congress*. New York: Crown Publishers, 1994.

Roberts, Jerry. *Never Let Them See You Cry*. New York: HarperCollins West, 1994.

Schroeder, Patricia. *Champion of the Great American Family*. New York: Random House, 1989.

Scobie, Ingrid Winther. *Center Stage: Helen Gahagan Douglas, a Life.* New York: Oxford University Press, 1992.

Shadegg, Stephen. *Clare Boothe Luce: A Biography.* New York: Simon and Schuster, 1970.

Smith, Margaret Chase. *Declaration of Conscience,* edited by William C. Lewis, Jr. New York: Doubleday and Co., 1972.

Swerdlow, Amy. *Women Strike for Peace: Traditional Motherhood and Radical Politics in the 1960s.* Chicago: University of Chicago Press, 1993.

Witt, Linda. *Running As a Woman: Gender and Power in American Politics.* New York: The Free Press, 1994.

Index

About the Authors

KAREN FOERSTEL is a senior reporter with *Congressional Quarterly*, specializing in political and legislative issues in the House of Representatives. Previously, she served as a staff writer with the Capitol Hill newspaper *Roll Call*.

HERBERT N. FOERSTEL is head of Branch Libraries at the University of Maryland. He is the author of *Surveillance in the Stacks: The FBI's Library Awareness Program* (Greenwood, 1991), *Secret Science: Federal Control of American Science and Technology* (Praeger, 1993), and *Banned in the USA: A Reference Guide to Book Censorship in Schools and Public Libraries* (Greenwood, 1994).